DIDEROT'S POLITICS

ARCHIVES INTERNATIONALES D'HISTOIRE DES IDÉES

INTERNATIONAL ARCHIVES OF THE HISTORY OF IDEAS

62

ANTHONY STRUGNELL

DIDEROT'S POLITICS

A STUDY OF THE EVOLUTION OF DIDEROT'S POLITICAL THOUGHT AFTER THE ENCYCLOPÉDIE

ANTHONY STRUGNELL

DIDEROT'S POLITICS

A STUDY OF THE EVOLUTION OF DIDEROT'S POLITICAL THOUGHT AFTER THE ENCYCLOPÉDIE

MARTINUS NIJHOFF / THE HAGUE / 1973

PRINTED IN THE NETHERLANDS

TABLE OF CONTENTS

PREFACE

It is only relatively recently that serious attempts have been made to rescue Diderot's political writings from obscurity and neglect, and ascribe to the ideas expressed therein their due place in the panoply of his intellectual and artistic achievements. This has been largely made possible by the transference of the Fonds Vandeul from Diderot's descendants to the Bibliothèque Nationale in 1954. This important collection of manuscripts and papers, to which scholars have previously had very inadequate access, contains the bulk of the political writings, most of which had either never been published, or were only obtainable in badly prepared or rare editions.

In recent years, however, excellent critical editions of the most important political texts have appeared; the *Textes Politiques* edited by Yves Benot, and the *Oeuvres Politiques* and the *Mémoires pour Catherine II* edited by Paul Vernière are all notable contributions. Meanwhile Jacques Proust has written a major thesis on *Diderot et l'Encyclopédie* which contains a detailed study of Diderot's political ideas during the years he devoted to the construction of that great intellectual monument. Most recently Yves Benot has published a general work with an important study of Diderot's hostility to European colonial policies, *Diderot, de l'athéisme à l'anticolonialisme*. Furthermore, Diderot's contributions to the three editions of Raynal's *Histoire des deux Indes* have been identified with virtual certainty by Michèle Duchet and Hans Wolpe, thereby opening up a further valuable source for his political ideas.

So with the abundance of material and critical work which has become available a full-scale study of the evolution of Diderot as a political thinker is now possible. This task has been partly fulfilled by Jacques Proust, but as he notes at the beginning of his thesis, "La pensée politique ne se diversifiera, et ne deviendra tout à fait intéressante qu'après 1765, lorsqu'il aura l'occasion, et le loisir d'étudier une série de problèmes très concrets"

(p. 341). The present study seeks to elucidate the complexity and at times apparent incoherence of Diderot's political thought as it evolves after the *Encyclopédie* and takes on a new richness and vitality. It also seeks to give it the place of importance in his *oeuvre* which it deserves.

We have been guided by a number of simple principles. Firstly, we believe that the political ideas of an unsystematic thinker such as Diderot are best studied and judged within their historical context. Secondly, in order to ascertain his originality and the extent to which he is representative of his age and milieu it is necessary to compare him with his main contemporaries. Thirdly, since every aspect of his thought is contained within an integrated conceptual structure, it is essential wherever possible to study his political writings in relation to the rest of his work. Only by attempting to fulfil these related aims can the developing response of a complex intellect and personality to the changing structures and forces of society be properly understood.

Having defined the aims of this study it remains to describe the method chosen. The whole tenor of Diderot's thought is hostile to the *esprit de système* which offends by its inability to apprehend the rich, multi-faceted nature of an ever-changing reality, and, moreover, fails to grasp man's constantly evolving perception of that reality. His political thought is no exception. Consequently only a chronological study can claim to make sense of the subject. A certain amount of systematisation is, however, inevitable, but we have tried to keep it to a minimum by dividing our study very simply into two parts. The first part examines those aspects of Diderot's philosophical and moral thought, and to a lesser degree his aesthetics, which provide the intellectual foundations for his political ideas. The second part is devoted to the evolution of his political thought proper. This approach has its limitations; in particular it could be argued that any artificial division of a body of ideas, which by common critical assent form an integrated whole, must necessarily falsify them. However if one wishes to highlight Diderot's distinctive development and achievement as a political thinker this risk must be taken, though limited as far as possible by the liberal use of cross-references.

I owe a considerable debt of gratitude to Professor Robert Niklaus of the University of Exeter from whom I have received unstinted encouragement and invaluable guidance during the writing and rewriting of this work.[1] I should also like to thank Professor J. H. Broome of the University of Keele for sympathetic criticism and advice on numerous points of sub-

---

[1] Originally presented in a different form, as a dissertation for the degree of Ph. D. in the University of Exeter, in 1971.

stance and detail. Among my colleagues at the University of Hull Professor J. C. Ireson read part of the manuscript and made a number of helpful suggestions, Dr. P. A. M. Taylor gave me bibliographical guidance on the history of the American Revolution, and Dr. J. L. Price unravelled for me some of the intricacies of 18th-century Dutch politics. Any errors or inadequacies which remain are naturally my own.

Finally I should like to express my gratitude to the Department of Education and Science for a State Studentship and to the French Government for a grant, which enabled me to undertake two years full-time research in Paris.

A.S.

Hull
April 1972

ABBREVIATIONS

A.T.: D. DIDEROT, *Oeuvres complètes,* ed. J. Assézat and M. Tourneux, Paris, Garnier, 1875-1877, 20 vols.

CORR.: D. DIDEROT, *Correspondance,* ed. G. Roth, vols. 13 to 16 with the collaboration of J. Varloot, Paris, Les éditions de minuit, 1955-1970, 16 vols.

CORR. LITT.: *Correspondance littéraire, philosophique et critique, par Grimm, Diderot, Raynal, Meister, etc.,* ed. M. Tourneux, Paris, Garnier, 1877-82, 16 vols.

ENC.: *Encyclopédie, ou Dictionnaire raisonné des sciences, des arts et des métiers, par une société de gens de lettres,* Paris, Briasson, etc. 1751-1780, 32 vols.

HIST.: G. T. F. RAYNAL, *Histoire philosophique et politique des établissemens et du commerce des Européens dans les deux Indes,* Paris, Berry, An III (1795-1796), 10 vols.[1]

MEL.: N. a. fr. 13,768, Diderot, Mélanges, Vol. XXXVIII of the bound volumes of the Fonds Vandeul.[2]

MEM.: D. DIDEROT, *Mémoires pour Catherine II,* ed. P. Vernière, Paris, Garnier, 1966.

O. PH.: D. DIDEROT, *Oeuvres philosophiques,* ed. P. Vernière, Paris, Garnier, 1956.

O. PO.: D. DIDEROT, *Oeuvres politiques,* ed. P. Vernière, Paris, Garnier, 1963.

O. RO.: D. DIDEROT, *Oeuvres romanesques,* ed. H. Bénac, Paris, Garnier, 1951.

P.D.: N. a. fr. 24,939. *Pensées détachées sur divers sujets extraites des manuscrits remis à l'abbé Raynal par Mr. Diderot,* Fonds Vandeul.[2]

P.W.: *The Political Writings of Jean-Jacques Rousseau,* ed. C. E. Vaughan, Cambridge, Cambridge University Press, 1915, 2 vols.

NOTE: In quotations taken from both manuscript and printed sources the original spelling has been respected.

---

[1] For reasons of accessibility we have used one of the many editions of *the Histoire des deux Indes* which were published during the Revolution. It differs in no significant respect from the more commonly used 1781 edition, 10 volumes in 8°, published by J. L. Pellet, Geneva.

[2] The page references to the *Mélanges* and the *Pensées Détachées* follow the original pagination of the manuscripts.

INTRODUCTION

The materialism which informs Diderot's political thought throughout the period with which we are concerned can be traced back to the *Pensées philosophiques*, written in 1746. Although the deistic view is still dominant in this short work, *Pensée XXI* contains an unambiguous statement of materialist belief. If, it is argued, one accepts the postulate that matter has been endowed with movement from all eternity, it follows that its combinatory possibilities are infinite, so it is reasonable to conclude that one combination has led to the formation of the universe.[1] This view is given greater prominence in the *Promenade du Sceptique* (1747), where Athéos argues that it is as reasonable to ascribe the birth of the world to chance as to a creative intelligence.[2] But in these early works materialism remains for Diderot a purely speculative philosophy, attractive for its simplicity and its value as a working hypothesis. It fails to gain his full adherence because he can see no way of constructing a moral system upon it, and morality had been his prime enthusiasm and concern since translating Shaftesbury's *Inquiry concerning virtue and merit*. With the *Lettre sur les aveugles* (1749), however, a radical change in Diderot's attitude to materialism becomes discernible. Although the work is tinged with scepticism, materialism emerges for the first time as something more than a speculative philosophy, being strengthened by reference to factual evidence and observation which invest it with a plausibility and authority that it had previously lacked. The figure of the atheist Saunderson, whose moral values are essentially determined by his physiological condition serves to weaken Diderot's belief in moral absolutes of vice and virtue, and brings him close to admitting that there is a necessary and subordinate relationship of the moral to the physical. The *Lettre sur les aveugles* then, marks the turning-point where Diderot's ethical reservations about ma-

---

[1] A.T., I, pp. 135-136.
[2] *Ibid.*, p. 231.

terialism are overcome and he is free to develop it into a sound and coherent intellectual system.

Jacques Proust remarks with reason that "c'est surtout son travail d'édi-
teur de l'*Encyclopédie* qui a permis à Diderot d'accumuler les observations
et les données expérimentales grâce auxquelles il a pu approfondir son
matérialisme, et le fonder sur les faits." [3] The type of speculative philosophy based simply on reason and practised by generations of thinkers from
Lucretius to Spinoza was valueless in itself. In the last analysis there were
no more substantial grounds for accepting it than for accepting any other
system reposing on reason. Materialism had to be founded on an objective
experimental science in order to raise its claim to credibility. A number
of articles in the *Encyclopédie* and the *Pensées sur l'interprétation de la
nature*, published at the same time as the third volume, give an indication
of Diderot's success in achieving this aim. In a supplement to the Abbé
Yvon's article *Ame* he dismisses the traditional view that the soul is situated in the pineal gland and argues that the body and the soul exist in an
indissoluable union; his argument is based on the latest scientific knowledge and is illustrated by the description of three pathological psychosomatic
cases which reveal the interdependence of mental and physical disorders.
In the article *Animal,* in which he comments on a series of texts from Buffon's *Histoire naturelle*, Diderot transforms the great naturalist's theory
of the continuous chain of beings from a purely static concept into a dynamic one. Buffon's observations thus set in a materialist perspective become a series of proofs of the material origin of all life, and of a natural
evolution of all living beings from the least to the most organised. Within
the context of the theory of the great chain of beings Diderot pinpoints two
problems: at what point does the transition from the inanimate to the
animate take place, and what is the essential difference between man and
the animals.

To the first question Diderot was already beginning to sketch out an
answer in the article *Animal* in which he reasons that if animals are distinguished from minerals by the greater number of relationships they
entertain with their environment, it follows that minerals by no means
all have the same number of relationships with the objects which surround
them, "en sorte qu'on peut dire qu'il y a des minéraux moins morts que
d'autres".[4] From there it is only a short step to the conception of potential

---

[3] Jacques Proust, *Diderot et l'Encyclopédie*, p. 286. The summary which follows
owes much to Jacques Proust's analysis of the development of Diderot's materialism
up to 1765. See *op. cit.*, pp. 284-293.

[4] ENC., I, p. 469. Quoted by J. Proust, *op. cit.*, p. 289.

or inert sensibility in matter. With the publication of the *Pensées sur l'interprétation de la nature* in 1753 which concludes with fifteen questions or rather propositions concerning the constitution of matter, the unity of nature, the evolution of the species, and the distinction of live and inert matter, the outline of a philosophy of monist materialism is clearly drawn. In 1765 Diderot proclaimed unequivocally one of the major tenets of his materialism that had been implicit almost from the beginning:

> La sensibilité (...) est une propriété universelle de la matière; propriété inerte dans les corps bruts, comme le mouvement dans les corps pesants arrêtés par un obstacle; propriété rendue active dans les mêmes corps par leur assimilation avec une substance animale vivante (...) L'animal est le laboratoire où la sensibilité, d'inerte qu'elle étoit, devient active.[5]

To the second question Diderot answers that man is qualitatively differentiated from the animals by language and his ability to associate ideas.[6]

The centrality of these two problems to Diderot's materialism endowed his philosophy with a much greater resourcefulness and flexibility than was to be found in the simpler mechanistic materialism of contemporaries such as Helvétius. However, until 1773 when Diderot first addressed himself seriously to elaborating a materialist explanation of human consciousness and judgment in the *Réfutation d'Helvétius* it is the first problem that dominated his materialism. The effect of this was to emphasise the all-enveloping continuity of a universe consisting of matter ranging in form from the simplest inert substance to the most highly developed living organism. As a consequence man at every stage of his development and in all his attributes is seen as an undifferentiated natural phenomenon, subject to the same inexorable laws that govern the rest of the universe. Whereas for Rousseau civil man has been alienated from his true nature by the artifices of society, for Diderot no such radical change has taken place. As early as the *Essai sur le mérite et la vertu* he had systematically placed the passions of natural and social man on the same level, thus implying that there was no essential difference between the two.[7] Elsewhere in the *Essai* Diderot notably failed to make the distinction made by Rousseau in the second *Discours* between a natural *amour de soi-même* and an artificial and selfish *amour-propre*. Although in the text of the *Essai* he uses "amour de son propre intérêt" [8] in the sense of natural self-interest,

---

[5] CORR., V, p. 141.
[6] ENC. I, p. 469.
[7] A.T., I, p. 64.
[8] *Ibid.*, p. 29.

in a footnote [9] he employs the terms "amour-propre" and "intérêt" in-
differently. While for Rousseau social man's inability to live without the
esteem and approbation of others is a sign of his alienation from his true
nature, for Diderot it is a wholly desirable characteristic, stemming in his
view from man's natural sociability. Between Diderot and Rousseau there
is an irreconcilable opposition which arises not simply from two different
temperaments, but from two wholly opposed conceptions of man.

The opposition can in the last analysis be narrowed down to the problem
of freedom and necessity. For it is in their widely differing answers to this
question that the two men reveal what it is that in their view makes man
man and not just a higher animal. Rousseau is quite clear where the difference lies:

C'est (...) pas tant l'entendement qui fait parmi les animaux la distinction spécifique de l'homme, que sa qualité d'agent libre.[10]

But Diderot in his *Lettre à Landois* rejects the concept of human freedom,
arguing that man like all other natural phenomena acts always and only
out of necessity. Free-will is an illusion, for every action, even if it is apparently voluntary, is determined by a combination of causes external to
the individual, namely his organisation and his education. What distinguishes man from the animals for Diderot is not freedom, rendered meaningless in a materialist content, but his reason. The only kind of freedom
which he finds meaningful is the liberty referred to in the article *Autorité
politique* where he writes:

La liberté est un présent du ciel, et chaque individu de la même espèce a
le droit d'en jouir aussitôt qu'il jouit de la raison.[11]

This is the natural liberty of social man whom no other man has the right
to oppress since all men are by nature, because of their similarity of organisation, equally reasonable.

Such totally opposed conceptions of human nature and human liberty
could not fail to produce wide divergences in the political philosophies
which were evolved from them. But before going on to describe Diderot's
political ideas as they developed in relation to Rousseau's during the time
with which we are concerned, we must first take note of his attitude to-

---

[9] *Ibid.*, p. 29.
[10] *Discours sur l'inégalité*, p. 80.
[11] O.PO., p. 9.

wards the major political thinkers of the 17th century to whose influence
he, along with all his contemporaries, was subjected.

The theoreticians of the 17th century approached the elaboration of
their systems in two distinct ways, as political philosophers and as jurists.
Whereas the former built their political theory on the foundations of their
philosophical assessment of the nature of man and of things, the latter
were more concerned with the legal justification of the principles they
formulated, and consequently the philosophical basis of their theory, although not absent, is relatively weaker. While the philosophers, Hobbes,
Locke and Spinoza, first sought to define the essential characteristics of
man's nature by replacing him in a hypothetical state of nature, the jurists,
Grotius and Pufendorf, contented themselves with several simple assumptions about man's nature, which they did not attempt to justify philosophi-
cally. But, however different their initial method of approach might be,
both philosophers and jurists constructed their systems around three basic
principles: natural right and its corollary natural law, contract and sovereignty. In so doing they established a highly satisfactory working method
which was subsequently adopted by their successors in the 18th century,
among them Diderot.

Of the political theorists mentioned above, Hobbes, Grotius and Pufendorf had the most significant influence on Diderot's thought. Spinoza
and Locke are of less significance. It is likely that the influence of Spinoza
is indirect, Diderot having assimilated the rudiments of his thought
through reading Meslier's *Testament*.[12] As for Locke, Diderot only takes
from his *Treatise on civil government* his theory of the right of property;
all the other ideas that could have interested him he had already found
in Grotius and Pufendorf.[13]

Diderot's attitude to Hobbes is characterized by an alternate attraction
and revulsion: on the one hand Diderot is drawn by Hobbes' genius and
profundity, on the other he is repelled by his extreme pessimism concerning
human nature. This ambivalence finds expression in the principles of
Hobbes' political thought. Man in his natural state is for Hobbes an
animal governed purely by an instinct for self-preservation, devoid of any
social sense, the first precept of nature being

That everyman ought to endeavour Pease as farre as he has hope of ob-

---

[12] J. Proust, *op. cit.*, p. 277, n. 114.
[13] See J. Proust, "La contribution de Diderot à l'Encyclopédie et les théories du
droit naturel."

taining it: & when he cannot obtain it, that he may seek, & use, all helps, & advantages of Ware.[14]

For Diderot the idea of the state of nature as a war of all against all is repugnant as it denies his theory that men are naturally sociable. In consequence he cannot accept Hobbes' negative, individualistic conception of natural law contained in his first precept. It is in Grotius and the natural law school that Diderot finds confirmation of his belief in man's natural sociability. For Grotius natural law, the foundation of his whole political doctrine, reposes on man's innate social instinct and is ascertainable by reason. It is

> Un décret de la droite raison indiquant qu'un acte, en vertu de sa convenance ou de sa disconvenance avec la nature raisonnable et sociable, est affecté moralement de nécessité et de turpitude et que, par conséquent, un tel acte est prescrit par Dieu, auteur de cette nature.[15]

Grotius' successor, the German jurist Pufendorf, further consolidated the theory of natural law by claiming it to be deducible by reason from the nature of things and therefore necessary and immutable. In so doing he freed the philosophy of law from all theological control for, since the laws of nature are immutable, they would be fully capable of constraining men even if God had not proclaimed them through his revealed word. The replacement of the divine by natural law in political philosophy could not fail to appeal to Diderot as a materialist.

Before turning to the theory of contract, it is necessary at this point to elucidate the relationship of the right of property to natural law in Diderot's thought. The two principal sources of Diderot's thinking on this matter are Grotius and Locke. Proust notes with regard to the former that in his *Droit de la guerre et de la paix* "on y lit en effet que le droit qui découle du principe de la sociabilité consiste 'd'abord', à 's'abstenir religieusement du bien d'autrui' ".[16] But while Diderot accepts the right of property as being inherent in natural law, he rejects the traditional theory which derives it from the right of the first occupant, replacing it by Locke's theory that property is acquired by work.

While Diderot does not accept the state of war as natural, like Hobbes he sees the formation of society as being a reaction against a state of anarchy which necessarily precedes it. For Diderot there are three stages in the

---

[14] *Leviathan*, p. 87.
[15] Quoted by J. Touchard, *Histoire des idées politiques*, Vol. I, p. 323.
[16] J. Proust, *Diderot et l'Encyclopédie*, p. 373, n. 155.

evolution of society, the age of the peaceful herd, the age of the pack of wolves and finally civilised society. So, although he rejects Hobbes' war of all against all at one stage, he appreciates its necessity as a premise for explaining the formation of society. However, when it comes to formulating a theory about the pacts by which men agree to institute a society and live according to certain fundamental laws, he once more turns from Hobbes to the natural law school, and to Pufendorf in particular, the reason being that Hobbes' theory of contract is totally unacceptable to him. As his second precept of nature Hobbes states:

That a man be willing, when others are so too, as farre-forth, as for Peace, & defence of himself he shall think it necessary, to pay down his right to all things, & be contented with so much liberty against other men, as he would allow other men against himself.[17]

Since man's right in the natural state consists in furthering his own interests by every possible means, a stable society can only be achieved if the members are prepared to give up their natural rights completely. This for Diderot is an impossibility, for if a man alienates his natural rights he automatically contravenes the law which is inherent in his nature. At this point Diderot also parts company with Grotius who is a partisan of the right of slavery.

Diderot does not refer explicitly to the pact of association which forms a society, the only one to interest him is the pact of submission. It is to Pufendorf that Diderot turns for his theory of contract and sovereignty, although it is likely that the doctrines of Grotius and Hobbes also exerted a certain influence. According to Pufendorf the contract between sovereign and people is made by consent, but in two different manners: either by force of arms or by freely accepting submission to the sovereign body. To this Diderot adds the condition that, in the first case authority remains as long as the conqueror is the stronger, unless it changes its nature and is freely consented to by the vanquished.[18] He further holds with Pufendorf that sovereignty is a transferable good owned by the nation:

En un mot, la couronne, le gouvernement, et l'*autorité* publique sont des biens dont le corps de la nation est propriétaire, et dont les princes sont les usufruitiers, les ministres et les dépositaires.[19]

---

[17] *Leviathan*, p. 87.
[18] *Autorité politique*, O.PO., p. 10.
[19] *Ibid.*, p. 15.

But whereas Pufendorf holds that in practice the people can in no circumstances free themselves from the obedience they have promised, Diderot, with Locke, does not accept the possibility of totally alienating the
rights of the individual. The authority that the prince exercises over his
subjects, he has obtained from them, "et cette *autorité* est bornée par les
lois de la nature et de l'Etat." [20] In theory, then, Diderot accepts the principle of popular sovereignty as opposed to the theory of divine right or
paternal power, but when it comes to applying it to a real political situation, his own country for example, the restricting qualifications he adds
to it, render it almost totally ineffective, as the nation cannot regain its
sovereignty until the ruling dynasty has been totally extinguished.[21] Any
idea of insurrection against the sovereign is inadmissible for the sovereign
is not only a private individual but also a moral body which represents the
general will of the society it governs.[22] Whereas Hobbes considers the
moral sovereign to be incarnate in the person of the individual or collective sovereign, Diderot carefully distinguishes between the prince as a
private person and as a moral being, the latter being sacred:

> Il y a des occasions où (le citoyen) se trouve sur la même ligne, je ne dis
> pas avec ses concitoyens, mais avec l'être moral qui leur commande à tous.
> Cet être a deux caractères, l'un particulier et l'autre public: celui-ci ne doit
> point trouver de résistance.[23]

So, although Diderot had formulated the principle of popular sovereignty
at such an early stage, it is not until after 1765 that it became fully realised within the pattern of his political thought. For throughout the whole
of the *Encyclopédie* period Diderot's main concern, influenced by Hobbes
and Grotius, was to ensure political stability and the indivisibility of sovereignty. In the article *Autorité politique* he will not admit that the
people have any right to resist the ruler:

> "Tous ces motifs qu'on croit avoir de résister ne sont, à les bien examiner,
> qu'autant de prétextes d'infidèlités subtilement colorées." [24]

Nor will he accept the limitation of sovereignty by a constitution or its
division in any way whatever. So we can conclude with Proust that:

[20] *Ibid.*, p. 13.
[21] *Ibid.*, p. 20.
[22] Art. *Cité*, A.T., XIV, p. 187.
[23] Art. *Citoyen*, A.T., XIV, p. 193.
[24] O.PO., p. 20.

"Diderot est, sans contestation possible, un absolutiste, au moins dans toute la période de rédaction de l'*Encyclopédie*. Il n'admet aucune condition politique au contrat qui lie le souverain au peuple, comme il est naturel pour un partisan convaincu de la souveraineté nationale: le roi peut tout, parce qu'il est l'interprète de la volonté de tous." [25]

In short, men in their natural state are sociable, this sociability leads them, after a necessary period of anarchy, to unite into a civilised society. Because of their similarity of organisation, they are equal and therefore enjoy an inalienable natural right to their liberty, but in society the natural rights of the individual members merge to form a sovereignty which is likewise inalienable. This sovereignty is entrusted to the ruler who becomes the moral representative of the general will of the nation. Although the nation theoretically remains in possession of its sovereignty, only the disappearance of the ruler, in the case of France the disappearance of the ruling dynasty, can justify the nation in reclaiming it. Even if the king is unjust, ambitious and violent, there is "un seul remède, celui de l'apaiser par leur soumission, et de fléchir Dieu par leurs prières," [26] the only legitimate one in the light of the contract of submission.

Among Diderot's contemporaries it was Rousseau who exercised the most influence on his political thought during its formative years, and even subsequently when the philosophical and personal divergences became so sharp that they led to a breaking off of all relations between the two, Diderot could not free himself entirely from the persuasive power of his old friend's ideas. While Diderot's interest in political matters had been slow to develop, Rousseau's had arisen spontaneously at a relatively early stage in his career and had developed at such a rate that only eight years separate the second *Discours*, the first of his political writings, from the *Contrat Social*, in which he defines a complete and coherent political doctrine. So it is more than likely that it was Rousseau himself who first directed Diderot's attention towards political philosophy, passing on to him information gleaned from his own reading, stimulating him with his conversation and inducing him to read for himself.

If we believe the *Confessions*, Rousseau's two *Discours* were appreciat-

---

[25] *Op. cit.*, p. 20. In his valuable study of the article *Autorité Politique* in *Essays on the Encyclopédie of Diderot and D'Alembert*, pp. 424-462, John Lough claims that "it is clear that (Diderot's) intention in the second part of the article was a purely tactical one" (p. 445). We show below that, far from being an exercise in diversionary tactics of which Diderot was admittedly an expert, it arises out of a combination of his insistence on the indivisibility of sovereignty, mistrust of the people which forced him to opt for absolutism, and a fascination with the *grande âme*.

[26] O.PO., p. 20.

ed by Diderot, the second even more than the first. Indeed, we find in the article *Agriculture* a theory of the history of society in which progress towards civilisation resulted in moral corruption, which reflects the argument of the first *Discours*. The second *Discours* too contains ideas shared by Diderot and developed in the article *Cité*. In it he argues that the birth and growth of vice and corruption accompanies the birth and growth of cities,[27] a view closely resembling the theory of the second *Discours*, developed from the first, that moral decay is inseparable from the progress of civilisation. In the article Diderot points out that life in society creates artificial needs which render people unhappy, an idea equally dear to Rousseau. But it was inevitable that the philosophical differences between Diderot and Rousseau could not be excluded from their political ideas, and from 1754 onwards the divergences in this field become apparent. Diderot still needed Rousseau's greater experience in political philosophy to guide him, but instead of incorporating Rousseau's ideas into his own theory, he tended more and more to define it in opposition to them.

The striking quality of Diderot's political thought in this period is the consistent logic with which it develops from his philosophical thought. This was possible because Diderot was dealing in purely abstract terms free from the consideration of political realities which would have rendered such a consistency more difficult to maintain.[28] Since, as we have seen, he started from an entirely different conception of man and nature from Rousseau, it was inevitable that the early agreement on certain political ideas could only be temporary. While Diderot considers natural man to be essentially reasonable and determined, and therefore without moral liberty, but with an innate propensity to unite with his fellow men, which expresses itself necessarily in the formation of society, Rousseau's natural man is essentially sensitive and a free agent, and is not naturally sociable, so that the formation of society is a chance occurrence which has no evident causes.

Diderot's theory of man's rationality and natural sociability led him to conclude that the pact of association which formed society resulted from the desire of its members to end the anarchy where the strong fought the weak, and to enjoy the advantages of mutual aid. In Rousseau's opinion this was an unjustifiable interpretation of the pact, for in the second *Discours* he demonstrated that immediately prior to the creation of society the inequalities which opposed men to one another were not phy-

[27] A.T., XIV, p. 188.
[28] Cf. Rousseau, "Commençons donc par écarter tous les faits; car ils ne touchent point à la question," *Discours sur l'inégalité*, pp. 68-69.

sical and moral but economic, and that the pact of association far from reducing this inequality had consolidated it. In fact the pact was a conspiracy of the rich against the poor to ensure that the former maintained their advantage over the latter.

Diderot and Rousseau agree that society, once formed, expresses itself as a whole by means of the general will. But, whereas Diderot holds that the general will of a particular society is part of a wider general will, which is found "dans les actions sociales des peuples sauvages et barbares; dans les conventions tacites des ennemis du genre humain entre eux, et même dans l'indignation et le ressentiment," [29] for Rousseau it is simply the will of any given political body, an artificially created community and it has no necessary connection with the general will of any other political body. It is the general will which formulates the laws, which are applicable to all members of the state without exception. The nation cannot alienate its sovereign right to legislate to a private person since this would mean destroying the freedom of the individuals who make up the political body. Diderot, as we have seen, equally believes in the principle of popular sovereignty; but all political power, including the right to legislate is conferred by contract in its entirety on the sovereign person, there being only one fundamental law, which stipulates the return of sovereign authority to the nation only in the event of the extinction of the dynastic line. So neither Diderot nor Rousseau accept the principle of shared sovereignty but to guard against it they apply diametrically opposed solutions, Diderot absolutism and Rousseau democracy. Although he rejected the theory of rule by divine right, Diderot nevertheless justified the principle of absolutism by the utopian assumption that the private person of the sovereign was capable of interpreting the general will and that it was naturally in his interest to legislate according to its dictates. Rousseau, on the other hand, insists that the general will by its very nature can only be expressed by the people as a whole, and that any transference of sovereignty to a single individual or group of individuals is a contradiction in terms.

If Diderot and Rousseau both arrived at the same theories of general will and popular sovereignty, however different the postulates from which they deduced them, and both agreed on the indivisibility of sovereignty, why is it that to maintain its integrity Diderot opted for an absolutist solution and Rousseau a democratic one? Why did Diderot concentrate his attention on the pact of submission, while Rousseau rejected it, identifying

[29] Art. *Droit naturel*, O.PO., p. 33.

the formation of society with the pact of association? Proust is of the opinion that Diderot's absolutism is a logical deduction from his general philosophy, because his political philosophy is "l'application stricte à l'ordre politique d'une conception du monde matérialiste, moniste, déterministe et rationaliste." [30] Elsewhere he states more precisely:

> Cette notion de *despotisme légal,* très importante dans la doctrine physiocratique, a aussi une place de choix dans la pensée politique de Diderot, car elle tient à la fois à sa conception générale du monde et à sa morale. On pourrait dire en effet que la théorie du despotisme légal n'est que l'aspect politique du monisme matérialiste de Diderot: en se soumettant au monarque absolu, le sujet ne se fait pas l'esclave d'un homme mais de la loi: et si cette loi est vraiment l'expression de la volonté générale du corps politique, elle ne peut être qu'une application particulière de la loi universelle qui régit le monde moral comme le monde matériel.[31]

However, although Diderot's theories of the general will and sovereignty are logically deduced from his monist view of the nature of man and society, it does not follow that his conception of the absolute monarch as interpreter of the general will and holder by usufruct of the sovereignty of the people is likewise a necessary conclusion drawn from his general philosophy. Without betraying his philosophical principles or being illogical he could have followed Rousseau and made the nation itself the holder and executor of its general will and sovereignty; indeed, such a step would have caused no difficulty, since for Diderot the existence of the nation as an organic entity was a reality. The reasons for safeguarding the integrity of national sovereignty and ensuring the expression of the general will through an individual, the absolute monarch, lie elsewhere: in his mistrust of the people and in his idealisation of the person of the ruler.

Proust provides the evidence for the first reason in his analysis of the *Réflexions sur un ouvrage publié à l'occasion de la renonciation volontaire de Rousseau au droit de Citoyen de Genève,*[32] in which he, quite rightly, refuses to see "le signe d'un glissement de Diderot vers l'idée démocratique." Despite Diderot's insistence that "quelque autorisés que soient les chefs, ce ne sont jamais que des citoyens et des commis du peuple; quelque fort que soit le peuple, il est toujours le maître," [33] it is evident that Diderot's main concern is to safeguard the integrity of the sovereign power, to the extent that he takes every precaution to prevent the people from exercising their sovereign right, transferring it in effect to their chiefs.

[30] *Op. cit.*, p. 510.
[31] *Op. cit.*, p. 433-434.
[32] *Op. cit.*, pp. 398-399.
[33] CORR. LITT., VI, p. 5.

For of the dual dangers of despotism and popular anarchy menacing the Genevan state, only the latter truly frightens him. He betrays his mistrust of the people and his desire to see political authority maintained with their chiefs when he states that the "tempérament," the system which supposedly will guard against excesses from either side, "tranquiliserait les esprits, sans trop prendre sur l'autorité des chefs." [34] In this context the term people is ambiguous, on one level it signifies the nation – the chiefs are the "commis du peuple" – but the whole tenor of the article implies a second meaning, that of the people seen as the ignorant multitude.[35] This latter conception is found in the article *Misère* [36] in which the people are equated with the populace; in the article *Populaire* [37] Diderot shows a marked hostility towards the demagogue who draws on popular support, and in the article *Multitude* [38] he further expresses his mistrust of the mass.

Since the nation was to a large extent made up of the ignorant multitude which, because of its inability to use reason would tend automatically towards anarchy if given its head, the only alternative for Diderot was to invest the sovereignty of the people and the interpretation of the general will in the ruler. By taking this step Diderot abandoned the common sense based on experience, on which is founded his mistrust of the multitude, for a utopian idealisation of the monarch quite unjustified by reality. For without this idealisation Diderot's absolute ruler would be no different from Hobbes' and he would lay himself open to the damning charge of justifying arbitrary despotism. But Diderot is not drawn towards the ideal ruler simply because he is unable to find any other way of safeguarding the integrity of popular sovereignty. The selfless monarch, whose interests are identified with those of the nation as represented by Henri IV in *Autorité politique*, is a projection of Diderot's preoccupation with the *grande âme* who is so attuned to the world around him through his reason and sensitivity that he is able to interpret its meaning directly. The portrait of Dorval, the poet communing with nature in the *Entretiens sur le Fils Naturel*, and the description of the scientific instinct of the great experimenters in the *Pensées sur l'Interprétation de la Nature* [39] are based on the same conception of the *grande âme*. In the *Encyclopédie*

---

[34] *Ibid.*, p. 5.
[35] Cf. the article "Diderot et la Notion de 'Peuple'" in which R. Mortier distinguishes three different meanings in the term *peuple* as used by Diderot: *peuple-nation, peuple-travailleurs, peuple-multitude*.
[36] A.T., XVI, p. 119.
[37] *Ibid.*, p. 383.
[38] *Ibid.*, p. 137.
[39] *Pensée* XXX, O.PH., p. 197.

period the portrait of Henri IV is the only instance where Diderot trans-
poses this conception into political terms, but as he elaborates his political
philosophy, the idea of the wise ruler increasingly occupies his attention,
for on it depends the integrity of sovereign power.

In short, Diderot is a partisan of absolutism, but unlike his principles
of general will and popular sovereignty, his choice of an absolutist system
is not a logical consequence of his monist materialism. Rather it is the
result, partly of his refusal, through mistrust of the people, to permit the
nation to exercise its sovereignty and interpret the general will as a political body in its own right, partly of his fascination by the superior intellect
and sensitivity of the genius, which introduces the utopian element into
his thought.

By 1765 Diderot has achieved a thorough grounding in the principles
of political philosophy through his close contact with Rousseau and the
intensive reading undertaken for the *Encyclopédie*. He has elaborated a
doctrine which is, admittedly, largely derived from the political theorists
of the 17th century and from Rousseau himself, but which has the virtue
of being logically constructed and firmly based upon his general philosophy. It is also a doctrine which is to a large extent abstract and utopian,
bearing little immediate relation to contemporary political realities. In
short, it is a political philosophy in embryo, awaiting the right conditions
in which to develop and mature. These conditions exist after 1765, when
Diderot, released of the burden of the *Encyclopédie*, in his middle age
launches himself with indefatigable energy into the centre of the political
problems, which are beginning to stir across France and Europe.

PART ONE

PHILOSOPHICAL AND MORAL FOUNDATIONS

CHAPTER I

MATERIALISM AND THE *MORALE UNIVERSELLE*

I. *MORALE UNIVERSELLE* AND *MORALE PARTICULIÈRE*

"Quelle notion précise," asked the author of the *Salon de 1767*, "peut-on avoir du bien et du mal, du beau et du laid, du bon et du mauvais, du vrai et du faux, sans une notion préliminaire de l'homme." [1] For Diderot an understanding of the nature of man and of his cognitive powers was the starting-point for speculation about ethics and aesthetics, and by extension about politics. He began his intellectual career under the influence of Shaftesbury as a rationalist deist, strongly inclined towards scepticism, but unable to take the final step to a radical negation of the transcendental. This philosophical limbo suited an antimetaphysician like Voltaire perfectly, but for Diderot it was a frustrating barrier to speculative thought. The *Lettre sur les aveugles* (1749), inspired by Condillac's sensationalism and founded upon an implicit atheist materialism, marked the turning-point. By opting for the only fruitful alternative to Catholic theology he was able to embark upon a sustained study of the origins of human knowledge which had previously been closed to him. The first steps in the *Lettre sur les aveugles* are hesitant; the arguments which make the individual's moral conscience dependent on the degree to which he is able to perceive the external world through his senses are either crude or faulty. So is the attempt to relate Saunderson's atheism to his blindness; his critique of the theist position could equally be made by a sighted man. The real value of the letter lies in its radical departure from the traditional view of the universe and of man's place in it. Saunderson, acutely aware of his own physical abnormality, rejects the view of the world as a static perfection created by God for man, since it fails to explain the existence of physical imperfections and misadaptations. In its place he offers a world of matter in motion in which physical organisms in

---

[1] A.T., XI, p. 124.

incessant variety have appeared, adapted and survived, or failed to adapt and disappeared. By reducing all phenomena to expressions of matter and motion the absolute doctrine of final causes disappears, and man loses his immutability, his centrality and his mystery to become an ephemeral mutant whose organisation and behaviour are open to scientific investigation.

It was now clear to Diderot that the way to a real understanding of man's nature lay through the biological sciences. The *Pensées sur l'interprétation de la nature*, in which he formulates a series of propositions, modestly couched in the form of questions on the organisation of inanimate and living matter, and his enthusiastic reading of Buffon and Maupertuis, all point to a growing interest in medical and zoological research sparked off in the *Lettre sur les aveugles*. Once the last pages of the *Encyclopédie* had been handed in to the publishers he was free to devote his energies to the assimilation of the latest discoveries in physiology through his contacts with the eminent physicians Tronchin and Bordeu, and by reading and annotating Haller's *Elementa physiologiae corporis humani*. By the summer of 1769 Diderot had acquired a vast documentation on human and animal physiology and pathology. The time had come to incorporate this material into a new and more all-embracing exposition of a materialist view of the world than had hitherto been possible. The result was unique; in the *Rêve de d'Alembert* Diderot combined a literary masterpiece with a remarkable exercise in scientific and philosophical speculation. In a series of three imagined conversations, in which he, d'Alembert, Julie de l'Espinasse and Bordeu participate, Diderot posits the theory of the universal sensitivity of matter, and develops from it a full explanation of living phenomena from the simplest organisms to man and his mental processes.

The *Rêve de d'Alembert* is a rich profusion of deductive thought, analysis and synthesis reaching its highest point in a profound imaginative vision of the universe. What is of particular interest to us in our attempt to determine the influence of Diderot's philosophical and moral thought on his political ideas is the explanation he gives of human physiology, its variations from individual to individual and the way it relates to emotional and psychological make-up, and ultimately its effect on men's moral conscience. Our understanding of man, both as a species and as an individual, maintains Diderot, is dependent on our knowledge of his organisation. As a species there is no essential difference between man and any other animal, it is simply a question of diversity of physical constitution. A canary and a musician consist of flesh, organised in different manners it is true, but with "une même origine, une même formation, les mêmes fonctions et la même fin." [2] In his *Encyclopédie* articles Diderot conceived of man, not as an individual but, as Jacques Proust has remarked, "(une) partie d'un système intégré lui-même dans un système qui l'enveloppe. Chaque homme fait ainsi partie d'une société restreinte, d'un corps qui, joint à d'autres corps, forme à son tour une société générale du genre humain, l'humanité, qui dans l'ordre moral, peut être considérée comme le *tout* où les individus et les sociétés particulières viennent se fondre." [3] Furthermore, since all men are identical in organisation they are naturally equal and sociable. These notions are contained implicitly or explicitly in the *Rêve de d'Alembert* and are given new force by the power of argument and evidence.

Where the work marks a new departure in Diderot's thinking is in the emphasis which is placed upon the factors which differentiate one individual from another. It was natural that he should wish to incorporate an explanation of human individuality into his understanding of man in order to make the latter complete and convincing. It was essential, too, that he establish the factors which make up the moral conscience of the individual in order to determine its relationship to the normative moral conscience which, as he maintains in a dialogue with an imaginary interlocutor in the *Salon de 1767*, is determined by the physical organisation of the species:

> La morale se renferme (...) dans l'enceinte de l'espèce... Qu'est-ce qu'une espèce?... Une multitude d'individus organisés de la même manière... Quoi! l'organisation serait la base de la morale!... Je le crois...[4]

Such a morality must necessarily be valid for all people at all times and in all places. One of the aims of the *Encyclopédie* had been to bring all men "à s'aimer, à se tolérer et à reconnaître enfin la supériorité de la *morale universelle* sur toutes les *morales particulières* qui inspirent la haine et le trouble, et qui rompent ou relâchent le bien général ou commun." [5] The *morale universelle* has a dual purpose: the conservation and the happiness of the human race, and as such it is more than an ethical system. By this term Diderot signifies the rules which should underpin all relations between men both private and public. It follows that the *morale universelle* provides the foundation for all political principles. The thread

[2] O.PH., p. 278.
[3] *Op. cit.*, p. 407.
[4] A.T., X, pp. 124-125.
[5] CORR., V, p. 84. Our italics.

leading from philosophy, through ethics, to politics is an unbroken one.

However, physiological variations between individuals are responsible for differences in intellect and temperament, which in turn lead to the formation of moral consciences which diverge in varying degrees from the norm of the *morale universelle*. Intellectual activities such as reason, memory and imagination, and the pathological and defective conditions of madness and imbecility are for Diderot simply "des conséquences du rapport originel ou contracté par l'habitude de l'origine du faisceau à ses ramifications." [6] It is the degree to which the *sensorium commune*, in other words the brain, exercises control over the nervous system from which it receives its information, that determines the temperament and intelligence of the individual:

Le principe ou le tronc est-il trop vigoureux relativement aux branches? de là les poètes, les artistes, les gens à imagination, les hommes pusillanimes, les enthousiastes, les fous. Trop faible? De là, ce que nous appelons les brutes, les bêtes féroces. Le système entier lâche, mou, sans énergie? De là les imbéciles. Le système entier énergique, bien d'accord, bien ordonné? De là les bons penseurs, les philosophes, les sages.[7]

Morally the members of the last category create no problems. Since they are physiologically perfect examples of the species their moral conscience is in complete accord with the *morale universelle*. Unfortunately they form only a small minority surrounded by a vastly greater number who are incapable of perceiving the desired norm and acting in accordance with it. Their deficient physical organisation is the cause of a defective moral vision, a *morale particulière* which differs from individual to individual, and which is the source of all forms of dissension and social disharmony.

Such an analysis of the condition of the human race would inevitably lead to an attitude of pessimistic fatalism towards the future of civilised society were it not for the notion of *modifiability* which Diderot holds to be a determining factor in the constitution of the human psyche. Reward is a means of encouraging to greater goodness the individual who had the good fortune to be born with a constitutionally beneficent disposition, while punishment serves to correct the ways of those who are naturally prone to maleficence.[8] Therein lies the means of reconciling the *morale particulière* and the *morale universelle*.

---

[6] O.PH., p. 354.
[7] *Ibid.*
[8] See CORR., I, p. 214 and O.PH., p. 364.

Diderot provides no immediate explanation of how the principle of modifiability can be reconciled with the concept of the morally predetermined individual. However, it is clearly assimilable with the mechanistic theories of memory and imagination which are expounded in the *Rêve de d'Alembert* and which are consonant with his materialism. Since man's mental processes control his behaviour, it is through the influence of external stimuli, designed to encourage or correct and received via the senses, that his attitudes and actions are modified to satisfy the tenets of the *morale universelle*. Diderot likens the interaction of the brain cells, or fibres as he calls them, when a series of ideas are recalled by the process of association, to a number of vibrating cords which are capable of setting up resonances in others.[9] Extending the analogy he compares the thinker to a sensitive harpsichord:

Comme sensible, il a la conscience momentanée du son qu'il rend; comme animal il en a la mémoire. Cette faculté organique, en liant les sons en lui-même, y produit et conserve la mélodie. Supposez au clavecin de la sensibilité et de la mémoire, et dites-moi s'il ne saura pas, s'il ne répétera pas de lui-même les airs que vous aurez exécutés sur ses touches. Nous sommes des instruments doués de sensibilité et de mémoire. Nos sens sont autant de touches qui sont pincées par la nature qui nous environne, et qui se pincent souvent elles-mêmes; et voici, à mon jugement, tout ce qui se passe dans un clavecin organisé comme vous et moi.[10]

The operation of the imagination is similarly explained:

L'imagination, c'est la mémoire des formes et des couleurs. Le spectacle d'une scène, d'un objet, monte nécessairement l'instrument sensible d'un certaine manière; il se remonte ou de lui-même, ou il est remonté par quelque cause étrangère. Alors il frémit au-dedans ou il résonne au-dehors; il se recorde en silence les impressions qu'il a reçues, ou il les fait éclater par des sons convenus.[11]

Since all the functions of the brain are open to the influence of impressions received through the senses mental patterns can be interfered with and altered.

The paradox of the individual both determined and modifiable is thus clarified. His physical organisation which determines his moral character also endows him with mental faculties which can respond to sense-im-

[9] O.PH., pp. 271-272.
[10] *Ibid.*, pp. 273-274.
[11] O.PH., p. 367.

pressions, actual or recalled.[12] Yet despite Diderot's ingenuity the description of the operations of the human brain, which emerges from the *Rêve*, and more specifically from the two passages quoted above, is unsatisfactory. By defining understanding in terms of memory and imagination, which are themselves seen as essentially mechanical reflex actions set off by the impulse of sensation, it confers on the brain a purely passive role. The notion of passivity is stressed by the choice of analogy: by comparing thinking man to a harpsichord whose strings are plucked to produce either a simple melody, or a series of chords and harmonics of varying complexity, depending on the type of thought process involved, Diderot fails to account for the faculty of judgment. Indeed, he does not mention it in the *Rêve*, preferring to use the term understanding (*entendement*), which is more amenable to interpretation as a passive function. Judgment, on the contrary, inferring as it does an active process of choice, comparison and collation, is not of the same order. Diderot, it would appear, is not entirely happy with the conclusions he has reached, for as Mademoiselle de l'Espinasse remarks,

Je dirais, qu'entre ces idées il y a du choix; je dirais ... que ce seul sujet traité à fond fournirait un gros livre.[13]

But for the time being he lets the matter rest. It will not be taken up again until Helvétius' provocative "Sentir, c'est juger" moves him to re-examine the whole problem in the *Réfutation d'Helvétius* in which he exposes the weaknesses of a mechanistic explanation of the more sophisticated human mental processes.

The conclusion reached by Diderot from his investigation into the nature of man and his moral attributes is that civilised man is faced, on the one hand with the desirability of a harmonious, well-ordered society governed in accordance with the *morale universelle*, in which the well-being of the individual and the public good are happily wed, on the other, with the reality of a society in which the vast majority of individuals follow patterns of behaviour which are at variance with the *morale universelle*. The transformation of society can therefore only be achieved by the merging of individual morality into the universal morality. The fact that

---

[12] Diderot does not consider all men to be modifiable and therefore socially redeemable. Some *malfaisants* are totally beyond recall. They are only of value to society in that their execution in a public place will act as a deterrent to others. See CORR., I. p. 214.

[13] O.PH., p. 368.

the individual is modifiable makes this operation a theoretical possibility, but what is to induce him to change his behaviour since his own nature both prevents him from obtaining a clear vision of the *morale universelle* and from conforming to it? In other words, how can the *morale universelle* be translated into a social reality, into "le bien général et commun"? The answer lies in legislation carried out by a suitably constituted form of government. The problem is in the last resort a political one and as such requires a political solution. The solution that Diderot proposes had already been outlined in the article *Autorité politique*, in the portrait of Henri IV, the archetype of the wise monarch who, guided by reason and equity, draws on the counsel of "les gens de savoir et de mérite," but who, nevertheless, is an absolute ruler, demanding from his subjects total obedience to his will. In this figure, who aspires to the title of liberator and restorer of his nation, and in his counsellors, Diderot places his hope for the salvation of society. The philosophical source of his conception of the wise ruler, who draws on the wisdom of his most enlightened subjects, as the political saviour of society lies in his conception of the creative artist and the *sage*, to which we now turn our attention.

II. *MORALE UNIVERSELLE* AND THE *SAGE*

Two years before the *Rêve* Diderot had posited the possibility of two contrasting moralities in the *Salon de 1767*:

Je pensais que s'il y avait une morale propre à une espèce, peut-être dans la même espèce y avait-il une morale propre à différents individus, ou du moins à différentes conditions ou collections d'individus semblables.[14]

The example that springs to his mind is "une morale propre aux artistes ou à l'art." [15] While Diderot admitted that man's constant aim was to achieve happiness, he equally felt within himself another need which could not be denied: the need formed by the creative impulse of the artist. Through his intimate personal experience of the processes of artistic creation, he knew that the creative impulse is restricted or subordinated at the risk of being destroyed. The striking heroic image of Dorval standing alone communing with the unchained elements is a symbol of the sovereignty of the artist through whom the creative impulse in man finds its fullest expression. The search for happiness, the prime occupation of the common man, cannot be the rule of life of the artist, for to achieve happiness one

[14] A.T., XI, p. 124.
[15] *Ibid.*

must "garder en tout un juste milieu," [16] striving constantly to reconcile personal happiness with the well-being of society. Such an attitude can only hamper the artist who, if he is to be true to the creative daemon within, must be prepared to "se jeter dans les extrêmes." [17] Sublimity in art and the attainment of happiness are two aims not easily reconcilable, in fact, "la morale aux artistes... pourrait bien être au rebours de la morale usuelle." [18]

The artist must, then, lead his life in accordance with an individualistic kind of morality which does not prevent him from giving free rein to his creative instinct. However, Diderot does not restrict the possession of this instinct to the artist in the commonly accepted sense of the term; it equally belongs to "tous ces rares et divins insensés (qui) font de la poésie dans la vie . . . les héros, les amants romanesques, les grands patriotes, les magistrats inflexibles, les apôtres de religion," and last but by no means least "les philosophes à toute outrance." [19] They are *insensés* because they do not seek happiness, indeed they cannot because this would involve compliance with the strictures of the *morale usuelle*. Their inability to reconcile their own moral perspective with that of society results inevitably in their condemnation to unhappiness:

La nature condamne au malheur celui à qui elle a départi le génie, et celle qu'elle a douée de beauté.[20]

The evolution of Diderot's conception of genius from the Dorval image of the poet afire with creative enthusiasm and condemned to an unhappy alienation from society, to the prototype of the great actor in the *Paradoxe sur le comédien*, the cold, uninvolved observer, has frequently been commented upon. It has not, however, been fully realised that the *Rêve de d'Alembert* marks the transition between the two. It is here that Diderot makes a *physiological* distinction between the Dorval genius and the *Paradoxe* genius. Discussing the relation of the brain to its nervous ramifications throughout the body, Bordeu remarks,

Le principe ou le tronc est-il trop vigoureux relativement aux branches?

---

[16] *Ibid.*, p. 125.
[17] *Ibid.*
[18] *Ibid.*, p. 124. Diderot understands by *morale usuelle* the body of principles on which a particular society has chosen to base its morality. It is not, therefore, synonymous with his ideal *morale universelle*.
[19] A.T., XI, p. 125.
[20] *Ibid.*

De là les poètes, les artistes, les gens à imagination, les hommes pusillanimes, les enthousiastes, les fous.[21]

The poet shares the same temperamental characteristics as enthusiasts and madmen, and in the portrait of Dorval the similarities are obvious. But a little further on Diderot points out that the "*grand* poète," like the "*grand* comédien" and all other men of great creative talent, will seek to "conserver à l'origine du faisceau tout son empire." [22] His emotions and instincts will at all times remain subordinate to his intelligence and as a result "il régnera sur lui-même, et sur tout ce qui l'environne. Il ne craindra pas la mort." [23] He is still separated from society but in a different way:

Les êtres sensibles ou les fous sont en scène, il est au parterre; c'est lui qui est le sage.[24]

Unlike the *rares et divins insensés* the *sage* is not an outsider condemned to alienation from society. He stands apart not because he is different, but because he is superior, the cold observer of the human comedy being played out by "les êtres sensibles, les fous."

The figure of the *sage*, which has appeared at frequent intervals in Diderot's writings, in his references to Aristus and to Socrates and embodied in the person of Saunderson in the *Lettre sur les aveugles*, becomes a focal point of his thought in the *Rêve*. In the interplay of the three characters it is Bordeu who dominates both by his personality and his intellect. D'Alembert appears as a direct successor to Dorval, the visionary enthusiast who attains to the sublime by entering a state of poetic ecstasy – the ecstasy being replaced by a feverish delirium. Mademoiselle de l'Espinasse is a *sensible*, a victim of her emotions she is the complete opposite of the *sage*. Bordeu stands out as being completely in control of the situation; he interprets and elucidates d'Alembert's feverish utterances, giving them the coherence which their author is unable to provide. While Mademoiselle de l'Espinasse is alternately moved to wonderment and apprehension at d'Alembert's behaviour, he remains quite calm and unmoved. Not only does Diderot use Bordeu as a mouthpiece to define the essential characteristics of the *sage*, he also portrays him as a *sage*. With consummate skill Diderot fuses philosophical discussion and character portrayal to-

[21] O.PH., p. 354.
[22] *Ibid.*, p. 357.
[23] *Ibid.*
[24] *Ibid.*

gether. It is only "à l'être tranquille et froid" such as Bordeu "qu'il appartient de dire: Cela est vrai, cela est bon, cela est beau." [25] Consequently it is he who comments with final authority on the issues arising out of d'Alembert's delirious utterances.

It is now possible to see why Diderot places his political faith in the wise absolute ruler who surrounds himself with advisers of equal wisdom and enlightenment. For the vast majority of men there is a divergence between their personal morality and the *morale universelle*: as their physiological organisation is imperfect they are not fully able to behave in a way which complies with the moral principles deducible from the organisation of the human race considered as a whole. This situation prevents the realisation of a harmonious, well-ordered society, both morally and politically. The *sage*, however, is fortunate in having "le système entier énergique, bien d'accord, bien ordonné." [26] He is, in fact, a microcosmic manifestation of the order and harmony of the physiological organisation of the species. Consequently there is no divergence between the private ethics of the *sage* and the *morale universelle*.[27] Therefore, only he is able to guide human society into confirming with the principles of the latter, as he alone enjoys an unrestricted vision of these principles. The *sage* is accorded this vision, not only through his intelligence, but because his whole being vibrates in unison with the universe, with nature in general, and with human nature in particular. With his fine insight into human affairs, afforded by his extraordinary powers of observation and co-ordination, with his instinctive vision of the principles on which the ideal society must be based, he is cut out by nature to bring it into being. This political *esprit de finesse* is summed up by Diderot in a passage from a fragment of a letter, possibly written to Madame de Meaux:

Il y a dans la nature ... des choses de pressentiments qui se sentent et qui ne se calculent point. Par la même raison, (les géomètres) doivent être mauvais politiques. Ils n'ont pas le nez avec lequel on évente ou saisit à la piste des phénomènes très fugitifs. Cela ne s'explique en x ou en y. Cela tient à un courant subtil des choses de la vie bien observées.[28]

[25] *Ibid.*, p. 359.
[26] *Ibid.*, p. 354   .
[27] This inherent moral quality of the ideal ruler had been defined by Diderot in political terms in his article, *Droit naturel*:
  Puisque des deux volontés l'une générale et l'autre particulière, la volonté générale n'erre jamais, il n'est pas difficile de voir à laquelle, il faudrait, pour le bonheur du genre humain, que la puissance législative appartint, et quelle vénération l'on doit aux mortels augustes dont la volonté particulière réunit et l'autorité et l'infaillibilité de la volonté générale. (O.PO., p. 34).
[28] CORR., IX, p. 245.

It is in the *sage* that Diderot's materialism ultimately escapes the inexorable necessity which bedevilled the mechanistic materialism of his time and drew it inevitably in the directon of political conservatism. For in the psychophysiological constitution of the *sage* the principle of modifiability is accompanied by an autodeterminative force which is absent in his fellow men. Admittedly the principle of modifiability itself is only admitted into Diderot's materialist view of man as the result of some dubious conceptual juggling. But from 1769 a new dynamism exists in his moral and consequently his political thought, although it is still countered by a recurrent fatalism which is a feature both of his philosophy and of his temperament.

III. PASSIVITY AND DYNAMISM

An odd alliance of a prodigiously aggressive energy and a characteristic passivity, even submissiveness, have made Diderot the most humanely attractive literary figure of his age. One can perceive in his exploitation by the publishers of the *Encyclopédie*, in his attitude to the authorities while imprisoned at Vincennes, and in his meek toleration of his wife's constant bickering, a peculiar readiness to submit to hostile forces. This passivity flows, not only from a realisation that it is pointless to oppose insurmountable odds, but also from a deep-seated longing for a life lived in peaceful harmony with his environment, whether this be his immediate relationships or the wider context of society.

The contrast between passivity and dynamism, which lies at the root of Diderot's personality, has a parallel in the opposing tendencies of his moral philosophy. His deterministic materialism has evolved a concept of man which paradoxically combines an intransigeant fatalism with a belief in man's capacity for self-modification. Similar contrasting tendencies are also to be found in his view of man's relationship to nature. On the one hand, Diderot, experiencing the powerful influence of the Rousseau of the *Discours sur l'inégalité*, holds that man should submit his destiny to the sovereign sway of nature:

Est bien mal, est bien méchant, est bien profondément pervers celui qui médite au milieu des champs. Il lutte contre l'impulsion de la nature entière qui lui répète à voix basse et sans cesse, qui lui murmure à l'oreille: Demeure en repos, demeure en repos, reste comme tout ce qui t'environne, dure comme tout ce qui t'environne, laisse aller les heures, les journées, les années, comme tout ce qui t'environne, et passe comme tout ce qui t'environne. Voilà la leçon continue de la nature.[29]

[29] CORR., IX, p. 186.

The opening thoughts echo the main theme of the *Discours*: man's reason, with which he strives to shape his destiny, is fundamentally evil, man can only achieve true fulfilment by returning to a life in harmony with the natural order. Yet we must not be deceived by the phrase "au milieu des champs"; "la nature entière" to which Diderot refers cannot be identified with the pastoral ideal which pervades the *Discours*, and in the lyrical passages in the *Confessions* and the *Rêveries*. The nature that Diderot has in mind is synonymous with the total reality in which man passes his hours, his days, his years, his whole life, and which it is futile, rather than evil, to combat. The efficacy of man's attempt to change the course of events is denied from the start in a world that is by its very nature determined, his only choice is to submit, to accept this world with its good and its evil, for both are equally necessary:

> Tout ce qui est ne peut être ni contre nature ni hors de nature.[30]

This passivity at times finds expression in a fatalistic acceptance of the contemporary world in which he lives, as when he writes in his letter to the readers of the *Encyclopédie*:

> Le monde a beau vieillir, il ne change pas; il se peut que l'individu se perfectionne, mais la masse de l'espèce ne devient ni meilleure ni pire; la somme des passions malfaisantes reste la même, les ennemis de toute chose bonne ou utile sont sans nombre aujourd'hui comme autrefois.[31]

Worn by fatigue and the constant battle against the powers that sought to prevent the completion of the *Encyclopédie* Diderot gives way to a feeling of pessimism and despondency, and submits to the belief that the struggle to improve man's condition is unavailing,[32] since the measure of good and evil in the world remain constant.

The opposing tendency, and much the stronger one, in Diderot's view of man's relationship to nature or reality, is his belief that man has an effective influence over the world he lives in, and that he can better his condition by aiding the forces for good and combatting the forces for evil. This belief corresponds to the dynamic side of his personality and to the aspect of his moral philosophy which admits man's capacity for

---

[30] O.PH., p. 380.
[31] CORR., V, pp. 80-81.
[32] A feeling echoed in a letter to Falconet: "On apprend peu de choses aux hommes. Ce n'est pas la ligne que nous écrivons qui les amende." (A.T., XVIII, p. 275).

self-modification. It is intuitive, gathering its strength from Diderot's ardent faith in the ultimate victory of truth, in the final ability of man to recognize his errors under their masks and thus overcome them. Whatever the obstacles, truth must out:

> Mais les avantages du mensonge sont d'un moment, et ceux de la vérité sont éternels; mais les suites fâcheuses de la vérité, quand elle en a, passent vite, et celles du mensonge ne finissent qu'avec lui.[33]

These opposing tendencies of Diderot's temperament, paralleled in the paradoxes contained in his moral philosophy account for the variations in his attitude to governmental authority. They are at the root of the vacillation between aggressive hostility towards the government, bordering on revolutionary fervour, and a fatalistic acceptance of the *status quo*, combined with a fear of the consequences ensuing from the disturbance of the political equilibrium, which characterises his political thought until he finally abandons his faith in the wise ruler.

The most noticeable and consistent feature, however, to emerge from the divergences of Diderot's moral thought is a contradiction between the requirements of the individual and those of society. Previously his reflections on the individual and society had remained in fairly watertight compartments so that the possibility of conflict or contradiction did not arise. In the *Lettre sur les aveugles*, for instance, there is little or no attempt to explore the problems of relating the blind man's morality to the ethical code of the sighted society in which he lives. Conversely, in his emphasis in the *Essai sur le mérite et la vertu* on natural sociability the individual is so completely subordinated to the collectivity that the question of exploring his relationship to it does not even arise. Now, however, the intuitive distinction that Diderot made between the individual and society has been incorporated into his moral philosophy.

It seems that Diderot was aware that this development risked impairing the monism essential to his materialism. At any rate he nullified any disruptive effect it might have, by restricting individuality to the person of the wise ruler whose own moral being is in harmony with the ideal moral being of society. Thus Diderot's monism remained intact on the philosophical, ethical and political planes of his thought. But however

---

[33] In the *Essai sur le mérite* Diderot does devote some pages to the possible contradiction between the interests of the individual and society, but rejects it (A.T., I, p. 66), because, as Proust points out, "Il ne raisonne pas sur ce qui est, mais sur ce qui devrait être. Il nie donc que l'intérêt particulier puisse croiser l'intérêt général parce qu'*en raison* il ne saurait en être ainsi." (*Op. cit.*, p. 412).

ingenious his efforts to maintain the unity of his thought a crack had appeared in the monolithic edifice which could only temporarily be sealed over. The conflict had been forced underground, but it continued nonetheless, creating a series of problems which preoccupied Diderot over the remarkably productive years from 1770 to 1773.

CHAPTER II

SOCIETY AND THE INDIVIDUAL

In 1770 Diderot's political thought entered a phase of swift and intense development culminating in the rejection of the figure of the wise ruler as the centre-piece of his doctrine. The abandonment of the belief that an enlightened absolute monarch could legislate to harmonise the life of the nation with the precepts of universal morality was forced upon him by the accumulation of irrefutable evidence hostile to it.[1] The radical changes taking place in Diderot's political ideas were paralleled by remarkable activity in the philosophical and literary fields. Between 1770 and 1773 he wrote the *Supplément au Voyage de Bougainville* and the *Entretien d'un père avec ses enfants*, both of them works concerned directly with philosophical and moral questions. Over the same period the fictional works of his maturity, the *Neveu de Rameau*,[2] *Jacques le Fataliste* and his best known *contes* approached their final form or were written in their entirety. These writings reflect in different ways Diderot's preoccupation with the relationship of the individual to society, and the divergent conclusions which emerge from the philosophical works on the one hand and the fiction on the other throw into relief the conflict going on in his mind.

In the *Entretien* and the *Supplément*, although his artistic concern is evident, Diderot's predominant aim is a polemical one. The dialogue technique and characterisation used in each of these works does minimise the possible stultifying effect of unadorned philosophical discourse, but the fusion between thought, character and situation which gives the

---

[1] See Part II, Chap. II.

[2] Allusions in the *Neveu de Rameau* to contemporary events show that Diderot must have started writing it in 1761 and redrafted and added to it until as late as 1776. It is difficult in a case like this to situate the work successfully in a chronological study of the author. However, as it is generally held that the most important passages were added or rewritten in 1765 and 1772, we feel justified in allowing a certain amount of latitude to include the *Neveu* for study in this chapter.

Rêve de d'Alembert its poetic profundity and persuasive power is missing. In the *Supplément* A. and B. are no more than shadowy exponents of a dialogue which lacks dialectic tension, the Aumônier is a cardboard caricature and the noble savages, Orou and the Vieillard, have dated badly since the 18th century. In the *Entretien* the balance between form and content seems at first sight to be more aesthetically satisfying: the situation is real enough, and there is a certain identity between the characters and the ideas they express. But a more critical investigation reveals that artistic considerations are outweighed by polemical aims. The potential dialectic between the arguments of father and son is upset by the fanaticism of the Abbé, and the lack of generosity shown by Moi to the sick criminal clashes sharply with his supposed wisdom as an advocate and disciple of natural equity. In each case Diderot's preoccupation with the formulation and expression of certain philosophical and ethical ideas causes him to neglect the aesthetic and psychological truthfulness of these two works.

In contrast Diderot's aims in the *Neveu de Rameau, Jacques le Fataliste* and the *contes* are essentially artistic; he is not primarily concerned to propose a particular philosophical or ethical point of view, but to create a self-justifying work of art. This is not to say that philosophical and moral issues are irrelevant to the works, on the contrary, with the characters and situations they are knitted into their very fabric. What is significant is that they are no longer seen by the reader in the persuasive context of a philosophical discourse but in the perspective of the work of art, which owes allegiance not to an external doctrine but to its own inner consistency and truth. Thus if the reader accepts the portrayal of character and situation as being psychologically and aesthetically true, then he will accept the judgment inherent in the work on the philosophical and ethical issues which the characters themselves hold or which are explored by Diderot in the *conte* or novel.[3]

While the *Supplément* and the *Entretien* pursue the inquiry into the relationship between the individual and society within the broad context of the *morale universelle*, exposed in the *Salon de 1767* and fleshed out in the *Rêve de d'Alembert*, the fiction focuses on strikingly individual characters, and plumbs for the first time the intricacies of the personal moral vision, the *morale particulière*, previously dismissed as imperfect and the source of division within society. Our task, therefore, in this chapter will be to analyse these two groups of tests in order to draw out the two sides

---

[3] We use the term "*novel*" for want of a better word, to designate the *Neveu de Rameau* and *Jacques le Fataliste*.

of the conflict going on in their author's mind between the claims of the collectivity and the rights of the individual living within it.

I. NATURAL MORALITY AND CIVILISATION

The *Entretien* and the *Supplément* provided Diderot with complementary perspectives for a critique of civilised society according to the criteria of natural morality. In the first Diderot takes up a critical position within society itself, whereas in the second the criticism derives from the contrast between civilised society and the utopian society of Tahiti where the *morale universelle* is shown in action. The effect of this dual perspective is to combine a discussion of specific aspects of civilised society: the application of justice, the attitude of the citizen towards the criminal, the role of the *sage*, with an appraisal of civilised society as a whole. In both the *Entretien* and the *Supplément* we will find that Diderot adheres strictly to the tenets of his materialism expressed in the *Rêve* and the ethical principles issuing from it.

As the *Entretien* deals primarily with the discussion of moral issues, there is little in it that can be interpreted as directly materialist in inspiration. However, some of Moi's remarks regarding the desirability of according medical attention to sick criminals give a clear indication that Diderot's view of human nature remains consistent with the biological materialism of the *Rêve*. Moi likens the criminal to "un chien enragé," "un monstre": [4] he is not morally responsible for his actions as they are due to accidental or congenital defects in his physiological organisation. The best solution for him and for society is to let him die, and the quicker the better; [5] indeed, natural equity and the good of society demand this,[6] since society can only achieve its true purpose, the conservation and happiness of its members, if the physiological organisation of the latter broadly complies with the norm of the species. Diderot's intransigeance towards the sick criminal, dictated by a thoroughgoing materialism, is here comparable to his attitude towards the unmodifiable *malfaisant* in the *Lettre à Landois*.[7]

But it is more in its assumptions regarding the question of the relationship of the individual to society that the *Entretien* is consistent with the philosophical and ethical concepts of the *Rêve*. These assumptions are expressed by Moi in the course of the discussion on the rights of the *sage* and the proper attitude to be taken toward the sick criminal.

[4] O.PH., p. 416.
[5] *Ibid.*
[6] *Ibid.*
[7] See CORR., I. p. 214.

It is Diderot himself who within the context of the *Entretien* assumes the role of the *sage* and expounds his attitude towards society and the laws governing it. When, for instance, he is criticised by his relatives for rejecting the legal ruling which was given on a particularly difficult case under discussion he points out that "la nature a fait les bonnes lois de toute éternité." [8] In other words legislation must reflect the *morale univer-selle*, the rules which permit the human race to achieve the fulfilment to which it is destined by nature. In the *Mémoires pour Catherine II* he proclaims the same idea in different terms: "La vertu se définit pour le législateur: la conformité habituelle des actions à la notion de l'utilité publique," [9] and he continues, "peut-être la même définition convient-elle au philosophe, qui est censé avoir assez de lumières pour bien connaître ce que c'est que l'utilité publique." Consequently the *sage* is only bound by the law in as far as it conforms with the dictates of nature of which he has an instinctive knowledge: "Je la cite au tribunal de mon coeur, de ma raison, de ma conscience, au tribunal de l'équité naturelle; je l'inter-roge, je m'y soumets ou je l'annule." [10]

The problem arising out of this situation – whether the *sage* should follow his own conscience and possibly infringe the law or remain sub-servient to it – had occupied Diderot's attention as early as 1767. In his *Satire contre le luxe*, inserted in the *Salon de 1767*, he had exposed two contrasting attitudes in the figures of Socrates and Aristippus. For So-crates there is no possible compromise; if the law is bad he will refuse to submit to it: "Ou je parlerai ou je périrai." [11] Aristippus, on the other hand, fearful of setting a bad example to the "multitude insensée" by such rebelliousness, is prepared to submit, but not passively: "Je ferai ma cour aux maîtres du monde; et peut-être en obtiendrai-je ou l'abolition de la loi mauvaise, ou la grâce de l'homme de bien qui l'aura enfreinte." [12] But Diderot gave no indication as to which attitude he considered to be more valid, the reason being, as we shall see, that the Socrates-Aristippus dilemma remained unresolved for him, so that according to circumstances he tended more to one side than to the other. Yet we can obtain a clearer understanding of Diderot's conception of each attitude if we read on from his definition of *vertu* in the *Mémoires pour Catherine II*. Again he evokes Socrates' unremitting hostility to a bad law and Aristippus' sub-mission and this time concludes "L'un parlait en souverain, l'autre en

[8] *Ibid.*, p. 430.
[9] MEM., p. 235.
[10] O.PH., p. 430.
[11] A.T., X, p. 123.
[12] *Ibid.*

citoyen." [13] Returning to the *Entretien*, we note that Diderot replies to his father's observation on the dangers of preaching the cult of autonomous action without reference to the law,

Je ne les prêcherai pas; il y a des vérités qui ne sont pas faites pour les fous; mais je les garderai pour moi.[14]

He freely admits that he claims no autonomy in the matter, it is for the wise ruler to legislate according to natural equity. But this does not mean that the opinion of the *sage* is of no consequence to the formulation of laws. In the article *Autorité politique* Diderot had pictured Henri IV prepared to admit to his presence "toutes sortes de personnes, de quelque état et condition qu'elles puissent être, afin que les gens de savoir et de mérite eussent le moyen d'y proposer sans crainte ce qu'ils croiraient nécessaire pour le bien public." [15] And in his political writings of this period we shall discover that he conceives of his wise monarch as absolute, but surrounded by wise counsellors who aid him in the task of legislation.[16]

But whatever his function may be as adviser to the ruler, in the *Entretien* Diderot holds that the interests and aspirations of the *sage*, similarly to those of every citizen must remain subordinate to the general good of society. The individual cannot ignore his total responsibility to the society in which he lives and any attempt to deny even part of that responsibility is tantamount to an assertion of the primacy of his individuality over and against society. This, in effect, is what Docteur Bissei does when he refuses to cast judgment on the sick criminal whom he has been called upon to cure, an attitude which provokes the following retort from Diderot:

Docteur, mais il y a une fonction commune à tout bon citoyen, à vous, à moi, c'est de travailler de toute notre force à l'avantage de la république; et il me semble que ce n'en est pas un pour elle que le salut d'un malfaiteur, dont incessament les lois la délivreront.[17]

In fact, nowhere in the *Entretien* is Diderot prepared to admit, even implicitly, that the individual has an inherent value of his own which can be appreciated outside the context of society. As we have seen, this doctrinaire opinion is most harsh in his attitude towards the sick criminal;

[13] MEM., p. 236.
[14] O.PH., p. 430.
[15] O.PO., p. 17.
[16] See Part II, Chap. II.
[17] O.PH., p. 414.

his condemnation of the felon is made in the name of the general well-being of society and not for one moment is he prepared to consider the criminal as an individual existing in his own right. The guilt a criminal may feel arises solely from the knowledge that he has transgressed society's laws and that he will be punished if his crime is discovered:

Le remords naît peut-être moins de l'horreur de soi que de la crainte des autres; moins de la honte de l'action que du blâme et du châtiment qui la suivrait s'il arrivait qu'on la découvrît.[18]

The hesitant tone of the argument does not arise from Diderot's uncertainty as to its validity, but from a desire to soften the blow of such audacious thinking on his reader. For audacious it is; Diderot rejects the idea that a man can be as much guided in his behaviour by the strength of his desire to maintain his own personal moral integrity as by the knowledge that his every action is open to acceptance or condemnation by society. The individual can only acquire significance and value by subordination to the society of which he is a member.

Whereas the materialism of the *Entretien* remains implicit, Diderot makes it abundantly clear in the *Supplément au Voyage de Bougainville* that his conception of man's nature, physical and moral, remains entirely consistent with that of the *Rêve*. In the dialogue between A. and B. the former states that the law of nature is "gravée au fond de nos coeurs." [19] B. in turn criticises A.'s remark for its incipient *innéisme*, and in so doing resumes the central philosophical and ethical themes of the *Rêve*:

Cela n'est pas exact. Nous n'apportons en naissant qu'une similitude d'organisation avec d'autres êtres, les mêmes besoins, de l'attrait vers les mêmes plaisirs, une aversion commune pour les mêmes peines; ce qui constitue l'homme ce qu'il est, et doit fonder la morale qui lui convient.[20]

Diderot's evocation of life in the primitive society of Tahiti gives substance to the principles contained in this passage. The inhabitants of Tahiti are the children of nature; the womenfolk are beautiful and fecund, the menfolk immensely strong and agile, and we are led to believe that they retain their natural capacities for a far longer span of time than is normal among Europeans. Their physical perfection goes hand in hand with a natural instinctive wisdom which pervades their personal relation-

[18] *Ibid.*, pp. 428-429.
[19] O.PH., p. 505.
[20] *Ibid.*

ship and directs the evolution of their society along lines designed to maintain it in close harmony with its natural environment. The whole moral code of Tahitian society is based simply and solely on the fulfilment of the natural physical requirements of its members, the satisfaction of the sexual instinct, the provision of food and shelter, and a regular amount of rest and sleep. The only restrictions placed on sexual activities are designed to prevent the association of the sexual act with mere gratification, rather than its true purpose, which is to increase the population and thus further the well-being of the society by strengthening its manpower. The islanders' labour is limited to providing sufficient nourishment and shelter for their needs, there is no question of working for superfluous luxuries.

In this portrait of the ideal primitive society Diderot seeks to demonstrate his belief, consistent with his materialist view of man, that the only desirable morality is one which is oriented towards the fulfilment and satisfaction of man's biological needs. It is therefore consistent that the disruptive influences of the European visitors lamented by the Vieillard should be in the first place of a specifically physical nature: the sailors' perverse sexual sophistication has aroused unknown desires in the native women leading to a flaring up of hatred and jealousy between them, and they have poisoned the blood of the race with venereal disease. By upsetting the harmony of the race in the physical sphere of their sexuality, they have introduced disharmony into the emotional, spiritual and social spheres as well:

L'idée de crime et le péril de la maladie sont entrées avec toi parmi nous. Nos jouissances autrefois si douces sont accompagnées de remords et d'effroi.[21]

The vice and immortality which the European sailors have introduced among the Tahitians may take on various psychological forms which are not directly related to their physical sources, but in the last analysis the symptoms can be traced back to an imbalance or disorder of a physiological nature. The same is true of European society; Orou, in a swift diagnosis of the ills of the civilised world successively details the various symptoms until he reaches their root cause:

La société, dont votre chef vous vante le bel ordre, ne sera qu'un ramas ou d'hypocrites, qui foulent aux pieds les lois; ou d'infortunés, qui sont eux-mêmes les instruments de leur supplice, en s'y soumettant; ou d'imbéciles, en

[21] *Ibid.*, p. 470.

qui le préjugé a tout à fait étouffé la voix de la nature; ou d'êtres mal organisés, en qui la nature ne réclame pas ses droits.[22]

The term *êtres mal organisés* is strikingly reminiscent of the language used in the *Rêve de d'Alembert* and furnishes unequivocal evidence that the moral and philosophical view of human nature contained in the *Supplément* is in strict conformity with the principles formulated in the *Rêve*.

The continuity of thought from the *Entretien* to the *Supplément* becomes all the more evident if we consider the history of their composition. The *Entretien* must have been written between Diderot's journey to Langres and Bourbonne in August 1770 and its publication in the number of Grimm's *Correspondance littéraire* which appeared on the 1st March 1771. Towards the end of that year Diderot composed an article on the *Voyage de Bougainville* which was to provide the starting-point for the *Supplément*, which in turn was completed by October 1772.[23] Bougainville's *Voyage* itself appeared early in 1771, the *privilège* is dated the 27th February; so it is possible that Diderot had read it before handing in his text of the *Entretien* to Grimm. What makes this seem likely is a passage from one of Diderot's speeches in the *Entretien*:

Est-ce que l'homme n'est pas antérieur à l'homme de loi? Est-ce que la raison de l'espèce humaine n'est pas tout autrement sacrée que la raison d'un législateur? *Nous nous appelons civilisés, et nous sommes pires que des sauvages.* Il semble qu'il nous faille encore tournoyer pendant des siècles, d'extravagances en extravagances et d'erreurs en erreurs, pour arriver où la première étincelle du jugement, l'instinct seul, nous eût menés tout droit.[24]

Whether this passage was inspired by his reading of the *Voyage* or not, it does provide a direct link between the *Entretien* and the *Supplément* and furnishes proof that these two works share a common philosophical perspective, the second continuing the discussion of the themes raised in the first. Diderot has used the debate in the *Entretien* to argue that the only good laws are those which are in accordance with a true assessment of the nature of the human race, and have been dictated by "la raison de l'espèce humaine," which, transposed into philosophical terms, becomes *la morale universelle*. In the *Supplément* he portrays an ideal society of savages in which the laws still comply with "la raison de l'espèce

---

[22] *Ibid.*, p. 484.
[23] Subsequent alterations made between 1778 and 1779 do not substantially change the text.
[24] O.PH., p. 436. Our italics.

humaine," in contrast with European society where this is no longer the case.

As the *morale universelle* carries with it an implicit rejection of the value of the individual, it may seem surprising that Diderot's main attack against Christian morality, in the *Supplément,* should be on the grounds that marriage violates the freedom of the individual. This violation is defined as a denial of human nature, for marriage rests on the assumption that "un être sentant, pensant et libre, peut être la propriété d'un être semblable à lui"; [25] it is also an institution which fails to recognise the continual change taking place within us, and which demands a constancy and fidelity which by our nature we cannot maintain. The diatribe ends with the striking picture of two beings of flesh swearing "un serment d'immutabilité . . . à la face d'un ciel qui n'est pas un instant le même, sous des antres qui menacent ruine; au bas d'une roche qui tombe en poudre; au pied d'un arbre qui se gerce; sur une pierre qui s'ébranle." [26] The universe undergoes constant change, so men, themselves material phenomena, cannot escape the common fate of the whole of which they are part. Orou, the Tahitians' spokesman, concludes that the institution of marriage has been one of the prime contributary factors to the dehumanisation of men in European society: "Crois-moi, vous avez rendu la condition de l'homme pire que celle de l'animal." [27]

But can we infer from this argument that Diderot, while remaining faithful to his materialistic philosophy, here admits that the individual has an inherent value which elsewhere he rejects? On the face of it, this would seem to be the case; the overall impression one receives is that by his condemnation of the dehumanising effect of marriage he is seeking to restore human personality to the fulness of its true nature. As Herbert Dieckmann points out:

Il apparaît clairement que la protestation contre les idées morales faussement attachées à certaines actions (. . .) signifie . . . la reconnaissance de la morale vraie, de la morale naturelle selon laquelle l'être humain n'est pas un objet mais une personne douée de libre arbitre.[28]

It is debatable whether *libre arbitre* is the right term to use here as technically it would imply that Diderot has rejected his determinism, which is not the case. Nevertheless it is true that through Orou he is fulminating

---

[25] *Ibid.,* p. 480.
[26] *Ibid.*
[27] *Ibid.,* pp. 480-481.
[28] *Supplément au Voyage de Bougainville* ed. H. Dieckmann, p. xxxvii.

against an institution which, in his opinion, deprives the individual of his humanity. Yet it would be unwise to assume that in a work which is pervaded by his materialism, a materialism that sets the collectivity before the individual, Diderot is now prepared to reverse the order, even partially, and concern himself with the individual for his own sake. Dieckmann has shown that the *Supplément* can be divided into two main parts with regard to the question of free sexual union, the critical and the positive.[29] The apparent reinstatement of the individual within Diderot's scheme of thought is situated in the first part, Chapter III of the *Supplément*, in which Christian sexual morality undergoes a scathing attack. However, to obtain a true picture of his thought on the matter we must turn to the second part, corresponding to Chapter V of the *Supplément* in which he sets out positive proposals on sexual union.

In this chapter Orou explains to the Aumônier the completely different rules which govern sexual relations in Tahiti. Fornication, incest and adultery are empty words, the only guiding lines are "le bien général et l'utilité particulière." [30] Orou gives a clearer idea of what these terms signify when he explains how "l'idée de richesse particulière ou publique, unie dans nos têtes à l'idée de population, épure nos moeurs." [31] Sexual relations are entirely subjected to the increase in material wealth which is brought about by an increasing population. As we have noted, the only restrictions placed upon free union are those levied against sexual activities simply intended to procure physical gratification. These apart, all kinds of sexual union are permissible, including those which would be considered incestuous in European society. Even the hospitality offered by the Tahitians has a practical purpose, the improvement of the race by the introduction of new blood, together with an increase in its numbers.

As a result of this purely utilitarian approach to sexual relationships, union is reduced to a simple physical act devoid of any emotional or spiritual overtones. Consequently, as the Aumônier rightly observes, such delicate and yet powerful emotions as marital tenderness and paternal love are foreign to Tahiti.[32] Orou's reply disturbs as much by its unconscious cynicism as by the sweeping generalisation it contains: he asks the Aumônier if "dans quelque contrée que ce soit, il y a un père qui, sans la honte qui le retient, n'aimât mieux perdre son enfant, un mari qui n'aimât mieux perdre sa femme, que sa fortune et l'aisance de toute sa

---

[29] *Ibid.*, p. xlii.
[30] O.PH., p. 495.
[31] *Ibid.*, p. 498.
[32] O.PH., pp. 498-499.

vie." [33] He refuses to accept that even the strongest and most intimate relationships can survive unless they are cemented by personal interest, and he continues,

Sois sûr que partout où l'homme sera attaché à la conservation de son semblable comme à son lit, à sa santé, à son repos, à sa cabane, à ses fruits, à ses champs, il fera pour lui tout ce qu'il est possible de faire.[34]

A purely materialistic self-interest governs human relations in Tahiti; a suffering child is wept over, a fertile woman, a nubile girl, an adolescent boy are highly prized, because "leur conservation est toujours un accroissement, et leur perte toujours une diminution de fortune." [35] The apparent attempt by Diderot to counteract the dehumanising effect of marriage and restore to the individual his essential humanity is effaced by a contradictory argument which more than ever transforms men and women into objects and means. With an uncompromising logic he has created a society in which the quality of human relationships depend upon the economic, utilitarian value of individuals, a society in which the old and the barren are looked upon as so much superfluous dross. Far from restoring to the individual the dignity and respect of which the corrupt morality of European society has deprived him, Diderot has succeeded in reducing him to complete subservience physically, emotionally and spiritually to the society of which he is a member.

Herbert Dieckmann has sought to defend Diderot by suggesting that his arguments for a social-utilitarian morality are motivated by a reaction against the celibacy of the priesthood and monasticism, and against the dangers of *libertinage* which threatened to destroy men's deep emotions and physical appetites.[36] Gilbert Chinard has also pointed to the influence on Diderot of the *économistes*, one of whose main concerns was the supposed depopulation of France.[37] These explanations contribute to our understanding of Diderot's conception of the relationship between the individual and society in the *Supplément*, but clearly they fall short of providing the whole answer. Dieckmann further argues that another motive can be found in Diderot's "penchant à s'échauffer sur les vertus bourgeoises, l'utilité sociale et le bien-être du genre humain" which were deeply rooted in his nature.[38] Although we agree that Diderot's enthusiasm

[33] *Ibid.*, pp. 499.
[34] *Ibid.*
[35] *Ibid.*
[36] *Op. cit.*, p. xliii.
[37] See *Supplément au Voyage de Bougainville* ed. G. Chinard, Introduction.
[38] *Op. cit.*, p. xliv.

for "l'utilité sociale et le bien-être du genre humain" has its source in his profoundly sociable and generous temperament, and contributed to the formation of his utopian vision of Tahitian society, we cannot see how they can be grouped together with his predilection for "les vertus bourgeoises," particularly as family loyalty and a belief in the value of individualism, bourgeois virtues par excellence are diametrically opposed to the collectivist society represented in the *Supplément*. Much as Diderot's reaction against the restrictions of contemporary society, the contemporary popularity of populationist thought, and his own natural inclinations to sociability may have influenced him, the main source of his inspiration lies in his monist materialism and the social ethics he derives therefrom. In the first part of Orou's conversation with the Aumônier Diderot's rejection of Christian sexual morality rests upon his contention that it ignores man's basic nature, his physiological nature. In the second part he replaces Christian morality by one which is based upon a true scientific understanding of man's nature. Tahitian morality is, in effect, an outstanding example of a society governed by the tenets of the *morale universelle* and untouched by the vitiating effects of the *morale particulière*.

The social values which flow from Diderot's materialist ethics are daunting in the extreme. Everywhere the individual is reduced to total subservience to the collectivity. He is no more than a utility, his acceptance and cultivation by the community being strictly proportionate to the services he is able to render. If through no fault of his own because of age or infirmity he is unable to fulfil the duties demanded of him, he is cast off and treated as a pariah. Worse still, if he commits a serious crime he can expect no mercy; since his behaviour is deemed to be the consequence of an abnormal organisation, rehabilitation is out of the question. There is no alternative to his destruction. Such are the social implications of Diderot's philosophical intransigency. If this were his last word on the matter it would be difficult to award him the title of humanist in any meaningful sense. However, other avenues of investigation lay open to a man of such varied talents. The art of fiction in particular enabled him to pursue his enquiries unhampered by the conceptual limitations of his speculative thought.

II. THE UNIQUENESS OF THE INDIVIDUAL

In the *Neveu de Rameau, Jacques le Fataliste* and the *contes* Diderot's approach is no longer governed by his philosophical and ethical preoccupations but by a desire to fulfil certain aesthetic criteria, namely that the tale told should provide through the plausibility of its characters and action a convincing though not direct reflection of the world. With the exception of two early works, *Les Bijoux Indiscrets* and *L'Oiseau blanc,* Diderot avoided forms of narrative fiction which did not satisfy these criteria. His hostility to the traditional novel, so noticeable in *Jacques le Fataliste*, arises from his distaste for its artificiality of style, the improbability of story and characters, and the temptation it presented to indulge in elaborate description and invention which contravene truth. The allegory, which as a genre is completely unrelated to the here and now, aroused his hostility even more than the novel if his scornful satire of it in *Jacques* is anything to go by.[39] As for the *conte*, in an epilogue to *Les Deux Amis de Bourbonne* Diderot distinguishes three kinds: the *conte merveilleux* or heroic tale, the *conte plaisant*, and the *conte historique*. The first two do not comply with the demands of reality and truth, the former because "la nature y est exagérée; la vérité y est hypothétique," in entering it "vous mettez le pied dans une terre inconnue, où rien ne se passe comme dans celle que vous habitez, mais où tout se fait en grand comme les choses se font autour de vous en petit." [40] In the second "le conteur ne se propose ni l'imitation de la nature, ni la vérité ni l'illusion; il s'élance dans les espaces imaginaires." [41] The author of the *conte historique* alone "a pour objet la vérité rigoureuse; il veut être cru," [42] and this is the aim of Diderot not only in his *contes* but in *Le Neveu* and *Jacques* as well.

The question arises as to how reality and truth can be reconciled with art. How can the artist who brings invention to the creative process, and who wants to captivate and move his reader, at the same time communicate reality and truth through his work? Diderot himself admits that the author cannot achieve his effect without eloquence and poetry, but eloquence is a kind of lie and nothing is more opposed to the illusion of reality than poetry.[43] The solution is to counteract the exaggerating effect of both by the introduction of natural incidents into the narrative which enable the author to maintain the essential link with reality:

Il parsèmera son récit de petites circonstances si liées à la chose, de traits si simples, si naturels, et toutefois si difficiles à imaginer, que vous serez forcé de vous dire en vous-même: Ma foi, cela est vrai; on n'invente pas ces choses-là. C'est ainsi qu'il sauvera l'exagération de l'éloquence et de la poésie; que la vérité de la nature couvrira le prestige de l'art; et qu'il satisfaira à deux

[39] O.RO., p. 514.
[40] *Ibid.*, pp. 790-791.
[41] *Ibid.*, p. 791.
[42] *Ibid.*
[43] *Ibid.*

conditions qui semblent contradictoires, d'être en même temps historien et poète, véridique et menteur.[44]

Thus while maintaining his freedom as an artist to exploit his creative powers Diderot also satisfies the fundamental dictum of his aesthetics, that the artist in order to be true must remain faithful to nature. In both his philosophical writings and his fiction, then, Diderot is engaged in what is essentially an objective study of human behaviour and organisation. But whereas in his philosophical writings he bases his investigation upon the data obtained from a scientific assessment of man's biological organisation and then deduces a system of ethics from it, his *contes* and novels are created out of the information gleaned from his observation of the people and situations belonging to the milieu in which he lived and moved. Furthermore, in the former he is seeking to establish generally valid principles and rules, whereas in the latter, unhampered by any *a priori* ideas about human nature and behaviour, his sole purpose is to tell a story in which characters and situations appear to be drawn from reality. There is no attempt to make the *contes* and novels vehicles for his philosophical and moral thought as happens in his theatre. Robert Niklaus has remarked on this essential difference between his dramatic and narrative fiction:

Son théâtre (...) n'est pas vraisemblable car il présente des personnages qui se définissent par ce qu'ils doivent être et jamais par ce qu'ils sont. Par

---

[44] *Ibid.* In a most perceptive article on the *contes*, *The Presentation of reality in Diderot's tales*, Herbert Dieckmann sets the reader on his guard against an uncritical acceptance of Diderot's remarks in the epilogue to *Les deux amis de Bourbonne*. In particular he argues that Diderot has established a fundamental antithesis which the device of studding the narrative of a *conte* with simple, natural incidents cannot solve. The antithesis arises from Diderot's claim that, as Dieckmann puts it, "the author of the "conte historique" aims at strict truth ("il a pour objet la vérité rigoureuse") and that he intends to deceive the reader." "Diderot," continues Dieckmann, "seems to have jotted down his ideas somewhat hastily: the question of truth and reality in the choice of plot and characters is amalgamated with that of the creation of illusion, and the author's tendency to "invent" is identified with his deliberate intention" (*Op. cit.*, p. 106). While we agree that Diderot has to some extent confused his terminology, we cannot altogether share Dieckmann's view that this passage contains an insoluble antithesis. In his argument Diderot uses the term *vérité* twice, but he endows it with different meanings. When he says that the "conteur historique a pour objet la vérité rigoureuse", he is referring to the underlying truth about men and things not always visible to the unpractised eye. This is the truth that he sets out to reveal in his *contes*, a truth distorted and hidden by layers of conventional wisdom and morality. This essential truth is not the same thing as reality ("la vérité de la nature"), whose illusion is ensured by the incorporation of naturalistic detail into the narrative. It is by this very marriage of reality with invention, by the imaginative transposition and reorganisation of events that Diderot seeks to grasp that "vérité rigoureuse" which no objective reporting of men's affairs can hope to convey.

contre les personnages des contes nous paraissent vivants parce que dans leur cas l'auteur n'a pas confondu le devoir avec la chose.[45]

However, although the *contes* and novels cannot be considered *pièces à thèse*, they are nonetheless connected in various ways with Diderot's thought. Much of *Le Neveu* consists of a moral and philosophical dialogue which deals with subjects which appear in Diderot's philosophical writings. In *Jacques* the main protagonist is an exponent of a fatalism which is a naive version of Diderot's own determinism. The *contes* themselves contain little discussion of moral and philosophical issues, but in the *Supplément* the fates of the various characters who appear in them, the depravity of the ones and the unhappiness of the others, are held to be the result of the sophistication of natural appetites in European society.[46]

Rameau and Jacques both project different aspects of Diderot's materialist determinism, but in these two novels the author dissociates himself from his philosophy and in so doing undertakes a test of its validity. Accepting that Rameau and Jacques are plausible characters, whose portrayal complies with a realist aesthetic, the credibility of the theories they hold will depend on the extent to which they themselves are consistent with them. In this way Diderot effects what Lester Crocker has called an "expérience morale," [47] whereby he seeks to verify the principles of his philosophy in an artistically created but nonetheless real world of characters and situations.

Rameau attempts to justify his moral depravity by arguing that forces outside his control have determined the nature of his personality. When Moi asks him why he should be so sensitive to the beauties of music and yet so blind to the beauties of morality and insensitive to the charms of virtue, he replies:

C'est apparemment qu'il y a pour les unes un sens que je n'ai pas, une fibre qui ne m'a point été donnée ... La molécule paternelle était dure et obtuse, et cette maudite molécule première s'est assimilé tout le reste.[48]

In this explanation of his moral depravity Rameau reasserts the biological materialism of the *Rêve de d'Alembert*. The moral nature of the individual is ultimately dependent on his physiological organisation: in his case a congenital defect which manifests itself in an inability to attach any

[45] "Diderot et le conte philosophique," p. 302.
[46] O.PH., pp. 514-515.
[47] See "*Jacques le Fataliste*," an "expérience morale" and "*Le Neveu de Rameau, une expérience morale*."
[48] O.RO., p. 473.

moral significance to life has infected his whole system. Indeed, not only does he share Diderot's materialist interpretation of human personality but he applies it in an extreme form. For when Moi asks him if he will not try to prevent his son from being affected by the "maudite molécule paternelle" he replies:

J'y travaillerais; je crois, bien inutilement. S'il est destiné à devenir un homme de bien, je n'y nuirai pas. Mais si la molécule voulait qu'il fût un vaurien comme son père, les peines que j'aurai pour en faire un homme honnête lui seraient très nuisibles.[49]

This is materialism in its most uncompromisingly deterministic mood. All attempts by the individual concerned, by those responsible for his education, or by society at large to change or modify his personality are bound to fail. Out of sheer biological necessity men are fated to keep the personality they received at birth.

Jacques equally holds a deterministic view of the world which he refers to by the quaint image of the celestial roll on which is written all the good and evil which occurs on earth. Similarly his conception of human nature is materialist, thought less explicitly so: human behaviour is not the result of the operation of free will but of an inner necessity imposed on the individual by his physical nature.

Il prétendait qu'on était heureusement ou malheureusement né ... Il croyait qu'un homme s'acheminait aussi nécessairement à la gloire ou à l'ignominie, qu'une boule qui aurait la conscience d'elle-même suit la pente d'une montagne; et que, si l'enchaînement des causes et des effets qui forment la vie d'un homme depuis le premier instant de sa naissance jusqu'à son dernier soupir nous était connu, nous resterions convaincu qu'il n'a fait que ce qu'il était nécessaire de faire.[50]

Jacques' naive fatalism is not as uncompromising as Rameau's more sophisticated biological materialism, as he does admit that men can be modified by reward or punishment. However, our interest lies not so much in the difference between Rameau's and Jacques' philosophies, as in the light which is thrown upon them in the respective works.

Rameau, as we have seen, believes that his turpitude has a physiological cause, an explanation which Diderot the philosopher would accept. Yet doubts arise when one attempts to verify the validity of Rameau's claim

[49] *Ibid.*
[50] O.RO., p. 670.

that he has complied with the inner necessity of his nature by attaining to a state of "parfaite abjection" [51] and has thus achieved the happiness which, according to his and Diderot's principles, must inevitably result from such compliance. For Rameau is not the "brigand heureux avec des brigands opulents" [52] that he purports to be. His present misfortune has come about because once in his life he dared to show "un peu de goût, un peu de raison," [53] thereby losing the favour of his protectors and the living he earned as their resident clown. He realises that by this momentary rebellion against his state of abjection he has refused to comply with what he considers to be his inner nature and he regrets it bitterly: "Rameau, mon ami, cela vous apprendra à rester ce que Dieu vous fit." [54] But there is something within him which prevents him from returning to the Bertin-Hus household and undergoing the debasing humiliation which would be required of him in return for the restoration of his living:

> Tenez, monsieur, cela ne se peut . . . je me sens là quelque chose qui s'élève et qui me dit: Rameau, tu n'en feras rien. Il faut qu'il y ait une certaine dignité attachée à la nature de l'homme, que rien ne peut étouffer.[55]

He knows full well that if he wants to have a full stomach everyday, to be clothed and sheltered and to enjoy the company of men akin to himself, then he has only to go back and apologise. But stronger than his physical needs and the inclinations of his temperament there exists an inextinguishable desire to preserve his personal integrity. Once a man abdicates his dignity against his will he loses all self-respect and ultimately his humanity. Rameau knows this "mépris de soi-même, ou ce tourment de la conscience qui naît de l'inutilité des dons que le ciel nous a départis; c'est le plus cruel de tous" and he concludes: "Il vaudrait presque autant que l'homme ne fût pas né." [56]

Jacques has not the complexity which makes Rameau one of the most profound and original creations of French literature, but there exists within him a similar conflict between his philosophical interpretation of human nature and his own actions. When, for example, his master submits to him that, in involving himself in a dispute without knowing how it originated, he had contravened the principles of his fatalism, Jacques admits: "Je pense d'une façon, et je ne saurais m'empêcher de faire d'une

[51] *Ibid.*, p. 474.
[52] *Ibid.*, p. 434.
[53] *Ibid.*, p. 409.
[54] *Ibid.*
[55] *Ibid.*, p. 411.
[56] *Ibid.*, p. 413.

autre." [57] While believing implicitly that men's hopes, joys and afflictions are all equally pointless, he is unable to prevent himself from laughing and crying.[58] He has tried a hundred times to become a consistent fatalist, to free himself from all care and accept life as it comes, willy nilly, and, indeed, his efforts are sometimes crowned with success, but, he adds, "le diable est que cela ne dure pas, et que, dur et ferme comme un rocher dans les grandes occasions, il arrive souvent qu'une petite contradiction, une bagatelle me déferre." [59] By an effort of will he can force himself to conform so far to his principles but no farther; a point is reached where, as with Rameau, unexplicable, irrational characteristics hidden in his personality reassert themselves.

Both Rameau and Jacques have discovered, partly by conscious reflection, partly by intuition, that a constant adherence to their deterministic philosophies, which involves a denial of what is most profoundly human in them, must finally lead to the destruction of their personalities. Furthermore, as Moi points out to Rameau when he asks why nature has not made men of genius as good as they are great, if we try to impose a perfect consistency on reality when it does not exist, then we logically renounce the right to our own existence as imperfect beings unable to achieve this consistency in our own lives.[60] Having reached this *impasse* on the level of experience and reflection both Rameau and Jacques opt naturally for existence rather than annihilation. The most important thing for each of them in the final analysis is not that the world or their own actions should conform with their deterministic views, but that they should *be* and be themselves. In concurring with Moi's argument Rameau says:

Le point important est que vous et moi nous soyons, et que nous soyons vous et moi. Que tout aille d'ailleurs comme il pourra. Le meilleur ordre des choses, à mon avis, est celui où j'en devais être, et foin du plus parfait des mondes, si je n'en suis pas. J'aime mieux être, et même être impertinent raisonneur, que de n'être pas.[61]

And he is echoed by Jacques who has renounced attempting to be a consistent fatalist:

J'ai pris le parti d'être comme je suis.[62]

[57] *Ibid.*, p. 579.
[58] *Ibid.*, p. 573.
[59] *Ibid.*, p. 574.
[60] *Ibid.*, p. 405.
[61] *Ibid.*
[62] *Ibid.*, p. 574.

In both cases experience has shown them that their determinism falls short of providing sufficient explanation of their personalities or of life as a whole. But it would be wrong to assume that as a result of their discovery either Jacques or Rameau abandon their philosophies or that in the perspective of each work determinism or the materialism on which it is based, stand condemned. Jacques does not abandon his fatalism as the result of his discovery, instead he expands it to include his personality as it stands with all its contradictions:

J'ai pris le parti d'être comme je suis; et j'ai vu, en y pensant un peu, que cela revenait presque au même, en ajoutant: Qu'importe comme on soit? C'est une autre résignation plus facile et plus commode.[63]

Similarly Moi, having demonstrated the weakness in Rameau's argument, does not condemn his materialism outright, but explains that it must accept reality as it is, and not impose upon it a pattern to which it manifestly does not conform:

Acceptons donc les choses comme elles sont. Voyons ce qu'elles nous coûtent et ce qu'elles nous rendent, et laissons là le tout que nous ne connaissons pas assez pour le louer ou le blâmer, et qui n'est peut-être ni bien ni mal, s'il est nécessaire, comme beaucoup de gens l'imaginent.[64]

What conclusions can we draw from Diderot's experiment in Le Neveu

---

[63] Ibid., Diderot's treatment of the theme of fatalism in Jacques le Fataliste is open, on the face of it, to strikingly contradictory interpretations. Arguing with Paul Janet ("Philosophie de Diderot, dernier mot d'un matérialiste"), who makes out a case for Diderot's abandonment of materialism in the latter part of his life, it might be claimed that Jacques is a satire on all forms of determinism, materialism included. On the other hand, it may be held with Paul Hazard (La Pensée européennee au dix-huitième siècle, II, p. 147) that at the end of the book victory lies with Jacques, and fatalism is thus vindicated. A third, more prudent view is that the novel is ambivalent, and that no clear case can be made out from it for or against fatalism. All three interpretations are mistaken in our view. Despite the temptation to attribute to Jacques le Fataliste a characteristic which is frequently held to give a novel in part its aesthetic letters of credence, the work is not ambivalent. But neither is it a simple attack on fatalism or a defence of it. Rather, as J. R. Loy has pointed out, it is "somewhere between (...). The answer ... lies in the direction of determinism and moral freedom" (Diderot's Determined Fatalist, p. 151); by the latter he means the freedom achieved by the mind or will-power acting on the determinant to change it and thus become part of that determinant, with the consequence that it is no longer effect but cause (Ibid., p. 131). This self-creating psychological causality is consonant with deterministic materialism, as the theory of consciousness developed by Diderot in the Réfutation d'Helvétius shows (see next chapter). In fact Jacques' expanded fatalism is a simply expressed form of the sophisticated determinism of the Réfutation, although Jacques himself does not understand its implications, and fails to appreciate that far from being "une autre résignation plus facile et plus commode," it constitutes an acceptance of the dynamic, constantly self-creating character of the human mind and personality.

[64] Ibid., p. 405.

and *Jacques*? The first is that without abjuring his deterministic materialism he comes to realise that in its present form it provides an insufficient
explanation of the contradictions and inconsistencies of human nature. A
dogmatic materialism which forces human behaviour into a falsely consistent pattern incurs three dangers. Firstly, it risks becoming entirely divorced from the reality on which it purports to be based. Secondly, by
formulating value judgments, by classifying human beings as *bienfaisant*
and *malfaisant*, by dividing natural phenomena into categories of normal
and abnormal, it unjustifiably implies the existence of an ethical dualism
inherent in nature itself, and thus contradicts the truth of the axiom, stated
by Diderot himself, that "il n'y a rien d'imparfait dans la nature, pas
même les monstres. Tout y est enchaîné, et le monstre y est un effet aussi
nécessaire que l'animal parfait." [65] Thirdly, and most dangerous of all,
by denying man's capacity for disinterested love and his inherent need
to maintain his dignity and self-respect it divests him of his essentially human characteristics and thereby reduces him to something less than human.

Their literary merit apart, *Le Neveu* and *Jacques* bear witness to Diderot's remarkable intellectual honesty and humility and to his uncompromising search for truth. For in these two works he has unflinchingly
put to the test the conclusion of years of arduous speculation, itself based
upon a vast amount of diligently acquired data. Having taken nature, in
the sense of man's physiological organisation as the foundation for his philosophy, he now returns once more to nature, in the sense of human personality and behaviour, in order to judge the validity of his deductions.
No scientific treatise, no philosophic discourse could ever carry out this
test successfully, for science and philosophy cannot conceive or grasp human personality and behaviour in all its dimensions. The artist's imagination alone is capable of investigating this reality in the process of recreating
it, hence Diderot could only realise his intentions in works of creative literature. This investigation has led to a partial collapse of the monolithic
edifice of his philosophical and ethical thought. The crack caused by his
attempt to reconcile his concept of the individual with his capacity for
moral modification into an overall deterministic view of man,[66] has widen-
ed into a great breach as a result of the confrontation between his philosophical and artistic, his rational and his intuitive conceptions of human
personality. One can search in vain among the *philosophes*, his contemporaries, for a man who possessed to an equal degree the same combination

[65] A.T., XV, p. 185.
[66] See pp. 29-30.

of intellectual powers, humility and love of truth, which enabled Diderot to resist the temptation of maintaining an intellectually satisfying system regardless of its credibility. He alone fully escapes Rousseau's scathing condemnation of the pride of the *philosophes* who were in the opinion of the Genevan more concerned with procuring their own glory than with serving the cause of truth:

Quand les philosophes seraient en état de découvrir la vérité, qui d'entre eux prendrait intérêt à elle? Chacun sait bien que son système n'est pas mieux fondé que les autres; mais il le soutient parce qu'il est à lui. Il n'y en a pas un seul qui, venant à connaître le vrai et le faux, ne préférât le mensonge qu'il a trouvé à la vérité découverte par un autre. Où est le philosophe qui, pour sa gloire, ne tromperait pas volontiers le genre humain? [67]

Diderot may have been carried away in a wave of indignant idealism when he countered Frederick II's cynicism with the claim that "l'homme cherche sans cesse la vérité; c'est le but de toutes ses études, de tous ses soins, de tous ses travaux," [68] but it never ceased to be true of his own aspirations.

We now turn to the challenge to Diderot's moral thought that *Le Neveu* and *Jacques* provided. Where Jacques finds the distinction between a physical and a moral world meaningless,[69] Diderot is now forced to recognise that the relationship between the two is far more complex than he was previously prepared to admit. The factors motivating human behaviour cannot so easily be reduced to the play of self-interest seeking to satisfy physical needs. Jacques, for instance, regrets an act of generosity towards an old woman, which left him in a state of penury with nothing to show for it. But his master insists that the principal merit of his charitable action lies in the forgetting of his own need, and that even if he had to die on a dunghill as a result, he would die satisfied with himself.[70] The realisation that virtuous acts are not always motivated by self-interest is firmly stated in a letter to Tronchin written while Diderot was working on *Jacques*:

J'ai bien reconnu que j'étais possédé du démon de la bienfaisance, puisqu' après l'avoir exercé dans toute son étendue, je n'en étais pas revenu. Est bien insensé celui qui secourt l'humanité, s'il s'en propose quelque retour. Malheur

[67] *Profession de foi*, p. 61.
[68] *Pages contre un tyran*, O.PO., p. 135.
[69] O.RO., p. 670.
[70] *Ibid.*, p. 571.
[71] CORR., XII, p. 92.

à celui qui s'est promis de ses bonnes actions d'autre récompense que celle qu'il a dû trouver au fond de son coeur.[71]

The magic formula inherited from Shaftesbury whereby virtue inevitably leads to happiness is discredited. Already in *Le Fils Naturel* characters had discovered that virtue often involves sacrifice. In the *Rêve de d'Alembert* Diderot had begun to question the identity of virtue with happiness. Yet still in his more polemical moments he tended to return to the old formula:

LUI: ... Mais, à votre compte, il faudrait donc être d'honnêtes gens?
MOI: Pour être heureux? assurément.
LUI: Cependant je vois une infinité d'honnêtes gens qui ne sont pas heureux et une infinité de gens qui sont heureux sans être honnêtes.[72]

Moi's retort, "Il vous semble," does little to lessen the weight of Rameau's argument. Happiness is a highly subjective phenomenon and it is false to assume that every individual can acquire it in the same way:

Tout être tend à son bonheur; et le bonheur d'un être ne peut être le bonheur d'un autre.[73]

This remark from the *Salon de 1767* refers to the happiness of different species or groups but it applies equally to each individual within a species. Happiness must be equated with maintaining the particular truth of one's own being even if this leads to the contravention of normal social behaviour. This is the case of Rameau for whom the only sure way to happiness is to follow his natural inclination to vice:

Puisque je puis faire mon bonheur par des vices qui me sont naturels ... il serait bien singulier que j'allasse me tourmenter comme une âme damnée pour me bistourner et me faire autre que je ne suis, pour me donner un caractère étranger au mien.[74]

The naive triple equation of virtue, self-interest and happiness, the fruit of a philosophical system wherein the moral derives directly from the physical, is found lacking in the face of human experience seen through the prism of a convincingly realist fiction.

The *Neveu* and *Jacques* herald the beginning of a considerable reorien-

[72] O.RO., p. 432.
[73] A.T., XI, p. 124.
[74] O.RO., p. 433.

tation of Diderot's philosophical and moral thought, which is accompanied by a parallel development in his political thought.[75] Whereas in the *Entretien d'un père avec ses enfants* and the *Supplément au Voyage de Bougainville* the interests of the individual are ruthlessly subordinated to the well-being of society, the fiction written over the same period points to a realisation that a philosophical *impasse* had been reached, and that a true explanation of human behaviour was being denied in favour of the advocacy of principles which, if put into practice, could only be detrimental. The truth with which Diderot the philosopher has been presented in *Jacques* and the *Neveu* is that man is not simply a collectivity, a homogeneous mass, but an assemblage of individuals, each with at the centre of their being a dignity and a self-respect which if destroyed robs them of their humanity, each with a need to fulfil their nature, which differs from man to man.

Armed with the knowledge that a true understanding of the human condition together with a desire to improve it cannot be achieved unless the reality of human individuality is respected, Diderot sets out in the *contes* to investigate the characteristics of individual behaviour in contemporary society. Unlike Rameau and Jacques the characters in the *contes*, including those which intersperse the narrative of *Jacques le Fataliste* do not attempt to interpret or regulate their actions according to a set of preconceived ideas. Their behaviour and attitudes are not the fruit of philosophical meditation, they arise directly out of the situation in which they find themselves or constitute their reactions to events which confront them. They all share a similar psychological characteristic in that they have primary temperaments, their reactions are spontaneous; they do not reflect before taking a decision or making a move. This what differentiates them from Rameau and Jacques who have secondary temperaments. The literary reasons for this choice of temperament are clear; the brevity of the *conte* demands characters who have an immediacy which is easily communicated to the reader and who spark off the action swiftly. But the portrayal of characters with a primary temperament also has considerable advantages for the study of individual human behaviour, as it avoids the complications created by reflection and meditation which often obscure the real motives for action.

The characters of the *contes* are convincingly portrayed individuals drawn from among his contemporaries, transformed by his art, it is true, but without any loss to their authenticity or individuality. Neither they

[75] See Part II, Chap. II, pp. 138-140.

nor their actions can be considered as typical or generally valid. In fact, characters such as Madame de la Pommeraye, Hudson, Madame Reymer, Gardeil, Tanié, Mademoiselle de la Chaux, and Madame de la Carlière are remarkable for their singularity. They do not fit into any particular psychological or social pattern and any attempt to provide a full explanation for their actions must necessarily fail. But most significant, none of them appear to conform to the norms of behaviour which Diderot has evolved from his philosophy. The *méchants* among them contravene the natural law without the slightest remorse or loss of tranquility, their victims continue to sacrifice themselves when to do so is evidently against their better interests. Changes in personality and attitude remain ultimately inexplicable. Why does Madame de la Pommeraye, a quiet, gentle, retiring woman, become suddenly transformed into a ruthless, coldly calculating seeker of the most cruel kind of revenge? What are the reasons for Gardeil's change of heart? Indeed, despite his callousness, one receives the impression that Gardeil himself is bewildered by the dramatic change in his feelings for Mademoiselle de la Chaux. And how is it possible that this charming girl from a good family could sacrifice her fortune and honour to become the mistress and slave of "un petit homme bourru, taciturne et caustique?" [76] Why is Tanié prepared to sacrifice himself entirely, only to be exploited by the most cynical of courtesans?

No final answer is forthcoming. None of these characters can be fully understood, not because Diderot fails to provide sufficient information about them but because of the opacity of their personalities. The *contes* provide us, not with a subtle analysis of the characters' actions and motivations, but with the proclamation of what Lester Crocker has called "la grandeur du moi." [77] In both the evil and the virtuous this *grandeur* manifests itself in a characteristic energy and irreducible inner unity, for as Dieckmann has written, "Diderot seems to be fascinated by the *individuum ineffabile* and to accept the enigma of the unique individual." [78] What is more, this quality of uniqueness, this *grandeur du moi* is not restricted to any particular social class, or level of mental ability; *Les deux amis de Bourbonne* demonstrates that they can be found among the most simple and humble of people:

Vous voyez, petit frère, que la grandeur d'âme et les hautes qualités sont

---

[76] O.R., p. 801.
[77] "*Le Neveu de Rameau,* une Expérience Morale," p. 148.
[78] Introduction to *Contes,* p. 18.

de toutes les conditions et de tous les pays; que tel meurt obscur, à qui il n'a manqué qu'un autre théâtre.[79]

Like the characters of the other *contes*, Félix and Olivier are lifted by their outstanding qualities above the common run of men. Yet they do mark the beginning of a definite democratisation of Diderot's moral thought which narrows the gap between him and Rousseau. The latter's constant criticism of the *philosophes'* concept of virtue, inherited from Socrates, Montaigne and Spinoza, had been that they considered it to be the fruit of learning,[80] thus restricting its acquisition to those privileged enough to have received the benefit of an intellectual training. Now Diderot through the portrayal of these two simple men implicitly rejects this intellectualistic concept of virtue for one which can be achieved by all men. Rousseau's exclamation in the *Profession de foi* might also apply to the ethical implications of *Les deux amis*:

Grâce au ciel, nous voilà délivré de tout cet effrayant appareil de philosophie: nous pouvons être hommes sans être savants; dispensés de consumer notre vie à l'étude de la morale, nous avons à moindres frais un guide plus assuré dans ce dédale immense des opinions humaines.[81]

For the idealist Rousseau this guide is the conscience of the individual; the materialist Diderot would reject this supposition, though what leads men to perform acts of virtue if it is not learning, he does not say.

Each of the characters in the *contes* we have mentioned at some time or other during the course of the story works from inner necessity, oblivious to the law, civil and natural, and to conventional ethics. Their prime concern is to achieve a self-fulfilment and liberation through the satisfaction of an impulse that wells up from the very core of their being, but only in the case of Félix and Olivier are a true fulfilment and liberation both achieved and maintained. The attempts of the other characters are either tainted with wickedness or vice (Madame de la Pommeraye, Hudson, Madame Reymer, and Gardeil), or finally end in misery (Mademoiselle de la Chaux, Tanié, and Madame de la Carlière). They are all victims of a malady which has spread throughout civilised society, a malady which Rousseau diagnosed in his second *Discours* and which Diderot pointed to towards the end of the *Supplément*:

Tant que les appétits naturels seront sophistiqués, comptez sur des femmes méchantes, (...) des hommes atroces, (...) des infortunés à propos de rien.[82]

[79] O.RO., p. 783.
[80] *Discours sur l'inégalité*, p. 99.
[81] *Profession de foi*, p. 117.
[82] O.PH., p. 514.

It would be impossible to find such examples of depravity and misfortune in Tahiti as are portrayed in the *contes*, adds one of the interlocutors.[83] But Diderot is gradually becoming aware that the construction of an imaginary ideal society is ultimately of little value when one is faced with the concrete problem of changing an existing social order. Philosophical speculation which is shown to be inadequate or erroneous must give way to knowledge born of experience. The principles which will bring about the establishment of a just and equitable society are to be found not in naturalistic utopias but in the actions and aspirations of real men. Men such as Félix and Olivier who, living beyond the reach of the corrupting influence of an artificial society, have been able to maintain the dignity and hence the freedom which becomes them as human beings. Men, too, like himself, creative minds who, in order to maintain their creative impulse, must constantly reaffirm their dignity and independence *vis-à-vis* a slave society which corrodes and eventually destroys human personality.

The role of fiction in clarifying a problem for which no philosophical solution was forthcoming can have few if any precedents. However, we do not wish to give the impression that this was Diderot's prime purpose in writing the *Neveu de Rameau, Jacques le Fataliste*, and the *contes*. On the contrary, we hope to have shown that his intentions were of an essentially artistic order, and that the clarification of the problem was itself an artistic one. But an artistic solution as such could not provide the basis for further development in the field of political thought. In order that this could take place the new insights into human nature granted by his fiction had to be reconciled with his philosophy. This was Diderot's main preoccupation as he entered on the last decade of his life.

[83] *Ibid.*, p. 515.

CHAPTER III

FROM INDIVIDUAL TO CITIZEN

Jacques le Fataliste marks a turning point in Diderot's literary and intellectual career, for never again was he to turn his hand to fiction; nor, as far as we know, did he ever contemplate doing so. Even in the broader field of aesthetics he seems to have exhausted his inspiration: the eighth *Salon* is a poor affair, and as early as 1769 he had told Grimm that he had very little left to say about art.[1] But if as a writer of fiction, an art critic and an aesthetician he had reached the end of the road, in the realm of his first love, philosophy, he showed a renewed vigour, enthusiasm and originality, which continued unabated throughout the last decade or so of his life. When visitors called they invariably found him eager to debate philosophical questions, and when death took him in 1784, although failing health had prevented him from writing for two years, he was busily engaged in preparing a complete edition of his works.

What were the reasons for this intensification of philosophical inquiry which led to such significant and even remarkable works as the *Réfutation d'Helvétius*, the *Commentaire de Hemsterhuis*, and the summum of his ethical thought, the *Essai sur Claude et Néron*, at an age when most men seek repose? Apart from the simple fact that Diderot was temperamentally incapable of finishing his life in a state of intellectual stagnation, the reasons are twofold. Firstly, his political thought, which had been slow to develop, was now reaching full if late flower and required a constant effort on the level of his moral and philosophical thought to sustain it. Secondly, the issues raised in his fiction could not be left in mid-air; he had to come to terms with them intellectually. Indeed, the two matters are integrally related, for only by attempting to solve within a philosophical context the problems posed by the creations of his literary imagination

---

[1] "Je suis devenu vieux et paresseux, j'ai vidé mon sac: ce qui me reste d'observations à faire sur l'art est si peu de chose qu'il sera facile de vous contenter," A.T., XI, p. 387.

could he see his way through to the successful elaboration of a post-abso-
lutist political doctrine.[2]

What were the problems with which his fictional writings presented
him? We have alluded to them in the previous chapter, but they require
further clarification if we wish to understand how he set about trying to
solve them. The *Neveu de Rameau*, *Jacques le Fataliste* and the *contes*
all bear witness, as we have seen, to the incontrovertible reality of the variety and uniqueness of human individuality. Although the complex mo-
tivational forces which animate Diderot's characters remain obscure, they
all share one overriding desire, the desire so to engineer or exploit circumstances, events and people, that they may rediscover or find for the first
time that happiness and sense of liberation that are concomitant with the
fulfilment of their personalities. Some succeed, though most fail. Those
who succeed do so because a combination of propitious circumstances and
judicious choice allows them to live and act in an atmosphere of freedom
in which their personalities gain complete release. This is true for the
Marquis des Arcis who fully assumes the situation in which Madame de
la Pommeraye's machinations have placed him; it is equally true for Félix and Olivier who achieve their freedom by opting out of a society
which oppresses their class. The same phenomenon of the individual free
to act can be seen in Diderot the author as he interrupts the narrative of
Jacques le Fataliste and defiantly proclaims his autonomous right to alter
the course of the story as he sees fit. Those who fail do so because the corrupt artificiality of society places them in situations which frustrate or
vitiate their attempts to achieve happiness and liberation. Both Madame
de la Pommeraye and Madame de la Carlière demand of their lovers a
fidelity which the amoral climate of society made it impossible to obtain.
Tanié and Mademoiselle de la Chaux are irretrievably in love with two of

---

[2] In the last years of Diderot's life there emerges the outline of what P. Vernière
and J. R. Loy have called respectively "une science totale de l'homme" (a) and "la
science humaine" (b), which transcends his more immediate preoccupations with moral
and political philosophy. A specifically scientific approach towards psychological and
economic problems is already discernible in the *Lettre sur les aveugles*, the *Rêve de
d'Alembert*, and the *Apologie de Galiani*. In the *Eléments de physiologie*, the *Voyage
de Hollande*, and in the questionnaires addressed to Catherine II and the Comte de
Munich (c) the scientific intention behind the amassing of a considerable amount of
data on physiological, psychological and economic matters is even more apparent. The
significance of Diderot's contribution to the beginnings of the social sciences has
been acknowledged by scholars in this field, but no serious study has been undertaken
on the subject. As it is an aspect of his thought which would require separate treatment
it is not dealt with in the present study.
  (a) O.PH., p. 559.
  (b) *L'Essai sur les règnes de Claude et de Néron*, p. 254.
  (c) M. Tourneux, *Diderot et Catherine II*, Appendices B et C.

the most vicious products of a perverse society. But with every character, whether he succeeds or fails, the power of his individuality and his implacable demand for happiness and fulfilment on his own terms strikes us forcibly.

Faced with the irreducible reality of human individuality Diderot recognized that to return to the old doctrine of the *morale universelle* with its strong absolutist connotations would be to avoid the issue. In fact, the *morale universelle* was no longer a practical proposition, since its political application, monarchical absolutism, was now increasingly discredited in his eyes. The movement towards the idea of popular sovereignty in his political thought [3] corresponded to the liberation of the individual in his fiction. A serious reassessment of his philosophical and moral thought was essential if the continuity between it and his political thought was to be maintained. This process would also enable him to investigate the nature, extent and variety of human individuality in a more thorough and systematic manner than fiction would permit. This, then, was the dual nature of the task that faced Diderot, philosopher and moralist, in the last years of his life.

I. MATERIALISM AND THE THEORY OF CONSCIOUSNESS

An opportunity for a re-evaluation of his philosophy presented itself during Diderot's stay at The Hague in the summer of 1773, at about the time when the evidence suggests that he began to work seriously on *Jacques le Fataliste*. In the spring of that year Marc-Michel Rey published *De l'Homme*, a posthumous work by Diderot's old Parisian friend and fellow *philosophe*, Helvétius, in which he set out to define man in the terms of a mechanistic materialism, strongly inspired by the sensualism of Locke and Condillac. Diderot acquired a copy of the work and set about studying it in characteristic fashion with pen in hand, annotating it as he read. By 1775 the annotations had grown into a major philosophical dissertation, the most important since the *Rêve de d'Alembert*, in which Diderot, drawing from his latest knowledge and experience, presented his own interpretation of man, the *Réfutation d'Helvétius*.

Why should Diderot wish to refute Helvétius? The two men with d'Holbach, whom Diderot had frequently aided in his writing, represented the extreme point of 18th-century thought, materialist atheism. Indeed, in the eyes of the public, Diderot was held to be in such great sympathy with Helvétius' views that the French ambassador at the Hague, the Mar-

---

[3] See Part II, Chaps. II and III.

quis de Noailles, thought it was he who had written the preface to Helvétius' treatise.[4] The reason for Diderot's rejection of Helvétius' views, stated
in its simplest terms, was that the latter denied man his supreme quality,
an essential individuality, substituting in its place an infinite modifiability
open to the influences of habit and education. This diminution of man's
greatness, Diderot was not prepared to brook; it was an act of dehumanisation against which his experience as a novelist and psychologist, indeed
his very being led him to cry out in horror. Besides, Helvétius' conclusions
were drawn in complete ignorance of the relation between human psychology and physical organisation, a fact which Diderot with the considerable scientific knowledge at his disposal could not view with equani-
mity.

It is generally agreed to-day that the view that Diderot renounced materialism in the *Réfutation* [5] is based on an erroneous reading of the work.
Far from condemning *De l'Homme* outright, Diderot intersperses his
criticism with lavish praise and recommends its reading to his compatriots, for it is a valuable counsel for rulers on the benefits of education, a
comfort for parents who despair of their children, and a timely corrective
for vain men convinced of their innate superiority. But his praise has a
sting in its tail, for he also recommends it as suitable reading for all writers,
". . . afin qu'ils s'étonnent de l'étrange absurdité où peut être conduit un
esprit d'une trempe qui n'était pas ordinaire, mais trop fortement oc-
cupé de son opinion, et qu'ils en deviennent circonspects." [6] Helvétius'
error lies not in his premises which are true, but in the conclusions that
he draws from them. It is his method which is at fault; lacking the open-
ness of mind and the humility which become the true philosopher, he ignores empirical evidence entirely and proceeds by means of purely rational deduction to the establishment of doctrines which are no more than
his own preconceived opinions in disguise. Consequently, his ideas are
stamped with a dogmatism and an *esprit de système* which Diderot could
not stomach, because they inevitably led to a considerable oversimplification of the truth and to the exclusion of vast areas of relevant data.

Proceeding from the postulate of general physical sensitivity Helvétius
argues that between man and other animals, and between individuals
within the human species itself there exists no qualitative difference. With
man as with all other animals both actions and mental processes are

---

[4] Letter from Noailles to the Duc d'Aiguillon, 14th September 1773 in *Diderot et
Catherine II*, p. 64.
[5] See P. Janet, "La Philosophie de Diderot, le dernier mot d'un matérialiste."
[6] O.PH., p. 603.

governed by simple physical desire and aversion. In the case of individuals differences that exist are the product of external conditions and influences; in fact, all men are potentially capable of the same achievements as they all share the same physical organisation. Diderot had already exposed this fallacy in the *Rêve de d'Alembert*. With the aid of solid scientific evidence he had demonstrated that differences in temperament and intellectual ability can ultimately be traced back to differences in physical organisation. However he had not as yet seriously considered the differences which separate man from the other animal species. Indeed, in the *Rêve de d'Alembert*, the tendency was rather the reverse: to minimise the differences and to show how closely man resembled the animals:

Il y a bien plus d'un morceau de marbre à un être qui sent, que d'un être qui sent à un être qui pense.[7]

Human understanding is no more than the combined operation of organic memory and judgment, which Diderot equates with sensation.[8] There is little if anything to distinguish between the interpretation of man's basic intellectual processes in the *Rêve de d'Alembert* and the one posited by Helvétius in *De l'Homme*. Both spring from an oversimplified materialism applied in too crude a fashion, and both are inadequate. Diderot, as we have seen,[9] was at least partially aware of this inadequacy in his materialism, but he was unable to transcend it, because his mechanist interpretation underestimated the complex functioning of the human mind and thus prevented him from seeing in it the decisive factor which establishes a firmly qualitative distinction between man and the rest of the animal world. As a consequence any possibility of founding a principle of individuation on the discovery relating to the differences in the physical organisation of individuals was barred. Only when a solution to the first problem had been discovered could he set about elaborating a theory of human individuality and investigate this phenomenon in the light of a scientific materialism.

It was Helvétius' brutal assertion "Sentir c'est juger," which finally confronted Diderot with not only the inadequacy but the absurdity of a philosophical interpretation which equated consciousness and intelligence with physical sensitivity.[10] It was absurd because it failed to recognise that

---

[7] *Ibid.*, p. 264.
[8] *Ibid.*, pp. 273-274.
[9] Part I, Chap. I, p. 22.
[10] Diderot himself had previously made this false equation in a passage in the *Eléments de physiologie* which closely resembles Helvétius' formula:
"Sentir deux êtres coexistants, c'est juger.

there is a hierarchy of animate existence, in which each level is separated
from the others by innate differences. To claim that the human faculty of
judgment has physical sensitivity as its direct cause is manifestly false,
since it implies that there is no real difference between man and the rest
of the animal world where behaviour is solely motivated by physical sensitivity. "Je suis homme," exclaims Diderot, "et il me faut des causes
propres à l'homme." [11] The operative word is "causes"; Helvétius has
committed a gross error in taking the conditions necessary for the development of consciousness and intelligence for their causes:

Sans doute, il faut être organisé comme nous et sentir pour agir; mais il
me semble que ce sont là les conditions essentielles et primitives, les données
sine qua non, mais que les motifs immédiats et prochains de nos aversions et
de nos désirs sont autre chose.[12]

Since the causes lie elsewhere it is essential to make a firm and clear distinction between the two orders, between sensation and reflexion, animal
and human, the physical and the moral:

La distinction du physique et du moral n'est-elle pas aussi solide que celle
d'animal qui sent et d'animal qui raisonne.[13]

Diderot had always made this distinction intuitively between the two series of terms, but his materialism as late as the *Rêve de d'Alembert* had
constantly denied it, and made man the slave of a crude determinism
which the introduction of the concept of a limited modifiability did little
to mitigate. Hence the unending battle between his head and his heart.
Until now he had been so preoccupied with the conditions governing the
emergence of consciousness that he had fallen into the same conceptual
trap as Helvétius and had failed to distinguish between its conditions and
its causes. But now that Helvétius had involuntarily helped him to isolate
this radical anomaly in his thought and overcome it, he could proceed to
integrate his earlier intuitions regarding human consciousness into an
overall philosophical structure and thereby transcend the previous restrictions of his materialism. This, in turn, would allow him to attain his
ultimate goal, the elaboration of a theory of human individuality of which
freedom is the essence. But this is to anticipate a little. Before we can

Voilà le jugement formé; la voix l'articule: l'homme dit mur blanc, et voilà le
jugement prononcé" (A.T., IX, p. 358).
[11] A.T., II, p. 300.
[12] *Ibid.*, p. 302.
[13] *Ibid.*, p. 303.

consider Diderot's conclusion regarding freedom and the individual, we must first examine the way in which his materialism evolved through the assimilation of a theory of human consciousness consistent with it.

In order to demonstrate the falsity of Helvétius' equation of judgment with sensation, Diderot turned again to the advanced knowledge of human physiology which he had already used in the *Rêve de d'Alembert*, but which the conceptual breakthrough he had now made allowed him to treat in a new and different manner. He agrees readily with Helvétius that the conditions of consciousness are the organs of the five senses. Reflexion is of necessity dependent on sensation: the faculty of judgment can only operate on data that has originally come from the exterior via the senses. But judgment is not a function of the sense organs, as Helvétius, ignorant of human physiology, implies; it is a separate "sixième sens" which resides in a central organ with which the other senses communicate. This central organ is the brain,[14] the "sensorium commune," and although little is known about it, and even concentrated study may do little to reduce the mystery surrounding it, there are two things regarding it that can be deduced from experience. First, its conformation varies from individual to individual and thus necessarily affects intellectual operations. Second, unlike the five senses it is not characterised by a purely passive receptive function; on the contrary, by the readiness with which it registers the information supplied to it by the senses, combines, compares and collates it, it proves itself to be the source of an active force.[15] The intellectual operations of the judgment and the memory which together form consciousness involve activity and not the mere receptive capacity which is implicit in Helvétius' premise.

Having established that consciousness is activity and that its mode varies from individual to individual according to the innate dispositions which arise from cerebral conformation, Diderot takes his investigation a step further in a key passage.[16]

> ... sans un correspondant et un juge commun de toutes les sensations, sans un organe commémoratif de tout ce qui nous arrive, l'instrument sensible

---

[14] *Ibid.*, p. 318. Cf. Rousseau, who writes of "un sixième sens, appelé sens commun, moins parce qu'il est commun à tous les hommes, que parce qu'il résulte de l'usage bien réglé des autre sens, et qu'il nous instruit de la nature des choses par le concours de toutes leur apparences. Ce sixième sens n'a point par conséquent d'organe particulier: il ne réside que dans le cerveau, et ses sensations purement internes, s'appellent perceptions ou idées," *Emile*, livre Second, *Oeuvres complètes*, p. 417.

[15] *Ibid.*, pp. 335-336.

[16] The importance and originality of this passage has been commented upon with considerable insight by I. W. Alexander in "Philosophy of organism and philosophy of consciousness in Diderot's speculative thought," p. 10.

et vivant de chaque sens aurait peut-être une conscience momentanée de son existence, mais il n'y aurait certainement aucune conscience de l'animal ou de l'homme entier.[17]

Consciousness differs radically from sensation because it provides the individual with a continuing awareness of himself. Sensation alone, since it is entirely occupied by the continuous inrush of information from the outside world, would not allow the individual to distinguish between his own existence and that of the world; the two would be completely identified. Consciousness, on the other hand, since it is an activity which selects and co-ordinates sense data, by this very process allows the individual to make this distinction. This phenomenon can be seen at its most elementary level in Descartes' "Cogito, ergo sum." Consciousness, furthermore, radically affects man's perception of the universe and places it in a fundamentally different category from that of the animal. The perception of the animal is made up of a succession of relatively unselected sense data and is therefore almost entirely objective. Man's perception, on the other hand, is produced by the combined activity of a selective faculty of judgment and a consciousness of self which interiorises sense data into a synthetic unity which *becomes* his existence. This is a process which continues throughout the life of the individual, so that with the further interiorisation of sense data the character of the synthesis and, therefore, of the individual's existence is constantly changing:

Tout s'est fait en nous parce que nous sommes nous, toujours nous et pas une minute les mêmes.[18]

This self which is being continually transformed is, then, none other than the universe constantly interiorised and reconstituted by the individual who perceives it:

... c'est toujours nous que nous apercevons, et nous n'apercevons jamais que nous. Nous sommes l'univers entier.[19]

So without abjuring his materialism and crossing into the idealist camp, Diderot, in the *Réfutation d'Helvétius*, is able to furnish a full and consistent philosophical interpretation of man's intellectual operations thereby restituting to men his full humanity, and providing his earlier intuitive

[17] A.T., II, p. 337.
[18] *Ibid.*, p. 373.
[19] A.T., XVIII, p. 115. Quoted by I. W. Alexander, *op. cit.*, p. 14.

insights with the sound philosophical basis which they had previously lacked.

The internal unity achieved through the activity by which man interiorises the world, and this activity itself are the two sources of happiness:

Il y a un bonheur circonscrit qui reste en moi et qui ne s'étend pas au delà. Il y a un bonheur expansif qui se propage, qui se jette sur le présent, qui embrasse l'avenir, et qui se repaît de jouissances morales et physiques, de réalités et de chimères, entassant pêle-mêle de l'argent, des éloges, des tableaux, des statues et des baisers.[20]

The first kind of happiness, the "bonheur circonscrit," arises from a pure sentiment of existence, of enjoyment of self, in a kind of psychological eternity outside of any spatio-temporal context. Diderot had already noted this psychic phenomenon in the *Rêve de d'Alembert* where he emphasises the intensity of the experience:

Qu'est-ce qui circonscrit votre étendue réelle? Rien. J'existe comme en un point; je cesse presque d'être matière, je ne sens que ma pensée; il n'y a plus ni lieu, ni mouvement, ni corps, ni distance, ni espace pour moi; l'univers est anéanti pour moi, et je suis nulle pour lui.[21]

and in the article *Délicieux* in which he describes the incomparable pleasure of the *rêverie*:

Il ne lui restait dans ce moment d'enchantement et de faiblesse, ni mémoire du passé, ni désir de l'avenir, ni inquiétude sur le présent. Le temps avait cessé de couler pour lui, parce qu'il existait tout en lui-même ... mais il en jouissait (de son existence) d'une jouissance tout à fait passive, sans y être attaché, sans y réfléchir, sans s'en réjouir, sans s'en féliciter.[22]

It is in this state of happiness that the individual knows the sublimity of self-fulfilment, the pure ecstasy which flows from the feeling of the unqualified completeness of his own being. But its achievement is dependent on the creative activity of the consciousness, itself a source of pleasure, which masters and comprehends the world. Man, therefore, in so far as he is truly man and not an animal, does not attain happiness through a mere mechanical process of desire and aversion, but by the creation of his

---

[20] A.T., II, p. 306.
[21] O.PH., p. 333.
[22] A.T., XIV, p. 277. Quoted by I. W. Alexander, *op. cit.*, p. 18. Cf. Rousseau, 5th *Promenade* of the *Rêveries du Promeneur Solitaire, Oeuvres Complètes*, I, pp. 1045-1047, in which he records and analyses a very similar experience.

own being through the recreation and subjectivisation of the world.

The stages of Diderot's thought, passing from a theory of consciousness, independent in its causality from physical sensitivity yet governed in its activity by innate inclinations and aversions, to the concept of self-creation, point clearly to a theory of individuality. This theory finds its final proof and illustration in Diderot's re-examination of the concept of genius.

In reply to Helvétius' claim that all men are born with an equal intellectual potential, and that it is only chance which brings forth the genius, Diderot retorts,

Si Helvétius avait exercé la profession malheureuse d'instituteur d'une cinquantaine d'élèves, il eût bientôt senti la vanité de son système.[23]

Common experience is further substantiated by biological fact:

C'est la nature, c'est l'organisation, ce sont des causes purement physiques qui préparent l'homme de génie.[24]

The genius through his organ of reason exercises a greater dominance over his senses than is the case for ordinary men.[25] His power of synthesis is such that he is able to gather up within himself the hidden unity of the world in a vast movement of intuition. However much a lesser man may try, he will never be capable of this operation simply because he lacks the innate capacity. Diderot has to look no farther than a comparison between Helvétius and himself to illustrate the truth of his argument:

Le système d'Helvétius est celui d'un homme de beaucoup d'esprit qui démontre à chaque ligne que l'impulsion tyrannique du génie lui est étrangère et qui en parle comme un aveugle en couleurs. Peut-être suis-je moi-même dans ce cas. Il y aura cependant cette différence entre nous, c'est que tout ce qu'il a fait, c'est à force de méditation et de travail . . . Il devine beaucoup de la contrée dont il parle, mais moi qui m'y suis promené, je vois qu'il n'y a jamais mis le pied.[26]

Helvétius' system is constructed by the analytical method; the evidence is to be found in his own words:

Les plus sublimes vérités, une fois simplifiées et réduites aux moindres termes, se réduisent en faits, et dès lors ne présentent plus à l'esprit que cette proposition: le blanc est blanc, le noir est noir.[27]

[23] A.T., II, p. 340.
[24] Ibid., p. 369.
[25] Ibid., p. 324.
[26] Ibid., p. 341.
[27] Quoted by Diderot, ibid., p. 351.

But analysis can never attain to true knowledge because it only consists in ordering ideas so as to demonstrate the identity of the conclusion with the premise. Since it cannot break out of this closed circle, it can never become creative, but must remain mere exposition. Knowledge of the real can only be attained by way of synthesis, that process of the mind which perceives truth, not as a series of logically related propositions, but through the intuitive grasp of the world as unity, as "enchaînement." [28] Hence Helvétius *knows about* reality but he does not *know* it. Knowledge of reality does not come about through its discovery but through its re-creation in the mind. Reality thus recreated is invested with sublimity and originality, but it must not be thought that the sublime is in itself original:

. . . il ne le devient que par une sorte de singularité qui le rend personnel à l'auteur.[29]

Recreated reality is, then, totally identified with its author; it is a projection of his self and as such bears witness to the irreducible uniqueness of the creative genius. The genius, therefore, is the supreme example of the process of individuation, the process whereby the individual in a unique and radically indeterminable manner creates his own being by an internal reconstruction of the world.

But although Diderot reproaches Helvétius for ignoring the link between individuality and physiological factors, he is far from underestimating the influences of social forces, such as education and legislation. Here again it is the genius who provides the perfect example of the degree to which these forces affect human personality:

. . . le génie est un germe dont la bienfaisance hâte le développement, et que la misère publique, compagne de la tyrannie, étouffe ou retarde . . . sous le despotisme l'homme de génie partage peut-être plus qu'un autre l'abattement général des âmes.[30]

For Diderot the emergence of individuality is dependent upon a dynamic and positive relationship between the subject and society. There can be no opposition between the individual and the social. The individual can only achieve his individuality and thus attain his happiness as a social being. But to attain this happiness society must allow him a freedom which is concomitant with self-fulfilment; social reform must be directed to the enhancement of this freedom. The genius is, then, for Diderot the perfect

[28] *Ibid.*
[29] *Ibid.*, pp. 331-332.
[30] *Ibid.*, p. 342.

example of the creative, self-fulfilling individual. By the very fact that he realises them to perfection the genius is the ideal representative of the aspirations of common humanity.[31]

An important change has taken place in the role of the genius in the matrix of Diderot's thought. Although his concept of genius, as Herbert Dieckmann argues,[32] goes against the postulate of the Enlightenment that general reason is accessible to all, no longer does he set the genius apart under the guise of the enlightened ruler or his counsellor to preside with absolute authority over the destiny of the nation, rigorously imposing the dictates of the *morale universelle* on his less endowed compatriots. On the contrary, in his demand to be his own master, to enjoy complete freedom to attain self-fulfilment and happiness on his own terms, he is completely identified with the ordinary citizen. So Diderot's re-examination of the concept of genius within the broader context of a theory of consciousness enabled him to establish a rational continuity between his fiction "(qui) témoigne incontestablement d'une rare puissance d'individuation," [33] and the increasingly democratic nature of his political thought. This continuity is further illuminated by a number of annotations in his *Commentaire de Hemsterhuis* to which we now turn our attention.

II. INDIVIDUATION AND SOCIALISATION

Georges May, who discovered and edited the *Commentaire de Hemsterhuis* contends that Diderot's thought is caught in a state of tension between the opposed philosophical poles represented by *De l'Homme* and Hemsterhuis' *Lettre sur l'homme et ses rapports*, and he continues,

Egalement repoussé de part et d'autre, (sa pensée) est mise en mouvement, elle acquiert son effervescence spécifique et s'oriente dans les directions qui lui sont propres, réussissant ainsi à sauvegarder toute son originalité.[34]

While there is truth in this general proposition, it does require some qualification. Hemsterhuis is manifestly not of the same intellectual calibre as Helvétius; his own homegrown version of Cartesian dualism lacks the originality, persuasive force and intellectual rigour which has secured Helvétius' thought, despite its shortcomings, a place of honour in the history of environmentalist psychology. Furthermore, the Dutch philosopher wields the French language in an ungainly manner and his idiosyncratic

---

[31] See G. Besse, "Observations sur la *Réfutation d'Helvétius* par Diderot," p. 44.
[32] "Diderot's conceptions of genius," p. 155.
[33] G. Besse, *op. cit.*, p. 41.
[34] Hemsterhuis, *Lettre sur l'homme et ses rapports* avec le commentaire inédit par Diderot ed. G. May, (*Commentaire de Hemsterhuis*), p. 16.

choice of imprecise and unaccustomed terms at key points in his exposition does not help to clarify his thesis. The net effect is that Diderot rarely receives stimulation from his adversary in dialogue sufficient to spark off any originality in his own thought. The *Commentaire de Hemsterhuis* is for the most part a routine reiteration of the materialist precepts that Diderot had previously set out in the *Lettre sur les aveugles* and the *Rêve de d'Alembert*. The tone is frequently that of a benevolent schoolmaster correcting the dissertation of a willing but not overtalented pupil for style and content. The main value of the annotations lies in their confirmation of the view that Diderot's adherence to materialism continued despite his reservations about Helvétius.

Two series of annotations do, however, re-emphasise and throw further light on the original themes developed in the *Réfutation*. In one passage Hemsterhuis explains the phenomenon of self-consciousness in a way which, despite the unscientific, vaguely scholastic terminology, attracted Diderot's attention because it showed a certain perceptiveness. Defining the heart as the organ which perceives "la face morale de l'univers," Hemsterhuis continues,

> Mais cet organe, ce coeur, qui me donne des sensations de cette face de l'univers, diffère de nos autres organes principalement, en ce qu'il nous donne une sensation d'une force dont notre ame (sic) notre *moi*, fait partie; ainsi, pour cet organe le *moi* lui-même devient un objet de contemplation.[35]

In his annotations, Diderot first points out that moral perception is not the function of a particular organ, but the effect of a specific kind of mental activity:

> . . . ce n'est toujours que la raison, ou la faculté intuitive appliquée à un nouvel objet.[36]

Having made this important rectification, he goes on to embroider the rest of the passage with which he is substantially in agreement with comments which refine Hemsterhuis's rather primitive notions and draw them in the direction of his own discoveries. Expanding Hemsterhuis's conception of self-consciousness, which is the view that man's faculty of moral perception leads to contemplation of self, he demonstrates that self is not only the object but also the creation of the individual's intellectual activity, and that the self thus created differs in essence from all other selves:

> Le *moi* est le résultat de la mémoire qui attache à un individu la suite de

[35] *Op. cit.*, p. 240.
[36] *Ibid.*, p. 241.

ses sensations. Si je suis un individu, c'est *moi*. Si c'est un autre individu, c'est *lui*.[37]

Although Diderot here places the emphasis on memory rather than on the combined activity of judgment and memory as the force which synthesises sense data into self, this annotation nonetheless bears a close resemblance to his theory of consciousness as it has evolved in the *Réfutation*. This close resemblance is further borne out by another annotation in which Diderot argues that the faculty of memory is essential to the individual's awareness of his own existence and that sensation alone fails to create this awareness:

Sans la mémoire qui attache à une longue suite d'actions le même individu, l'être, à chaque sensation momentanée, passerait du réveil au sommeil; à peine aurait-il le temps de s'avouer qu'il existe. Il n'éprouverait que la douleur ou le plaisir d'une sensation un peu forte, la surprise des autres, à chaque secousse qui exercerait sa sensabilité, presque comme au sortir du Néant.[38]

This is almost a direct transposition, with a few elaborations, of the key passage in the *Réfutation* quoted and discussed above. The fact that it appears to have been written later than the other annotations on the same page,[39] suggests that Diderot added it after writing the original passage in the *Réfutation*.

So far Diderot has done little more than reaffirm the theory of individuality that we found in the *Réfutation*. But in his next annotation he takes his thought a stage further, and shows more precisely than he had done in the *Réfutation* the manner in which the individual's quest for happiness, synonymous with self-fulfilment, should determine the nature of his relationship to society:

Ce *moi* veut être heureux. Cette tendance constante est la source éternelle, permanente, de tous ses devoirs, même les plus minutieux. Toute loi contraire est un crime de lèse-humanité, un acte de tyrannie.[40]

Self-fulfilment and the fulfilment of social duty, or virtue to give it its other name,[41] are two sides of the same coin, though neither is possible in a society which does not grant to the individual the freedom to act accord-

[37] *Ibid.*
[38] *Ibid.*
[39] G. May notes that this annotation was written in a different hand and ink from those that precede it on the same page.
[40] *Op. cit.*, p. 243.
[41] "Le devoir et la vertu sont synonymes; ou s'il y a quelque différence, c'est que la vertu n'est que le devoir rempli," *Ibid.*, p. 297.

ing to his own inner promptings. Diderot makes it quite clear that duty, although it derives from the notion of individual happiness, does not mean a narrow duty to self, as is apparent in a later annotation in which he defines the *méchant* as

... un homme qui veut son bonheur, et qui fait le contraire de ce qu'il veut. Il ne voit pas plus loin que son nez; il calcule mal; il fait à tout moment de faux marchés.[42]

The self-seeking *méchant* is *par excellence* the type of individual who has failed to integrate with society and whose desire for self-fulfilment is thus constantly frustrated.

It would appear from this that Diderot has reverted to his earlier virtue-happiness formula which had been discredited in the *Neveu de Rameau*.[43] But this contradiction is more apparent than real; for whereas previously the formula was no more than an observation on the actual relationship between the individual and society, which experience proved to be groundless, he now presents it as a speculative theory based on an ideal relationship between the two. Diderot knows full well that in existing society there are "... une infinité d'honnêtes gens qui ne sont pas heureux et une infinité de gens qui sont heureux sans être honnêtes." [44] Crime rewarded by happiness, virtue by misery, Père Hudson and Mademoiselle de la Chaux: these situations are inevitable in a society which vitiates the individual's desire for self-fulfilment by a corrupting legislation which denies him his freedom and thus prevents him for realising his social nature. The happiness of the *méchant* is obtained at the expense of those he misuses. Only a society which will encourage in the individual the free and simultaneous development of self and social commitment can ensure the happiness of the greatest possible number. But – and here Diderot closes the gap between his moral and political thought – it is incumbent upon the individual as citizen, exercising his social duties to the full, to establish and preserve freedom in the State. He must constantly affirm the right of the people to oppose the will of even the most authentically enlightened and beneficent despot and reject the happiness of the "gras pâturages" to which the latter would lead his flock.[45]

In the *Réfutation* and the *Commentaire* Diderot has achieved a remarkable understanding of the problem of the individual in his relation

---

[42] *Ibid.*, p. 297.
[43] See pp. 51-52.
[44] O.RO., p. 432.
[45] A.T., II, p. 381.

to society, more profound than that of any other contemporary thinker with the exception of Rousseau. Arguing against Helvétius' theory of the individual's absolute modifiability in favour of innate differences, he nonetheless demonstrates that differentiation and self-fulfilment are dependent on the individual's relation to society, but to a society of whose freedom the individual is with his fellow citizens the guarantor. Despite Guy Besse's negative conclusion [46] it is not an exaggeration to claim that Diderot's thought has evolved to the point where he is able to discern, albeit in relatively simple terms, that the processes of individuation and socialisation are interrelated, that a man's individuality can only flourish in a society in which he can be fully active as a social being. The idea is, of course, not original to Diderot; it lies at the very core of most if not all of Rousseau's writings. Rousseau's defiant and uncompromising display of individualism in the *Confessions*, the *Rêveries* and the *Discours sur l'iné-galité* is an attempt to preserve individuality intact in the face of a society that seeks to destroy it, while awaiting the day when it may flourish, freely joined to a truly social nature, in the new society of the contract. Diderot, of course, along with almost everybody else, failed to understand that Rousseau's seemingly intemperate individualism and his unsparing social criticism were a necessary prelude to a philosophy of society more radical and all-embracing than any since *The Republic*. For Diderot Rousseau's ideas were at worst a series of sophisms, at best a tissue of contradictions unlikely to impress a reasonable man:

Rousseau croit l'homme de la nature bon . . .
Rousseau croit que la société n'est propre qu'à dépraver l'homme de la nature . . .
Rousseau s'imagine que tout est au mieux dans les forêts et tout au plus mal dans les villes . . .
Rousseau écrit contre le théâtre, et fait une comédie; préconise l'homme sauvage ou qui ne s'élève point, et compose un traité d'éducation. Sa philosophie, s'il en a une, est de pièces et de morceaux.[47]

Yet depite these severe strictures Diderot felt bound to observe that although Rousseau's principles were false, the conclusions he drew from them were true.[48] No remark could illustrate more clearly the extent to which Diderot had moved towards Rousseau's advanced position in his understanding of the relationship between the individual and society. But it also indicates the vast temperamental and intellectual gulf which

[46] *Op. cit.*, p. 43.
[47] A.T., II, pp. 316-317.
[48] *Ibid.*, p. 316.

still separated them, and always would. Rousseau's demands for a radical renewal of society were primarily inspired by the non-rational promptings of his own frustrated ego. His sublime misanthropy precludes us from viewing his social philosophy as the fruit of his commiseration for the sufferings of his fellow-men in a society which oppresses them. His introspection, his belief in a *philosophie de la conscience* are ultimately incompatible with a formal theory consistent with a rational interpretation of political realities. Rousseau's revolt, in both its negative and positive aspects sprang from an existential need within him and gave birth to a body of thought whose unity is more organic than rational, and which depends on persuasive eloquence rather than logical proof for its exposition. Diderot, who had been his most intimate friend, knew this well:

Il se soucie bien plus d'être éloquent que vrai, disert que démonstratif, brillant que logicien, de vous éblouir que de vous éclairer.[49]

But Diderot could not accept that a political philosophy could be anything other than a logical deduction from intellectually verifiable premises. Both principles and consequences must stand up to rational scrutiny. In the *Réfutation* and the *Commentaire* he had succeeded in re-establishing this consistency which had temporarily been lost when his political thought had evolved more swiftly in a democratic direction than his philosophical and moral thought. But it is in the relaxed and intimate atmosphere of the *Essai sur les règnes de Claude et de Néron* that Diderot's thought attained the profound unity free of ambiguities and hesitations, which permitted him to adopt a position of firm political commitment and so at last to bridge the gulf separating theory from action.

III. SENECA AND THE IDEAL CITIZEN

The *Essai* is without doubt the most intensely personal of all Diderot's works. Unfortunately it is also the least approachable. Its forbidding length and highly discursive style have so far discouraged any sustained critical analysis of the text, though recently a monograph and two essays have appeared which treat certain limited aspects of the work.[50] Of these three

---

[49] *Ibid.*, p. 292. Cf. Rousseau's admission to Dom Deschamps: "Vous êtes bien bon de me tancer sur mes inexactitudes en fait de raisonnements. En êtes vous à vous apercevoir que je vois très bien certains objets mais que je ne sais point comparer; que je suis assez fertile en propositions sans jamais voir de conséquences; qu'ordre et méthode qui sont vos dieux, sont mes furies; que jamais rien ne s'offre à moi qu'isolé et qu'au lieu de lier mes idées dans mes écrits, j'use d'une charlatanerie de transitions qui vous en impose tous les premiers à vous autres philosophes," (*Correspondance Générale*, VI, p. 209).

[50] Douglas A. Bonneville, *Diderot's "Vie de Sénèque." A Swan Song Revised.* Fritz Schalk, *Diderot's Essai über Claudius und Nero.*

studies J. R. Loy's examination of the philosophical and moral content of the *Essai* is of most immediate interest to us. Douglas Bonneville's comparison of the earlier and later versions could form the starting point for a detailed study of work, but it is unfortunately flawed by a number of misconceptions relating to Diderot's political thought [51] and Fritz Schalk's essay contains what is essentially a literary study of the text, and is therefore not directly relevant here.

A further difficulty arises from the significant difference between the 1778 and 1782 editions due to the sizeable additions made by Diderot, mainly to defend himself from the violent attacks launched against the first edition by the anti-philosophic journals, with Fréron's *L'Année littéraire* in the lead. These additions are responsible for most of the lengthy digressions, expatiations and general confusion and disorder which Grimm first pointed to as the main weakness of the work; although he added that he did not think it made the work any the less piquant or original.[52] Diderot's editor, Assézat, while agreeing with Grimm, would nevertheless have preferred that "au lieu d'intercaler, quelquefois sans souci des transitions, sa défense dans le texte primitif, Diderot eût conservé ce texte sans remaniements et donné à part sa réponse aux critiques." [53]

This is the crucial problem facing the critic who wishes to explore Diderot's last major work in any depth. Should he treat the first edition and subsequent editions separately or refer himself only to the second edition? His decision will depend partly on the reasons which prompted him to examine the *Essai* in the first place, partly on his interpretation of Diderot's intentions in writing the work in its first and final forms and on his assessment of its place in Diderot's *oeuvre*. Our purpose in examining the *Essai* is to define the intellectual principles which underly it and place them in the evolving train of the philosophical and moral thought which sustains his political ideas. This approach, taken on its own, would require a separate, chronological treatment of the two editions. However, this

[51] Notably Bonneville points to a marked increase in bitterness in the political content of the second edition as compared with the first, and concludes that Diderot is "negative in all the socio-political comments interpolated into the second edition ... Only the philosopher-public-servant is exempt from criticism, and then, apparently, only if he is Seneca or Diderot, especially Diderot" (*op. cit.*, p. 28). He further argues that since Diderot vilifies the people (i.e. the proletariat) in the second edition, thereby considerably diminishing the public whom he claims to be the final judge of morality, his final stance is politically Machiavellian, and morally Nietzschian (*op. cit.*, p. 32). Bonneville's broad conclusion on the *Essai* appears to be that "if this be the "retreat of the sage," it is less stoic than misanthropic or even nihilistic" (*op. cit.*, p. 32). Such views can, in our opinion, only be reached as the result of an over-simplification of the ideas contained in the *Essai*.

[52] Quoted by J. Assézat, A.T., III, p. 6.

[53] *Ibid.*, p. 7.

would be to neglect the second set of considerations stated above which must affect our decision. In order to take these into account we can do no better than take note of Diderot's dedicatory letter to Naigeon which prefaces the second edition of the *Essai* and in which he explains in clear and precise terms his reasons for undertaking the *Essai* and its meaning in relation to his own life and work.

At the beginning of the letter Diderot describes the atmosphere in which the *Essai* was written:

Cet essai (...) est le fruit de mon travail, ou pour mieux dire, de mon loisir pendant un des plus doux intervalles de ma vie. J'étais à la campagne, presque seul, libre de soins et d'inquiétudes, laissant couler les heures sans autre dessein que de me trouver le soir, à la fin de la journée, comme on se trouve quelquefois le matin après une nuit occupée d'un rêve agréable. Les années ne m'avaient laissé aucune de ces passions qui tourmentent, rien de l'ennui qui leur succède.[54]

The contrast with the working conditions that Diderot had known for most of his life could not be more complete, nor could the image that he now presents of himself be more different. The overworked, underpaid director of the *Encyclopédie* grinding away in Le Breton's office, the erupting genius working feverishly into the small hours in his booklined study at the top of the house in the rue Taranne, the enthusiastic conversationalist of the urbane and brilliant society of the rue Royale and Grandval, the colicky traveller prepared to endure the unending rigours of a journey by stagecoach across Europe to visit his "Sémiramis du Nord" and entirely revamp her state policies for her, these are no more. Old age and rural calm combine to free him from the worries and disquieting passions which he had known most of his life. The conditions are ideal for a period of reverie, reflexion, meditation and summing up after a life spent combating for an ideal of truth and goodness constantly menaced from every side. And what more satisfying way of achieving this than by entering into dialogue with Seneca? For it was a dialogue which could fulfil a double purpose: Seneca too had devoted his life to an ideal of truth and virtue in a corrupt age in which that ideal was constantly threatened and maligned, but destiny had also placed him in a position in which he could play an active role in society; ideals in Seneca's hands could and did become realities, meditation could and did lead to action. Diderot saw in Seneca a *sosie* of Antiquity, a Classical counterpart whose life and values mirrored his own. In commenting upon the works of the Latin author he was pointing to the principles and values which never ceased to inspire and sustain his

[54] *Ibid.*, p. 9.

own life's work, in portraying Seneca as well as the other players on the
stage of Antiquity with who he was connected, Diderot was portraying
himself:

> ... si l'on jette alternativement les yeux sur la page de Sénèque et sur la
> mienne, on remarquera dans celle-ci plus d'ordre, plus de clarté, selon qu'on
> se mette plus fidèlement à ma place, qu'on aura plus ou moins d'analogie
> avec le philosophe et avec moi; et l'on ne tardera pas à apercevoir que c'est
> autant mon âme que je peins, que celle des différents personnages qui s'of-
> frent à mon récit.[55]

But Diderot also saw in Seneca something that he had never been, something which circumstances had prevented him from being: a man of action directly involved in and directly influencing the life of the nation.
Seneca had achieved the kind of fulfilment that Diderot would never
know, the transformation on an immediate and personal level of ethical
preoccupations into direct social and political action. Seneca provided
Diderot with a mirror for himself, but he also enabled him to experience
vicariously the kind of direct involvement in the life of the nation which
had been refused him, with, perhaps, the somewhat ironical exception of
his stay at Vincennes and other minor brushes with the authorities. In this
respect Seneca was also a practical teacher whose moral philosophy had
been refined in the fire of continuous experience. Diderot, while identifying himself with Seneca, nevertheless recognised with characteristic humility at the end of this close acquaintance that he was also his disciple; and
he ends his letter with this final piece of advice to Naigeon and to himself:

> ... il ne vous (suffit) pas d'avoir éclairci les passages les plus obscurs du
> philosophe; (...) il ne me (suffit) pas d'avoir lu ses ouvrages, reconnu la
> pureté de ses moeurs, et médité les principes de sa philosophie: prouvons que
> nous avons su, l'un et autre, profiter de ses conseils.[56]

By concluding his life's work with an apology of Seneca Diderot finally
vindicated his contention that those things which we really believe in are
the ones to which we return most frequently. Diderot's lasting concern
throughout his long and varied career was for the moral life: "la morale,
carrefour de toutes ses connaissances, de toutes ses expériences et de toutes
ses recherches" as J. Thomas had eloquently put it.[57] The *Essai* replaces,
in a sense, the systematic treatise on morality that Diderot had never been

---

[55] *Ibid.*, p. 10.
[56] *Ibid.*, p. 14.
[57] *Histoire des littératures*, III, p. 738.

able to write. His description of his approach to his subject indicates that his preoccupation with the moral aspect of Seneca and his writings transcends all other considerations:

> J'aurais pu ne recueillir des règnes de Claude et de Néron que les endroits où Sénèque est en action, et ne montrer que cette grande figure isolée; mais il m'a semblé que, placé au centre du tableau, on sentirait plus fortement la difficulté et la dignité de son rôle: le gladiateur antique serait plus intéressant, s'il avait en face son antagoniste.[58]

Diderot has no wish to portray the aesthetic grandeur of his hero in splendid and peerless isolation as he did once with Dorval. His aim is not to recreate Seneca in a portrait *à la Van Dyck,*[59] but to present a defence and illustration of the man, his life and work, and, through Seneca, of himself. The *Essai* is on Diderot's admission, not a great creative work but a relaxed, intimate study written in a subdued register:

> Ce livre, si c'en est un, ressemble à mes promenades. Rencontré-je un beau point de vue? je m'arrête, et j'en jouis. Je hâte ou je ralentis mes pas, selon la richesse ou la stérilité des sites: toujours conduit par ma rêverie, je n'ai d'autre soin que de prévenir le moment de la lassitude.[60]

It is not a work of genius concerned with the problem of genius as was the *Neveu de Rameau*, nor did Diderot intend it to be. Rather it is the work of a moralist which takes the form of an intimate study of another moralist, with particular emphasis on his relationship with society. With disarming sincerity Diderot finally renounces the mantle of genius preferring to it the humbler but to him more pleasing cloak of virtue:

> ... je serais, je l'avoue, beaucoup moins flatté que l'homme de génie se retrouvât dans quelques-unes de mes pensées, que s'il arrivât à l'homme de bien de se reconnaître dans mes sentiments.[61]

So it would no doubt prove an interesting exercise in textual scholarship to compare the first and second editions of the *Essai*, but it would fail to grasp the essential spirit of the work as outlined by Diderot in the dedicatory letter to Naigeon, a spirit of communion between Seneca and his apologist so intimate that it borders on a fusion of the two personalities and the values which they embody. Given this coalescence of character

---

[58] A.T., III, p. 11.
[59] *Ibid.*
[60] *Ibid.*
[61] A.T., III, p. 10.

and purpose it is understandable that when Diderot found himself under vicious attack for his apology of Seneca he did not hesitate to intercalate his own defence into the original text of the *Essai*. It was to him entirely logical to identify his own justification with that of Seneca; all the more so since the vituperation, calumny and vicious insults directed against the work by its foremost critic, Geoffroy, in *L'Année littéraire*, were equally divided between subject and author, one letter being devoted to each.[62] No contemporary, least of all the enemies of the *philosophes* could fail to perceive the subtle identity of interest linking Diderot to Seneca in the first edition; by the second edition it is blatantly obvious. The additions to the 1782 edition then, are an integral part of the whole work and, *pace* Assézat, should be treated as such.[63]

In the *Réfutation d'Helvétius* and the *Commentaire de Hemsterhuis* Diderot had defined the nature of the relationship between the individual and the society in which he lives. Without genuine social integration the happiness and self-fulfilment of the individual must remain incomplete. Furthermore only by exercising his social duties to the full as a citizen, can the individual hope to bring about the free and just society which will permit him to attain that happiness and self-fulfilment which are his reasons for living. But who is this citizen? What are his essential qualities? Rousseau had created Emile, the archetypal citizen tailormade for the society of the contract. Where was Diderot's Emile? As with Rousseau the answer is that Diderot's ideal citizen lay within himself; as with Rousseau it was a *rêverie* which drew him forth and gave him substance. Diderot's *rêverie* was the *Essai sur Claude et Néron*, his ideal citizen the *homme de bien*. But we must be careful not to draw too close a parallel between the ways in which these two ideal citizens emerged from the consciousness of the two men. In Rousseau's case Emile is, indeed, the child of a *rêverie* experienced in isolation, in Diderot's the *homme de bien* emerges from a *rêverie-dialogue*, from an intimate communion across the centuries between Seneca and himself.

But why should Diderot now offer the *homme de bien* as the formula for the ideal citizen, when only a few years earlier in the *Réfutation* he had held up the genius as the truest representative of the aspirations of common humanity? Indeed, both he and Seneca could equally well have lent themselves to a protracted examination of the nature and qualities of the genius. Be this as it may, Diderot knew full well that the genius, how-

---

[62] *L'Année littéraire*, 1779, Letters II and IV.
[63] D. A. Bonneville reaches the same conclusion in the course of a study of the style in the two versions of the *Essai, op. cit.*, pp. 38-39.

ever much he might incarnate the ideal of the creative, self-fulfilling individual, could never truly be presented as a model of citizenship to the common man. The profound, innate intuition of the genius frequently allows him to transcend morality and grasp the unity of truth, goodness and beauty in a strange and mysterious way. The ordinary citizen, less endowed by nature, must work his way along "le chemin de la vertu (. . .) taillé dans un roc escarpé" [64] through a constant application of the will, sustained mental effort and frequent sacrifice to reach his goal. Only the morality of the *homme de bien* could give him the guidance he required.

Even in the *Réfutation* Diderot had indicated that this allegiance, which had oscillated throughout his life between the genius and the *homme de bien*, was already beginning its final swing back to the latter, that at the deepest level it was morality and virtue which he cared for above all else:

... je suis convaincu (...) qu'à tout prendre, on n'a rien de mieux à faire pour son bonheur que d'être un homme de bien ... C'est une question que j'ai méditée cent fois et avec toute la contention d'esprit dont je suis capable.[65]

He might not have felt himself equal to the task of composing a formal treatise defending virtue [66] but in becoming Seneca's apologist he could nevertheless in some measure satisfy the deepest of all ambitions. For Seneca was *par excellence* the *homme de bien*: "Notre philosophe," says Diderot, "avait rencontré la vraie base de la morale. A parler rigoureusement, il n'y a qu'un devoir: c'est d'être heureux: il n'y a qu'une vertu: c'est la justice." [67] The imperative call to duty and virtue incarnated by Seneca finally convinced Diderot that ethics, the province of the *homme de bien*, and aesthetics, the province of the genius, could not weigh equally in the balance of human values, that a fine action has greater merit than a fine page.[68] With Montaigne he does not hesitate to place the moral purity of Seneca above the stylistic elegance of Cicero, and laments the fact that popular preference for the latter had prevented him for most of his life from appreciating the superior qualities of the former:

Ah! quel mal on m'a fait! pour rendre le littérateur meilleur écrivain, on a empêché l'homme de devenir meilleur." [69]

---

[64] A.T., III, p. 288.
[65] *Ibid.*, p. 345.
[66] *Ibid.*
[67] *Ibid.*, p. 312.
[68] *Ibid.*, p. 285.
[69] *Ibid.*, p. 372.

This scale of values, the preference of moral rectitude to artistic creativity, of the *homme de bien* to the genius is sustained with unrelenting vigour throughout the *Essai*. The Voltaire who defended the Calas family is placed above the Voltaire who wrote *Mahomet*; [70] the writings of Lucan, had the author been superior to Homer, would forever remain closed to Diderot in whose eyes nothing can expiate the vileness of his denunciation of his mother in order to save his own skin.[71] And in the conclusion to his own apology which completes the second edition of the *Essai* we find that when Diderot does at last fleetingly refer to Seneca's genius, the term has been emptied of the meaning which previously opposed it to the concept of the *homme de bien* to become completely assimilated with the latter:

> Sénèque a-t-il du génie . . .?
> A-t-il parlé de la vertu comme un homme qui connaissait la douceur et la dignité . . .? [72]

Here it is evident that the genius, taken in this sense, is synonymous with the *homme de bien* . . . And if any further evidence is required to demonstrate the extent to which morality has replaced genius at the head of Diderot's scale of values we need only observe the transformation undergone by one of the most powerful of those recurring images which characterize his style: the symbol of the tree. In the *Neveu de Rameau* Diderot had used it to describe Racine, the archetype of the genius whose sublimity takes him out of the range of normal moral judgment:

> C'est un arbre qui a fait sécher quelques arbres plantés dans son voisinage; qui a étouffé les plantes qui croissaient à ses pieds; mais il a porté sa cime jusque dans la nue; ses branches se sont étendues au loin; il a prêté son ombre à ceux qui venaient, qui viennent et qui viendront se reposer autour de son tronc majestueux; il a produit des fruits d'un goût exquis et qui se renouvellent sans cesse.[73]

In the *Essai* Diderot returns once more to the tree symbol, but this time he uses it to express the vast ramifications of morality:

> . . . cet arbre immense dont la tête touche aux cieux et les racines pénètrent jusqu'aux enfers, où tout est lié, où la pudeur, la décence, la politesse, les vertus les plus légères, s'il en est de telles, sont attachées comme la feuille au rameau, qu'on déshonore en le dépouillant.[74]

---

[70] *Ibid.*, p. 285.
[71] *Ibid.*, p. 137.
[72] *Ibid.*, p. 406.
[73] O.RO., p. 404.
[74] A.T., III, p. 217.

However much Diderot may admire the genius he is too frequently guilty of dishonouring the tree of morality, so he must be set aside in favour of the *homme de bien*, for only the latter can accede to virtue through a constant effort of will and intelligence.

But if in Diderot's estimation the genius must fare poorly against the *homme de bien* as a candidate for the title of model citizen, the proletarian is not in the running at all. With regard to the masses Diderot is quite adamant:

L'homme peuple est le plus sot et le plus méchant des hommes: se dépopulariser, ou se rendre meilleur, c'est la même chose.[75]

The author of *Les deux amis de Bourbonne* knows full well that the *homme-peuple* is sometimes capable of grasping the truth through instinct and compassion, and that in this he is superior to the *philosophe-homme de bien*:

Souvent il faudrait un long discours au philosophe pour démontrer ce que l'homme du peuple a subitement senti.[76]

But the instinct of the people is unequal to the task of attaining happiness; lacking a developed faculty of reason they are too easily misguided. The question "What is happiness?" cannot be answered by referring to the judgment of the masses, for the masses are no more than a flock of slaves.[77]

Pour être heureux, il faut être libre: le bonheur n'est pas fait pour celui qui a d'autres maîtres que son devoir.[78]

Duty, the path to virtue and ultimately to happiness, can only be perceived and obeyed by the individual in whom the voice of reason guarantees his freedom from all other masters. The voice of the *philosophe,* which gainsays that of the people, is that voice of reason.[79]

In the case of Rousseau the *rêverie* from which his ideal citizen emerges and the treatise on the type of education which will form him are contained in one and the same work. In the case of Diderot they are separate; the *Essai* is his *rêverie*, but for his educational treatise we must turn to his *Plan d'une université russe* completed two years earlier. This work

[75] *Ibid.*, p. 263.
[76] *Ibid.*, p. 314.
[77] *Ibid.*
[78] *Ibid.*
[79] *Ibid.*, p. 263.

constitutes an exact transposition of the values of the *Essai* into educational terms, for, as J. R. Loy has pointed out:

> ... bien que l'éducation soit traitée sous tous ses aspects, on trouve encore une insistance sur le développement de l'homme de bien – non pas comme médiocrité mais comme coeur essential d'une nation.[80]

Education for citizenship requires the enhancement of those qualities, namely effort and intelligence, which enable a man to know and practise virtue.[81] The encouragement of genius must be sacrificed if it is incompatible with the prime purpose of such an educational programme:

> Il vaut mieux risquer d'égarer le génie que d'enlever aux professions subalternes une multitude d'enfants pour les livrer à tous les vices qui suivent l'ignorance et la paresse.[82]

The pious belief that the virtuous life is as accessible to the slave and the primitive as it is to the educated citizen is dismissed as a groundless myth:

> Combien de vertus délicates que l'esclave et le sauvage ignorent! Si l'on croyait que ces vertus, fruits du temps et des lumières, sont de convention l'on se tromperait; elles tiennent à la science des moeurs comme la feuille tient à l'arbre qu'elle embellit.[83]

So in the *Plan* as in the *Essai* the rare, intuitive comprehension of the genius on the one hand and the animal sensitivity, natural conscience or instinct of the people on the other, so close to that of natural man, are dismissed as qualities unsuited to the citizen. There remains the solid if unspectacular rational intelligence of the *homme de bien*, these qualities alone can provide the citizen with the resources he needs in order to climb the wearing path of duty to virtue and happiness.

In his study of the *Essai* J. R. Loy argues that Seneca's moral philosophy attracted Diderot because it maintains a precarious balance between the doctrines of Lucretius, Zeno and Epicurus, and that similarly Diderot highlights the inadequacies of the moral philosophies of three corresponding contemporaries, La Mettrie, Helvétius and Rousseau, and in the *Essai* attempts to synthesise them.[84] Drawing together the threads of his argument J. R. Loy concludes that

---

[80] *Op. cit.*, pp. 250-251, n. 9.
[81] Il faut plus de raison, plus de lumières et de force qu'on ne le suppose communément pour être vraiment homme de bien. Est-on homme de bien sans justice, et a-t-on de la justice sans lumières? ... (A.T., III, p. 433).
[82] *Ibid.*, p. 526.
[83] *Ibid.*, p. 430.

En effet, tout est lié dans la morale si on arrive à voir qu'aux catégories *génie-homme raisonnable-peuple* correspondent les trois catégories (...) *biologique-intellectuel-affectif*.[85]

and that

...la morale qui ne comprendra pas que l'homme est à la fois matière, sensibilité et intellect (...) n'aura rien compris.[86]

This interpretation of the *Essai* is very tempting as it suggests that Diderot did in fact achieve the synthesis of the differing facets of his philosophical and moral thought which had constantly eluded him throughout his life. There is no doubt some truth in the interpretation, but it is unfortunately too convenient, too systematic to be entirely true. To claim that the *Essai* constitutes a fusion of the three categories mentioned above is to ignore one obvious fact, namely the centrality of the morality of the *homme de bien* to the work. As we have seen, in choosing his ideal citizen Diderot specifically rejects the genius and the proletarian in favour of the *homme de bien*; there is no attempt at a reconciliation of the three concepts, implicit or otherwise. Furthermore he represents both Seneca and himself as exemplary *hommes de bien*, exercising will and reason in the pursuit of virtue, and not as men acting upon a vast and comprehensive vision of the moral complexity of society.

Diderot admires the eclecticism of Seneca's philosophy, not because it results in a global synthesis of contrasting doctrines, but because it succeeds in producing a morality which relates the meditation of the philosopher to the action of the citizen. It is a combination of the stoicism of Zeno and the disciplined worldliness of Epicurus.[87] There is no reference, direct or implied, in the section which deals with the *Questiones naturales* or elsewhere to the inclusion of Lucretian materialism in Seneca's doctrine. So one can only conclude that J. R. Loy's argument that Diderot sees Seneca's philosophy as a synthesis of all three Classical thinkers is based more on bold speculation than on solid evidence.

A further instance of this critic's tendency to oversimplify is his equation of Seneca's attitude towards Epicurus with Diderot's attitude towards Rousseau. It becomes apparent from a reading of the relevant passages in the *Essai* that these attitudes differ considerably. Whereas Diderot is vehement in denouncing the "méchant artificieux" who had been his

[84] *Op. cit.*, p. 249.
[85] *Ibid.*, p. 252.
[86] *Ibid.*, p. 254.
[87] See A.T., III, pp. 315-316.

friend, Seneca is unequivocal in proclaiming that beneath the sensual pleasure apparently advocated by Epicurus' doctrine lies a profound moral integrity:

> ... la morale de ce philosophe est saine, et même austère pour celui qui l'approfondit; sa volupté est renfermée dans les limites les plus étroites. La loi que nous (les stoiciens) prescrivons à la vertu, il l'impose à la volupté; il veut qu'elle soit subordonnée à la nature: et ce qui suffit à la nature, est bien mince pour la débauche.[88]

Seneca's and Diderot's condemnation is reserved for those who have perverted Epicurus' doctrine by using it to justify their own moral depravity. If there is a parallel between Epicurus and Rousseau in Diderot's mind – though it is not clear from the *Essai* that there is – then it is a parallel between the master, for whom pleasure must be compatible with the demands of virtue, and his corrupt disciple, for whom pleasure means unrestrained self-indulgence. For undoubtedly the *Confessions* were for Diderot an example of the worst kind of self-indulgence which sacrifices the confidences of friends and acquaintances together with their reputations to an imperious need for self-advertisement. Rousseau's voice of conscience, the keystone of his moral philosophy and the motivating force behind the *Confessions*, was no more than a transparent façade for his own egoism. Diderot is prepared to admit that Rousseau had one great talent: eloquence; but he devoted it exclusively to the service of a dangerous demagogy and insidious persuasiveness which appeal to the passions but not to the mind, and which thus encourage vice and stifle virtue. As an *anti-philosophe* he had acted as an inspiration to all those whose own moral depravity had aroused in them a fanatical hatred for those severe moralists "qui osent préférer les talents et la vertu à l'opulence et aux dignités." [89]

There is, then, no attempt on the part of Diderot to incorporate Rousseau's opinions, even in their mildest form, into his own moral vision. He execrates both the man and his principles. No less does he detest the person and doctrine of La Mettrie. The faithful servant of Frederick II is "dissolu, impudent, bouffon, flatteur, (. . .) fait pour la vie des cours et la faveur des grands." [90] The simple determinism of his materialistic philosophy is dangerous in its implications:

> ... (ses) principes, poussés jusqu'à leurs dernières conséquences, renver-

[88] *Ibid.*, p. 316.
[89] *Ibid.*, p. 97.
[90] *Ibid.*, p. 218.

seraient la législation, dispenseraient les parents de l'éducation de leurs enfants, renfermeraient aux Petites-Maisons l'homme courageux qui lutte sotte-
ment contre ses penchants déréglés, assureraient l'immortalité au méchant
qui s'abandonnerait sans remords aux siens.[91]

Both Rousseau and La Mettrie, in their persons and in their doctrines,
are a denial of the ethical principles which Diderot is at pains to present
in the *Essai* as the only viable basis for citizenship.

The relatively moderate criticism of Helvétius in the *Réfutation* bears
no comparison with the outright rejection of Rousseau and La Mettrie in
the *Essai*. Diderot's main purpose in the *Réfutation* was to expose the
false consequences of Helvétius doctrine, in particular with regard to his
interpretation of the nature of the genius, and not to attack the man whom
he admired or his principles which he accepted. Indeed, in the man and,
subject to certain reservations, in his doctrine Diderot saw an outstanding
example of virtuous living and an apology for education in citizenship.
Helvétius was no doubt wrong in thinking that all men at birth possessed
the same potential and that subsequent differences were due solely to
variations in environment and education, nonetheless he was right to
emphasise the role of education in cultivating virtue and wisdom in the
individual. As an attempt to understand the nature of the genius the
Traité de l'Homme is undeniably a failure, but as an autobiographical
and philosophical portrait of reasoning man, of the *homme de bien*, it
is a success, and as such it earned Diderot's enthusiastic praise:

Il y a cent belles, très-belles pages: il fourmille d'observations fines et
vraies . . .[92]

It is, therefore, difficult to maintain with Loy that in the *Essai* Diderot's
moral thought achieves the synthesis which he claims for it as the whole
work is built around one central, exclusive theme: the morality of the
homme de bien. It is an ethical doctrine which excludes the moralities
of the genius and the *homme du peuple*. In Seneca it is an eclectic combination of the philosophies of Zeno and Epicurus. In Diderot it leads to a
rejection of Rousseau and La Mettrie and induces the same respect for the
values of reason and education as are to be found in Helvétius.

Having established the *homme de bien* as the ideal citizen whose endeavours would bring about and sustain a free and just society, it remained for Diderot to clarify the function of the *philosophe* in the fight for the

[91] *Ibid.*
[92] A.T., II, p. 315.

emergence of that society. As we have seen, in the *Essai* he closely associates the *philosophe* and the *homme de bien*: they have the same virtues
and the same aspirations, and use the same means to satisfy those aspirations. In a sense all *philosophes* are *hommes de bien* and vice versa. But
Diderot acknowledged that not all men, however worthy they might be as
citizens could or would wish to lay claim to the special title of *philosophes,*
that small group of citizens who were marked out from their brethren by
their particular gifts of abstraction and argument, and their ability to
express themselves cogently. It is to Diderot's attempts to define their
role in the light of the values exemplified by the *homme de bien* that we
finally turn our attention in this chapter.

Diderot recognised that the case of the *philosophe* was particularly
problematic:

> Vaut-il mieux avoir éclairé le genre humain, qui durera toujours, que d'a-
> voir ou sauvé ou bien ordonné une patrie qui doit finir? Faut-il être l'homme
> de tous les temps ou l'homme de son siècle? C'est un problème difficile à ré-
> soudre.[93]

For a man strongly attached to the idea that immortality is assured by the
acclaim of posterity, it could not be an easy matter to reject the praise of
future generations for the gratitude of his contemporaries. Yet in the
circumstances it was a problem that pressed for an answer, it demanded
a decision on the relation of thought to action. Were the *philosophe's*
meditations to bear indirect fruit in the profit to be drawn from them in
centuries to come? Or were they to provoke effective action in the immediate situation? In other words was the *philosophe* to exercise his mind upon the eternal issues facing mankind and remain aloof from contemporary battles, or was he to descend into the arena as a committed thinker? In
claiming that the *philosophe's* state was one of war, that he was dealing
not only with error and vice but with their perpetrators,[94] Diderot had
already moved half way to a solution. In a later passage in which he re-
primands Seneca, who in a moment of weakness states his preference for
the sublimities of philosophy to direct involvement in the affairs of men,
he is quite explicit; the philosopher, he writes, is in all places worthy of
esteem,

> Mais plus au sénat que dans l'école, plus dans un tribunal que dans une
> bibliothèque, et la sorte d'occupations que vous dédaignez est vraiment celle

[93] A.T., III, p. 325.
[94] *Ibid.*, p. 271.

que j'honore, elle demande de la fatigue, de l'exactitude, de la probité; et les hommes doués de ces qualités vous semblent communs! Lorsque j'en verrai qui se seront fait un nom dans la magistrature, au barreau, loin de croire qu'ils ont perdu leurs années pour qu'une seule portât leur nom, je serai désolé de n'en pouvoir compter une aussi belle dans toute ma vie.[95]

The *philosophe* who professes "une philosophie de la valeur, une morale aboutissant à l'action"[96] is the image and ideal that Diderot leaves as his legacy in the *Essai*. It is in this ideal that the philosophical, ethical and political dimensions of his thought at last achieve that synthesis which had constantly eluded him throughout the greater part of his life. All Diderot's intellectual efforts in the last few years of his life are devoted through his writings, particularly his contributions to the *Histoire des deux Indes*, to the inculcation of a new revolutionary spirit and mentality in his readers.

But it is a synthesis which is reached at a price; for Diderot, in common with so many other theorists and exponents of revolution, all but sacrificed his aesthetic interests for the utilitarian preoccupations of his moral and political doctrine. We have to look no further than the *Essai sur les règnes de Claude et de Néron* to recognise how far Diderot had departed from his concern for beauty. We have already mentioned its formlessness, its lack of stylistic distinction. Within the work itself we have noted his preference for other writers' moral qualities against their creative capabilities, for the fine action against the beautiful page. A further instance is to be found in his changed attitude to the Socratic ideal. This is doubly significant as besides providing confirmatory evidence of Diderot's declining interest in the aesthetic dimension it also demonstrates how far he had progressed beyond the rather naïve Aristippus-Socrates polarity in his understanding of the type of influence a man such as himself could exercise upon the authorities.

Jean Seznec has remarked of the dialogue between Aristippus and Socrates which Diderot included in the *Salon* of 1767:

(Il) a dû retentir plus d'une fois dans la conscience de Diderot; mais le dernier mot est resté à Socrate ... L'intrépidité sied mieux au vrai philosophe que la prudence tactique. Il est grand, il est beau de s'exposer comme Socrate, et de souffrir pour la vérité au lieu de la taire ou de la rétracter.[97]

If we take as Diderot's last word on the subject his outburst in the *Lettre*

---

[95] *Ibid.*, p. 338.
[96] A remark made by J. Fabre during a discussion at the annual congress of the A.I.E.F., June 1961. See *Résumé des Discussions* in the *Cahiers*, p. 398.
[97] "Le Socrate Imaginaire" in *Essais sur Diderot et l'Antiquité*, pp. 10-11.

apologétique de l'abbé Raynal à M. Grimm, then Seznec is right. In this letter a violent attack on the life-long friend who in his old age had thrown in his lot with those rulers who had cosseted him with titles and pensions, and who had become "un des plus cachés, mais un des plus dangereux anti-philosophes," Diderot proclaimed defiantly:

> Celui qui a pris le manteau de Socrate, et qui aime la vérité et la vertu plus que la vie, dira, lui: "Philosopher d'abord, et vivre ensuite." Si l'on peut . . .[98]

But it must be remembered that the letter is a spontaneous, highly emotional reaction of a man whose own self-respect has been deeply injured, for the passages in the *Histoire des deux Indes* against which Grimm had particularly directed his criticism were precisely those that Diderot himself had contributed. This, and the sudden realisation that his closest colleague had ranged himself in the camp of his adversaries account for the tone of the letter and the passionate defence of the Socratic ideal of truth pursued uncompromisingly in the face of all opposition to the point of self-sacrifice in its service. However, against this letter written *ab irato* we must set Diderot's conclusions on the same subject in the *Essai*, much of which was written in the pastoral calm of Sèvres far away from the polemical turmoil of the capital. These conclusions are far more nuanced and subtle, and in our opinion express more truly Diderot's final attitude on the role of the *philosophe* than does the rather infantile invective of the *Lettre apologétique*. Once more it is Seneca himself who serves as model and provides the answer to the Aristippus-Socrates debate. Seneca, albeit a faithful servant of the truth throughout his life, had not looked upon the sacrifice of his life as the best way of serving it, preferring the less spectacular but more effective way of prudently exploiting his position so as to minimise the evil and corruption of the masters whom he served. Only when no other means was possible did he finally resolve to take his own life. Seneca's was the adult idealism, tempered by a sense of practicality, of a man of experience, but as his death showed, this practical idealism did not degenerate into pragmatism. He lived an Aristippus and died a Socrates. His concern was not for the beauty and nobility of his own actions, but the unremitting service of truth and satisfaction of the needs of others. In applauding Seneca's attitude Diderot notes that the beauty and grandeur associated with self-immolation are essentially false:

> Le sacrifice de la vie donne aux actions un éclat qui prouve moins la force

[98] O.PH., p. 629.

de celui qui s'y résout que la faiblesse de celui qui s'en étonne. Un autre mon-
trerait sans doute du courage à mourir; vous en montrerez davantage à
vivre: un autre ne penserait qu'à lui; Sénèque se souviendra de ses concitoyens: un autre s'illustrerait par sa résistance; votre condescendance sera
blâmée, vous n'en doutez pas, et c'est par cette raison que vous en serez plus
grand.[99]

This is Diderot's own position in the last years. Circumstances prevented
him from exercising a direct ameliorative influence upon French society.
But if he was denied the position of magistrate or functionary he did towards the latter end of his life seek every available opportunity to combat
oppression and injustice, and call upon his fellow citizens to take the destiny of their nation into their own hands. He exerted his influence
through his writings, in the *Essai sur Claude et Néron*. Following Seneca's
example he allied tactical prudence with an unrelinquishing pursuit of the
truth which expressed itself in an irreconcilable hostility to the rulers who
had usurped the rights of their subjects. Like his master he imitated the
caution of Aristippus, unlike him he was spared the sacrifice of Socrates.

[99] A.T., III, p. 377.

PART TWO

THE EVOLUTION OF DIDEROT'S
POLITICAL THOUGHT

CHAPTER I

A COHERENT ABSOLUTISM

I. ABSOLUTISM AND ENLIGHTENMENT

In 1765 twenty years of unremitting toil on the *Encyclopédie* came to an end. By July of that year the last manuscript pages had been completed, and publication, held up since the revocation of the *privilège* in 1759, could go ahead. Distribution of the eagerly awaited volumes to subscribers began early in the following year despite the prohibition of Sartine, acting on the orders of the *dévot* party at court. The flouting of the prohibition order did lead to action on the part of the authorities, but the effects were minimal and did little to stem the outflow of the bulky folio volumes. Le Breton, the head of the publishing syndicate, was despatched to the Bastille to reflect on his incautious enthusiasm, and copies of the last ten volumes were seized from courtiers at Versailles who had been so indiscreet as to subscribe to the dangerous publication. These half-hearted efforts at suppression were the last vain blows struck in the bitter war waged by the authorities against the *Encyclopédie* and all those connected with its production.

The triumph was a personal one for Diderot, for without his tenacity the great project must necessarily have failed. For twenty years he had worked on against odds that would have made a lesser man give in. Abandoned by his co-editor d'Alembert at a time of considerable danger, he took over complete editorial responsibility. When the work was suppressed, he nonetheless continued to write and edit articles in semi-clandestinity; and when, the end already in sight, he was reduced to the depths of despair by Le Breton's cowardly censorship of the last volumes, carried out without his knowledge, he managed to pull himself together and finish the task. His unsparing devotion to the great enterprise had brought him little financial reward, and on several occasions it had nearly resulted in his having to leave the country or risk imprisonment.[1]

[1] CORR, V. p. 64.

The history of the editing and publication of the *Encyclopédie* is the history of Diderot's political awakening. At the outset of the venture neither temperament nor circumstance inclined him to take a great interest in political matters. His efforts were restricted to satisfying the claims made upon him as a father and husband, while trying to achieve the at times conflicting ambition to become a *philosophe* and an artist worthy of the name. Consequently his sole desire was to be allowed to work in peace and unhindered, as was the right of any honest, law-abiding citizen pursuing his innocent daily course. The demands of the *Encyclopédie* and his conversations with Rousseau did lead to the extension of his philosophical speculation into the field of political theory, but the results were relatively unimportant. They amounted to little more than a set of principles, largely derivative, which supported and justified the rule of the absolute monarch as the only suitable form of government for France. Here was nothing that by its practical implications could on the face of it be considered in any way subversive.

Yet if Diderot's prudent conservatism was accompanied by a political orthodoxy which was apparently above suspicion, the assumptions on which he based his theory of absolutism made him the target of the traditionalists. By stating that "le prince tient de ses sujets mêmes l'autorité qu'il a sur eux" [2] and that he holds his authority by usufruct alone,[3] Diderot denied the traditional theory of divine right, thereby incurring the wrath of the Church, which saw its privileged position as the chief ideological support of the Throne come under attack.[4] The criticism levelled against the article *Autorité politique* was symptomatic of the hostility aroused by the *Encyclopédie* from its earliest days until its completion. The foremost adversaries of Diderot and his colleagues were not the government proper (witness the unwillingness of d'Aguesseau, Malesherbes and Sartine to intervene against them), but the ranks of the Church and the *Parlement*, the guardians of orthodoxy. The *Encyclopédie* was, therefore, not so much politically dangerous as ideologically subversive. To all intents and purposes orthodox in his politics, it was Diderot's philosophical heterodoxy which led to his involvement in the growing turmoil of the political scene, and with involvement came, inevitably, political awareness. Rousseau was born dispossessed, he grew up a social misfit, as

---

[2] O.PO., p. 13.
[3] *Ibid.*, p. 15.
[4] See J. Lough, "The Article *Autorité Politique*" in *Essays on the Encyclopédie of Diderot and d'Alembert* in which the *Instruction Pastorale* of Charles de Caylus, Bishop of Auxerre, which condemns *Autorité politique* as a seditious article, is quoted and discussed at length.

a man he was highly sensitive about his underprivileged status. For Jean-Jacques a political conscience was in the nature of things. In contrast, the deprivations which Diderot had experienced as a young man had been temporary and in a measure self-imposed, and they had not left any mark. He had to undergo prolonged and vicious persecution of his most dearly held beliefs before acquiring a political conscience approaching the same intensity as that of his contemporary. It took twenty years of trial and tribulation for him to realise that the aims of those in power rested on values which were incompatible with his own beliefs.

In a short passage from his letter to the subscribers of the *Encyclopédie*, which accompanied the final volumes, Diderot revealed his understanding of the contemporary political situation and outlined his hopes for the future. Looking forward to the day when education on a national scale would enable all men to profit from the vast compendium of knowledge contained in the *Encyclopédie*, he wrote,

C'est aux Maîtres du monde à hâter cette heureuse révolution. Ce sont eux qui étendent ou resserrent la sphère des lumières. Heureux le temps où ils auront tous compris que leur sécurité consiste à connaître des hommes instruits! Les grands attentats n'ont jamais été commis que par des fanatiques aveugles.[5]

The significance of these few short sentences is considerable, as they contain the essence of Diderot's political thought at a critical time when politics were moving quickly from the periphery to the centre of his attention. They represent the merging of the political theory evolved from his philosophy with the lessons learned from his experiences as the principal editor of the *Encyclopédie*.

The remarks in the passage are of general application but Diderot does not deceive his readers; it is clear that his words are primarily inspired by the political situation in France and the struggle that has been engaged between ignorance and enlightenment. If we read between the lines we will see that essentially Diderot is arguing that man is reasonable, and that it is only through the unhindered exercise of his reason that his well-being will be achieved. It is in the ruler's interest to bring about this happy revolution, for reason will lead "les hommes instruits" to the conviction that the only satisfactory form of government is one in which sovereignty, which belongs of right to the people, is unequivocally vested in the ruler. Only in this way will the monarch ever be secure. While he continues to rest his authority on Church and *Parlement* he will never feel

[5] CORR., V, p. 84.

assured of his safety. These two institutions are dedicated to the maintenance of ignorance and intolerance. Their prime aim cannot be to serve the king, for the welfare of the king depends on the nation being enlightened by reason and knowledge – and here Diderot can turn to the evidence of history to support his argument. Beneath a semblance of loyal service to the Crown their real concern has always been the advancement of their own interests. The attempts by religious fanatics to assassinate monarchs, the frequent endeavours of the Paris *Parlement* to infringe royal authority since the death of Louis XIV, and the machinations of the Society of Jesus which led to its dissolution in France in 1764, all give weight to Diderot's contention that the monarch could not rely on them for either practical or ideological support.

The new pattern of power as conceived by Diderot thus emerges. The monarch must remain absolute; in him alone can national sovereignty be vested, he alone can express the general will of the nation. But his authority and power should no longer issue from a meaningless theological doctrine, nor should it rest on institutions whose loyalty is more than dubious, but upon the confidence of an educated nation whose loyalty to him is born of reason. These are the main features which characterise Diderot's political thought over the time bounded on one side by the completion of the *Encyclopédie* and on the other by his meeting with Catherine II in 1773-74, when it acquires a new orientation.

With the exception of two stays at d'Holbach's country home, Le Grandval, in the summer and autumn of 1767, Diderot stayed in Paris for a period of five years which was eventually broken by a journey to Bourbonne and Langres in July and August, 1770. During these five years his reflexions on political matters became characterised by an increasing optimism which contrasted strongly with the increasingly oppressive atmosphere on the home front, as Choiseul in league with the *parlements* made a determined attempt to suppress all forms of heterodoxy. In the person of Catherine II, and in the revelation accorded to him by the physiocrat, Mercier de la Rivière, and the idiosyncratic utopian Dom Deschamps, Diderot found a confirmation and extension of his own ideas, developed in the *Encyclopédie* articles, and an antidote to the pessimism caused in him by the domestic situation. These years also saw the beginning of his fruitful association with the abbé Raynal, in whose *Histoire des deux Indes* he was to find a platform for his most uninhibited and daring political ideas.[6] His contributions to the 1770 edition of this work, though

---

[6] H. Wolpe in *Raynal et sa machine de guerre* (viz. Appendice II, *Diderot et l'Histoire des deux Indes*) and more recently M. Duchet in an article "Diderot Colla-

rare compared with those to later editions, together with his correspondence constitute the most important source of information from which we can establish the evolution of his political thought at this time. The fact that Diderot wrote no self-contained political works before 1770, the year in which he drafted his *Apologie de l'abbé Galiani*, indicates that although he had a good grounding in political thought he was not yet satisfied that he had acquired an adequate corpus of ideas to launch out independently. Until 1765 he had not disposed of sufficient time or energy to concentrate on such matters; in the five years to which we now turn our attention he was able to complete his political apprenticeship.

Diderot's attitude to the domestic régime at the beginning of this period alternates between a fatalistic acceptance of the *status quo* and a naive faith that the situation will improve. The twenty years battle of the *Encyclopédie* had drained him of his militancy, and once more the passive side of his temperament reasserted itself.[7] The world grows older but it does not change, the measures of good and evil in the human race remain the same.[8] Sharing the contemporary disenchantment with the English parliamentary ideal, he turns to the government of his own nation and views it with a fatalism tinged with despondency.

Nos ministres ne sont peut-être pas trop bons; mais tâchons de nous en contenter, puisqu'ils ne sont pas meilleurs ailleurs. Notre société est peut-être assez mal administrée, mais c'est la condition commune de toutes les sociétés.

A flame of reforming idealism flickers briefly,

Il est certain que toute puissance qui n'est pas dirigée au bonheur général est illégitime,

borateur de Raynal: A Propos des "Fragments Imprimés" du Fonds Vandeul" have proved beyond any reasonable doubt the extent and nature of Diderot's contribution to Raynal's work in its three editions of 1770, 1774 and 1780. Most of the passages which were written by Diderot and actually incorporated in the *Histoire* were joined together as a continuous text in two MS volumes of the Fonds Vandeul: N. a. fr. 24.939 (*Pensées Détachées*) and N. a. fr. 13.768 (*Mélanges*, Vol. XXXVIII). Further passages published in the *Histoire de deux Indes* were inserted in MS versions of *Sur les Femmes* (N. a fr. 13.768, art. 23, pp. 357-382) and of the *Observations sur le Nakaz* (N. a. fr. 24.939). Three more sources complete the list of Diderot's known contributions to Raynal's work, which were published: *Sur la civilisation de la Russie* (N. a. fr. 13.766), *Philosophie des Brames* (N. a. fr. 24.940[1], frag. 17-44), *Eloge d'Eliza Draper* (N. a. fr. 24.940[1], frag. 164-166). Finally, four further passages, intended for the *Histoire* but not published, have come to light over the years: *Fragments Politiques*, A. T. IV, pp. 41-50, *Fragments Echappés*, A.T. VI, pp.444-457, and two passages published in the *Correspondance Littéraire* of the 1st October 1772 and 15th November 1772, which were rediscovered by H. Dieckmann, see his article "Les contributions de Diderot à la *Correspondance Littéraire* et à l'*Histoire des deux Indes*."
    [7] See Part I, Chap. I, pp. 27-30.
    [8] CORR., V, p. 80.

but it is quickly dowsed and his thought is once more pervaded with a fatalistic gloom:

Mais qu'on me nomme sur la terre une seule puissance légitime en ce sens. Serions-nous assez déraisonnables pour exiger qu'il y eût une administration unique, faite tout exprès pour nous. Ma coutume est de me consoler de tous les maux que je supporte avec tous mes concitoyens; pourquoi ne me consolerais-je pas d'un mal commun à tous les hommes? [9]

Ten months later the savage and unjustifiable execution of the young Chevalier de la Barre woke Diderot out of his torpor. Not only did it sting him into a vigorous and indignant denunciation of the barbaric act,[10] but it also served to remind him that his own life would be in danger if the persecuting ardour of the *parlements* continued unabated. The ferocious animal had tasted human blood, it had eaten up the Jesuits, and looked now as if it would pounce on the *philosophes,*

Je sçais bien qu'elle a les yeux tournés sur moi, et que je serai peut-être le premier qu'elle dévorera.[11]

But, with the exception of several incidents like the execution of the Chevalier de la Barre, society had an air of outward calm, so that a tired soul like Diderot could delude himself into believing that he could live innocently and obscurely, intent only on improving himself.[12] However, he realised, albeit unwillingly, that this was no more than a dream. He knew that his waking hope that the world had come to its senses overnight was just stupid generosity on his part.[13] The wicked do not change, the fanatics are as active as ever, and the rulers of the world, and particularly of France, are no nearer to appreciating that their real interests lie with their subjects. Diderot's endeavour to free himself from involvement in the philosophic battle and live in quiet anonymity was at an end. After a year's rest in which passivity had been the keynote of his relations with the authorities and fatalism had been preponderant in his political thought a new energy began to stir in him and reinvigorate his interest in political matters.

Once more Diderot's faith in knowledge and education, the very things the *Encyclopédie* had sought to propagate, came to the fore. In his letter to the readers of the *Encyclopédie*, he had proclaimed that the salvation of

[9] *Ibid.*, p. 173.
[10] CORR., VI, p. 254.
[11] *Ibid.*, p. 334.
[12] *Ibid.*, p. 336.
[13] *Ibid.*

the nation lay with the ruler whose authority rested upon an educated population. But the victory in the fight of enlightenment against ignorance, represented by the triumphant publication of the last volumes of the great work was only momentary. Governmental oppression was once more on the increase, and Diderot records his detestation of Choiseul, whose avowed policy was to prevent the spread of knowledge:

Un freluquet sans lumière et sans pudeur dit intrépidement à sa table que l'ignorance fait l'honneur des peuples.[14]

A year later, writing once more to Falconet who is at St. Petersburg, he informs him that the situation has deteriorated even further:

L'intolérance du gouvernement s'accroît de jour en jour. On diroit que c'est un projet formé d'éteindre ici les lettres, de ruiner le commerce de librairie et de nous réduire à la besace et à la stupidité.[15]

By the end of the decade the effects of the government's renewed efforts to suppress the dissemination of information and free comment on issues such as government, religion and morality were only too evident to Diderot. Enthusiasm had been lost; the crusading zeal which had previously existed in a significant section of the population had waned, to be replaced by a calculating spirit and a taste for easy living.[16] There could be no hope of great changes being brought about in a nation whose populace had been reduced to voluptuous indolence by the alliance of Throne and Altar which imposed its tyranny by the silencing of ambition and the cramping of intellectual activity.

II. MERCIER DE LA RIVIÈRE AND EVIDENCE

His experience with the *Encyclopédie* and now the renewed intolerance of the authorities had led Diderot to the conviction that free access to knowledge and information of all kinds was a political issue of the first importance. Tyranny could only flourish if ignorance were maintained; apathy and self-seeking were the inevitable consequences of a society whose members were not permitted to comment freely on matters of national import, and thus associate themselves with the furtherance of the public good. As early as 1751 in the article *Autorité politique* Diderot had commented approvingly on Henri IV's practice of admitting freely to his presence all kinds of people, "afin que les gens de savoir et de mérite

---

[14] CORR., VII, pp. 56-57.
[15] CORR., VIII, pp. 44-45.
[16] *Salon de 1769*, A.T. XI, p. 450.

eussent le moyen d'y proposer sans crainte ce qu'ils croiraient nécessaire pour le bien public." [17] But he had never developed the idea of the freedom of knowledge as a means of creating an informed citizenry into a formal article of his political creed. It required the stimulus of another thinker of inferior quality to enable him to integrate this aspect of his thought into the body of his political ideas. The effect of the stimulus was dramatic, not to say revolutionary; politics, from being one of Diderot's more peripheral intellectual activities, became the centre of his attention, the focal point on which all his other intellectual interests converged. For the first time in his life Diderot's own political ideas took on a significance and an immediacy which they had never before attained.

The thinker in question was Mercier de La Rivière. The transformation he wrought in Diderot's thinking was by the intermediary of his book *De l'Ordre naturel et essentiel des Sociétés politiques,* which itself was inspired by the principles of Quesnay and the physiocratic school. Ironically Diderot had been asked by his old school friend Sartine to act as official censor for the book when it appeared anonymously in June 1767. Diderot's reply was favourable and the book was duly published, *sans privilège.* The effect of the book on its unexpected censor was immediate:

Tous les écrits, toutes les conversations, toutes les lectures m'avoient tellement embrouillé la tête sur les questions d'économie et de politique, que j'ai dit cent fois que la plus mince de ces questions étoit plus difficile qu'un problème de calcul différentiel et intégral. Voilà le premier qui m'ait éclairé, qui m'ait instruit, qui m'ait convaincu et qui ait dissipé les fantômes que les autres m'avoient faits.[18]

La Rivière succeeded where others had failed because his system incorporated a number of significant features which bore a close resemblance to the basic principles of Diderot's own thought, set out in a persuasively logical order. "Une logique dont je ne connais aucun exemple" [19] commented Diderot enthusiastically.

The main argument of *De l'Ordre naturel et essentiel des Sociétés politiques* is straight forward. The principal weakness of the book, and an indication of La Rivière's limitations as a political theorist, lies in its repetitiveness. The author is clearly so delighted at having formulated a set of principles which he regards as the definitive blueprint for the perfect society that he is not satisfied with simply expounding them and leaving

[17] O.PO., p. 17.
[18] CORR., VII, p. 77.
[19] *Ibid.*, p. 76.

it at that. In chapter after tedious chapter he juggles and toys with them, without throwing any further light on his thesis in the process. However, this very repetition does have the advantage of endowing La Rivière's ideas with a clarity, consistency and lack of ambiguity which in turn enabled Diderot finally to clarify his own ideas and rid himself of the confusion which, on his own admission, had arisen in his mind whenever he turned his attention to political matters.

The argument of La Rivière's book goes as follows: Man is destined by nature to live in society. Only in the social order can he find the happiness which is the final aim of all his activities. This being so, the laws which constitute the social order should be a part of the general and immutable laws of creation. Our misfortunes spring from our ignorance of the nature of these laws. However, there indubitably exists a natural order for the government of society which will necessarily assure us of all the temporal happiness to which we have been called. So that we may discover this order nature has endowed us with "une portion suffisante de lumières." It is an order which, once known, will be observed. In it the happiness of each member is inseparable from that of every other, from the sovereigns down to the last of their subjects. Finally, it is an order which demonstrates God's goodness, and thus disposes men to love and adore him.[20]

Leaving aside the references to the divine, which are extraneous to the argument and which La Rivière seems only to have included for orthodoxy's sake,[21] the main ideas are closely related to Diderot's, though they lack the philosophical foundation of the latter.[22] Diderot equally believes in man's sociability; the social instinct is inscribed in the very structure of each individual. He also holds that all laws are or at least should be a particular application of the universal law which rules the moral as well as the physical world.[23] With La Rivière he holds that man is essentially reasonable and it is his faculty of reason which enables him to perceive and apply the universal law in its different ramifications, not least in the context of society. And it has been one of Diderot's most strongly held beliefs since the Essai sur le mérite et la vertu that general

---

[20] De l'Ordre naturel et essentiel des Sociétés politiques, Discours préliminaire, pp. v-vii.

[21] Catherine II was not deceived: "Je commence à croire que cet homme-là ne croit pas en Dieu. Il arrange son ordre naturel comme les athées arrangent la création du monde, et puis il vous plante là." Quoted by G. Roth in CORR., VIII, p. 52.

[22] La Rivière does, however, refer to "la nécessité physique de la société," so that the philosophical premises of his political thought are implicitly materialistic. Diderot emphasises this aspect of his thought in a letter to Falconet in which he refers to "ses principes, tous appuyés sur l'ordre physique et l'enchaînement général des choses." (CORR., VII. p. 94).

[23] See J. Proust, op. cit., pp. 405-408.

and individual wellbeing are integrally related.

According to La Rivière the natural and essential order of society is determined by the evidence of the physical order.[24] This evidence is perceived by the reason, or to use the author's own expression, "une portion suffisante de lumières." La Rivière's conception of evidence is essentially rationalistic, as is clear from the following definition:

> Une chose évidente est une vérité qu'un examen suffisant a rendu tellement sensible, tellement manifeste, qu'il n'est plus possible, à l'esprit humain d'imaginer des raisons pour en douter, dès qu'il a connoissance de celles qui l'ont fait adopter.[25]

Only if the physical order of nature is first investigated and analysed by rational processes and the information or evidence gained is applied to the laws governing society will its vices be rectified and the social order be established on a sound and lasting basis. The role of evidence is to enlighten opinion, to replace irrational prejudices and preconceptions, which are always a danger to society, by hard, incontrovertible facts. In this way, opinion will be united and fixed, leading to the replacement of an arbitrary social order by one which is natural and therefore necessary.

La Rivière goes on to argue that the natural and essential order of society will only subsist if sovereignty is exercised by an individual and is hereditary.[26] His objections to the division of sovereignty, whether it is vested in a few or in the nation as a whole stems from his belief in the right of property, which he considers sacrosant and the very basis of society.[27] The right of property necessarily excludes equality and therefore causes men's interests to vary widely, consequently it would be impossible to achieve a unanimity of opinion on the laws to be promulgated. A further but less significant objection is that it would be impossible to assemble the nation in one place at one time for the purpose of legislating; here La Rivière obviously has Rousseau in mind.[28] The sovereign must be hereditary and not elective since, in order to possess the power necessary

---

[24] *Op. cit.*, p. 40.
[25] *Ibid.*, p. 60.
[26] *Ibid.*, p. 66.
[27] "Les hommes (. . .) en se réunissant en société, n'ont eu d'autre objet que d'instituer parmi eux des droits de propriété commune et particulière, à l'aide desquels ils pussent se procurer toute la somme du bonheur que l'humanité peut comporter" (*Discours préliminaire*, p.v.) Both La Rivière and Diderot follow Locke in considering property to be the fruit of the individual's work, but the right of property occupies a more important place in the thought of the former, as is the case of all the physiocrats, than it does with Diderot.
[28] *De l'Ordre essentiel*, 2e Partie, Chap. XVI.

to preserve his authority, he must be the co-proprietor of the net product of the land under his domination.[29] It therefore follows that wherever "une connoissance évidente et publique de l'ordre naturel et essentiel" reigns, this form of government is the one most advantageous to society as it establishes a truly legal despotism,[30] based on a relationship of mutual necessity between the sovereign and his subjects; for sovereignty could not exist without the nation, nor the social order without the sovereign power.[31] La Rivière is careful to make a sharp distinction between legal and arbitrary despotism:

> Le despotisme arbitraire n'est point le vrai despotisme; (. . .) il est à tous égards contraire aux intérêts de celui qui l'exerce; (. . .) il n'est que factice, précaire et conditionnel, au lieu que le despotisme *légal* est naturel, perpétuel et absolu.[32]

Whereas under a system of arbitrary despotism the sovereign rules according to his private whim and fancy, under legal despotism the "Chef unique," who exercises both the legislative and executive powers is

> l'organe de l'évidence; (. . .) il ne fait que manifester par des signes sensibles, et armer d'une force coercitive les loix d'un ordre essentiel dont Dieu est l'Instituteur.[33]

The operative force in government is not the sovereign but evidence; the sovereign is simply the instrument through which the evidence is channeled so that it can impose an essential and natural order on society. Obviously the sovereign will wish to call men of knowledge and wisdom to help him in his deliberations and furnish him with the evidence he requires, but they will act in a purely consultative capacity. His will alone will order and dictate the laws.[34]

This summary of La Rivière's system serves to show how close he is to Diderot in the final application of his principles if not in all his underlying suppositions. The main difference between the two men lies in their conception of sovereignty. Diderot theoretically believes that sovereignty belongs by right to the nation and that it is conferred by contract on the ruler who becomes sovereign by usufruct.[35] In practice there would ap-

---

[29] *Ibid.*, 2e Partie, Chap. XIX.
[30] *Ibid.*, p. 66.
[31] *Ibid.*, p. 201.
[32] *Ibid.*, p. 66.
[33] *Ibid.*
[34] *Ibid.*, pp. 85-86.
[37] See Introduction, p. 11.

pear to be no disagreement on this matter; both men are absolutists and partisans of a hereditary monarchy. But if La Rivière brought nothing original to Diderot's political thought why should the latter have welcomed his book with such enthusiasm and gratitude? And why should it have brought about such a transformation in Diderot's attitude to political matters? The reasons are twofold.

At the time La Rivière's book appeared Diderot's political thought existed in fragmentary form, dispersed among a number of articles in the *Encyclopédie,* certain passages in his correspondence, and other minor texts. He had never had either the occasion or the inclination to produce a single, continuous exposition of his ideas. Indeed, it seems doubtful whether he was fully aware that his disparate thoughts did constitute a coherent philosophy. Now, at a time when he felt a growing sense of anger and frustration at the political bankruptcy of an increasingly tyrannical government, he found in *De l'ordre essentiel* the first complete and cogent exposition of the principles to which he himself adhered. The value of La Rivière's influence on Diderot was that it enabled him to refurbish his political ideas, to perceive their relationships, and to view them, not as a number of isolated concepts, but as a unified system. Diderot's political thought after reading *De l'ordre essentiel* does not differ to any marked degree from his thought when writing *Autorité politique.* What does differ is his attitude to his own political ideas; now he sees them as a coherent set of principles which, if applied, would free the nation from the oppression which is the inevitable outcome of arbitrary despotism, and set it on a sound footing.

The second valuable contribution of La Rivière to the clarification of Diderot's political thought at this stage lies in his stress on the role of evidence. Even in the early days of the *Encyclopédie* Diderot considered specialist knowledge and enlightened opinion to be invaluable aids to the ruler in his task of legislating for the well-being of the nation. In his thesis Jacques Proust devotes an important section to the study of Diderot's conception of the relationships of the *philosophes* with the authorities.[36] From a careful analysis of several of his articles and allied writings Proust deduces that Diderot sees the solution to the political problem in a revolution of opinion, brought about by the intellectual élite of the nation who simultaneously act in an advisory capacity to the monarch and other public bodies, and contribute to the formation of enlightened opinion in the nation as a whole. Proust then goes on to raise an objection:

---

[36] *Op. cit., Le pouvoir et les philosophes,* pp. 438-448.

Il reste qu'en plaçant ainsi la solution du problème politique sur le seul plan de l'opinion, Diderot s'est enfermé dans un cercle vicieux ... Comment peut-il être vrai à la fois que l'homme soit le "produit du milieu social" où il vit, et que ce milieu soit "forgé par l'opinion publique, c'est-à-dire par l'homme"? Si le prince et les membres du corps politique sont aveuglés par les préjugés de l'opinion au point de prendre le mal pour le bien et d'oublier la loi de leur propre nature, comment cette même opinion pourra-t-elle se changer en son contraire pour éclairer le prince et progressivement tout son peuple? [37]

Since Diderot did not express himself very clearly on the matter at that time Proust is perhaps justified in claiming that his concept of the role of opinion contains an antinomy. But the subsequent contact with La Rivière helped Diderot to clarify his ideas. In the course of a long letter to Falconet he speaks out vehemently against the group of *philosophes* led by Mably who decried the theory of evidence. If evidence is useless, he argues, then the creators of evidence are importunate gossips, more useless and despicable than the least of citizens. And he points to the main fallacy in their argument:

Ils disent que l'opinion est la reine du monde; et ils nient que la vérité, qui n'est que l'opinion démontrée, accrue de la force de l'expérience et de la raison, puisse quelque chose! [38]

In this counter-attack against the anti-evidence movement, Diderot exonerates himself from the charge made against him by Proust. Opinion, as he conceives it, is not subject to the arbitrary and changing pressures of social environment. It is, in fact, no less than the inviolable, unchanging truth of the universe, which is revealed by the process of rational and empirical investigation. It is the truth which the *sage*, whether he be the king or his advisors, perceives through the exceptional powers of observation and co-ordination accorded him by his privileged physiological organisation. The synthesis of Diderot's political and his philosophical and moral thought is complete.

La Rivière's book claimed Diderot's attention as a most opportune moment. At a time when his morale was low, when the struggle to spread enlightenment through the nation seemed a failure in the face of increasing governmental oppression, La Rivière gave him new courage and a new hope. He enabled him to order his scattered thoughts and his own personal experience into a unified political vision which was the culminat-

---

[37] *Ibid.*, p. 447.
[38] CORR., VIII, p. 113.

ing point of his moral and philosophical thought. Central to this vision are the "créateurs de l'évidence" the dispensers of the rationally verifiable knowledge and informed opinion which is the true safeguard against tyranny and the real guarantee of the well-being of the nation. If the intellectual élite is not free to form public opinion and to counsel the monarch effectively, then the nation is lost; for

il ne s'est rien opéré de constamment bien dans ce monde que par l'évidence. Il n'y a rien de bien dans les gouvernements qu'où la notion de l'utilité publique est évidente. Tant que le maître ignore le bien, tant qu'il est ignoré des sujets, quelque nom qu'on donne au gouvernement, il est mauvais.[39]

The revolution in public opinion brought about by the unhindered dissemination of knowledge and freedom to comment on matters of public interest would create an ever growing body of enlightened individuals whose function would be to represent the general will of the nation. But the body would have no political power; Diderot remained convinced that a strong and undivided sovereignty vested in the person of the ruler was necessary to preserve the nation against the destructive forces of personal interest. His conviction was reinforced by the disenchantment with the English parliamentary ideal, popularised in France by Montesquieu, which was general among the *philosophes* in the 1760's.

D'Holbach had returned from a stay in England in September 1765 bringing back with him a thoroughly jaundiced view of everything English, and not least the political system. His bitterly critical attitude was reported faithfully by Diderot in his correspondence with Sophie Volland.[40] In their conversations that followed his return to France, d'Holbach had convinced his friend of the bankruptcy of the English political system. The famous balance of powers of which Montesquieu had spoken so highly was a sham. It had been rendered ineffective as a barrier against tyranny by the wholesale corruption which pervaded the electorate and the Parliament, with the result that

le monarque paroît avoir les main libres pour le bien, et liées pour le mal; mais il est autant et plus maître de tout qu'aucun autre souverain. Ailleurs la cour commande et se fait obéir. Là elle corrompt et fait ce qu'il lui plaît, et la corruption est peut-être pire à la longue que la tyrannie.[41]

The English parliamentary system stood condemned on two counts: be-

---

[39] CORR. LITT., XVI, pp. 224-225.
[40] CORR, V, pp. 125-126, 129-135, 170-173.
[41] *Ibid.*, p. 129.

cause it provided no protection against the arbitrary personal despotism
of the ruler, and because it was instrumental in the moral depravation of
the citizens – veritable anathema for a thinker who believed that

La politique et les moeurs se tiennent par la main.[42]

It would doubtless have astonished Diderot that the system he depre-
cated so strongly has survived remarkably little changed to the present
day. But then the pragmatism which is the key to the longevity of the
British Parliament had little place in the politically extreme situation in
18th-century France which provoked in its antagonists a thoroughly un-
pragmatic idealism. Diderot, imbued as he was with a political idealism
based on a highly intellectual moral and philosophical vision of the world,
could not be expected to understand that the English system contained
within it the necessary robustness which would enable it to surmount temporary perversions of its democratic, libertarian principles. Hence his inordinate adulation of La Rivière at the expense of Montesquieu:

Ce livre m'a fait plus de plaisir et m'a été cent fois plus utile que l'*Esprit
des Loix*.[43]
Je vous déclare que pour les bons penseurs, il n'y a nulle comparaison à
faire de son ouvrage et celui de Montesquieu. Je vous déclare que cent mille
points et autant de phrases ingénieuses de celui-cy n'équivaudront jamais à
une ligne solide, pleine de sens, et grave du premier.[44]
Tout ce qui se fera de bien, ici ou ailleurs, se fera d'après ses principes.
Le Montesquieu a connu les maladies; celui cy a indiqué les remèdes; et il
n'y a de vrais remèdes que ceux qu'il a indiqués.[45]

But if these principles were to be applied so that the remedies might be
forthcoming the necessary actors had to be found in real life to fill the
roles established in theory. The intellectual élite, the potential representatives of enlightened opinion, were present in abundance, but where was
the wise ruler who, for the public good, would welcome their counsel in
his deliberations and submit himself selflessly to the rule of evidence, thereby bringing about a revolution in monarchic absolutism? The political
situation in France made the hope of the revolution occurring there no
more than a pipe dream. But in 1762 a remarkable woman had mounted
the Russian Imperial throne. Soon after her accession Catherine II showed
unmistakable signs of sympathy for the ideals of the Enlightenment, and

[42] CORR., III, p. 130.
[43] CORR., V, p. 77.
[44] CORR., VIII, pp. 36-37.
[45] *Ibid.*, pp. 112-113.

in so doing captured the imagination of the *philosophes*. When it became apparent that she intended to carry her enlightened principles into the realm of politics, her intentions were greeted with unbounded praise and jubilation. Catherine would fill the role of the wise ruler and give reality to Diderot's political ideal.

Diderot's first contact with Catherine came in March 1765 through the intermediary of General Betzki, when she offered to buy his library, so that he might provide a dowry for his daughter. The extent of her generosity is well-known; she insisted that the library remain in his possession during his lifetime, and she subsequently nominated him her official librarian with a handsome stipend to match his title. A gap in Diderot's correspondence with Sophie deprives us of his initial response to her benevolence, but it was certainly no less ecstatic than Voltaire's when he became acquainted with the news:

Par ma foi, j'embrasse aussi l'impératrice de toute Russie. Aurait-on soupçonné, il y a cinquante ans, qu'un jour les Scythes récompenseraient si noblement dans Paris la vertu, la science, la philosophie, si indignement traitées parmi nous?
Illustre Diderot, recevez les transports de ma joie.[46]

The first expressions of Diderot's enthusiastic devotion to Catherine available to us appear in his letters to Falconet after the arrival of the latter in St. Petersburg in October 1766. By now Diderot had become Catherine's unofficial cultural attaché in Paris and was instrumental in sending Falconet to Russia to execute that statue of Peter the Great which she had projected.

It was at this time that Voltaire leaked the news to an astonished and delighted audience of Catherine's grand design to convoke the States General of the Russian Empire in the summer of 1767 for the express purpose of establishing a new code of laws. It would replace the antiquated *Ulozhenie* of 1649 and would have as its aim "le bonheur de tous et de chacun." As a guide and a prologue to the activities of the legislative commission Catherine had prepared a *Nakaz* or *Instruction,* in which, using ideas drawn mainly from the *Esprit des Lois* and Beccaria's *Dei delitti e delle pene*, she set forth her general view upon all the principal problems of legislation. As a result of her sympathy for enlightened constitutional and juridical thought her *Nakaz* embodied the most liberal and humane ideas on government ever advanced by a ruling monarch. Briefly, the *Nakaz*

---

[46] Quoted by G. Roth in CORR, V, p. 27.

advocated an autocratic government, it sponsored the principle of a separation of powers and made suggestions for penal reform which re-
pudiated torture and questioned the wisdom of capital punishment and
cruel penalties. But as Catherine's *Instruction* was not available in translation until 1771,[47] and for some unknown reason Diderot does not seem
to have read it until his journey to the Imperial Court in 1773, the interest for him and his contempories lay less in the detail of the contents
than in the general tenor of the work and, above all, in the fact that she
had called upon the representatives of the nation to determine the needs
and desires of the people and to aid her in her deliberations.

The first indication that Diderot had been informed of Catherine's
plans comes in a letter to General Betzki.[48] Following a lapse in the pay-
ment of his librarian's stipend Betzki had informed him that his sovereign
had decided to send in advance the sum she intended to spend on the up-
keep and improvement of her library over the next fifty years. Diderot
is effusive in his gratitude, including in his letter an ode to Catherine's
glory, written by his friend Devaines. He concludes his protestations of
undying loyalty, respect and admiration with the following remarks:

> Je sçais que tous mes jours seront marqués par des voeux; et ces voeux,
> vous croyez sans doute qu'ils seront faits pour elle? Non, monsieur, ils seront
> tous pour le peuple qu'elle gouverne. Lorsque la Providence destine à un
> trône, c'est toujours un malheureux qu'elle condamne à des travaux infinis.
> Il n'y a presque pas une journée pure pour le père d'une si nombreuse fa-
> mille. Et puis, quels redoutables engagements Catherine n'a-t-elle pris avec
> l'univers! Il a les yeux attachés sur elle. La voilà dans la nécessité de montrer
> que la nature n'a fait des obstacles que pour discerner les grandes âmes des
> âmes communes; et on le verra.[49]

In Catherine Diderot had discovered the *grande âme*, the *sage* of whom
he had given a precise philosophical and moral definition in the *Rêve de
D'Alembert*.[50] The wisdom bestowed upon her by nature, he claims, has
led her to the conviction that in order to legislate for the ideal society she
must consult the will of her people. Hence the "redoutables engage-
ments" she has undertaken. The freedom she allows Falconet in his interviews with her is further proof to Diderot that she conforms with his

---

[47] The *Nakaz* was originally published in a French translation by the Academy of
Sciences of St. Petersburg in 1769. A further edition was produced without name of
author by a Dutch editor in 1771. It was banned by the French censor as one more
subversive anonymous treatise.
[48] CORR. VI, pp. 355-361.
[49] CORR. VI, pp. 360-361.
[50] See Part I, Chap. 1, pp. 24-27.

vision of the ideal monarch, represented in history by his hero, Henri IV. In fact, for the first time he draws a direct parallel between a reigning monarch and Henri; writing to Falconet he remarks,

Je ne suis point étonné du récit de la liberté de vos séances au palais. On disoit à Henry quatre tout ce qu'on vouloit. La morgue du rang est toujours en raison de la petitesse de celui qui l'occupe. Plus le souverain se distingue de l'homme, plus il confesse qu'il est un pauvre homme.[51]

The resemblance in Diderot's mind is even more apparent when one compares the imaginary speech to her subjects that he ascribes to Catherine and part of Henri IV's speech to the assembly of *notables* which he incorporated into his article *Autorité politique*.

Henri addresses his subjects thus:

Je ne vous ai point ici appelés, comme faisaient mes prédécesseurs, pour vous obliger d'approuver aveuglément mes volontés; je vous ai fait assembler pour recevoir vos conseils, pour les croire, pour les suivre; en un mot pour me mettre en tutelle entre vos mains.[52]

Diderot has Catherine address her people in similar fashion:

Nous sommes tous faits pour vivre sous des loix. Les loix ne sont faites que pour nous rendre plus heureux. Personne, mes enfants, ne sçait mieux que vous à quelles conditions vous pouvez être heureux. Venez donc tous me l'apprendre. Venez vous en expliquer avec moi.[53]

These laws will be the product of the general will of the people, channeled through Catherine. However, this is not the autonomous will of an artificially created community, as Rousseau conceives it, but the will of a natural collective being, the human race.[54] The general will of the Russian people which Catherine will consult is one aspect of the universal morality which stems from the physiological constitution of mankind conceived as a whole.[55] The general will is none other than the evidence of La Rivière, the laws it imposes, no less than the natural and essential order of society.

It may seem surprising that in his references to Catherine's grand design Diderot does not evoke the *philosophes* and the men of learning who have been so prominent in his thought up to now. He always pictures her

[51] CORR., VII, p. 61.
[52] O.PO., p. 18.
[53] CORR., VII, p. 87.
[54] See Introduction, p. 10 and J. Proust, *op. cit.*, pp. 338-339.
[55] See Part I, Chap. 1.

seeking the advice of the nation as a whole; [56] any reference to *notables* of any kind is conspicuously absent. It would be wrong to deduce from this that Diderot's ideas have suddenly grown more democratic and that he now believes the necessary advice required by the sovereign is forthcoming from all citizens irrespective of education or intelligence. The more likely answer is that Diderot believed Russia to be a backward nation in every respect and unlikely to harbour the profusion of intellectuals and specialists that existed in France. Consequently, since she was deprived of an enlightened élite, the task of investigating the requests, petitions, and advice of her people in order to discover the essential general will, the true evidence, fell more heavily upon Catherine than it would have done on a Western monarch.

But if there were no indigenous counsellors worthy of Catherine's trust, Diderot was more than willing to send her some from among his friends and acquaintances, although modest about his own ability to co-operate with her in her great work. When he looks at himself he sees that he has the necessary qualities of the *sage*:

> J'ai l'âme haute, (...) il me vient quelquefois une idée forte et grande, (...) je sçais la présenter d'une manière frappante, (...) je sçais entrer dans les âmes, les captiver, les émouvoir, les entraîner.[57]

Unlike d'Alembert his *esprit de finesse* enables him to inspire in men a love of virtue and truth. But his native candour and simplicity would be out of place in a court.[58] The man to aid Catherine was La Rivière and on Diderot's instigation he travelled to St. Petersburg in order to unfold to the Empress the secret he had discovered, "le véritable secret, le secret éternel et immuable de la sécurité, de la durée et du bonheur des empires." [59]

In sending La Rivière to Catherine, Diderot thought that he had engineered a glorious encounter between the designer of the perfect political system and the enlightened ruler of a great nation, who would be willing and able to turn that system into a reality. It was an encounter which would revolutionize the world. The failure of La Rivière to impress Catherine, his dismissal and return to France in June 1768 under a cloud of imperial disapprobation must count as one of Diderot's greatest disap-

---

[56] See also CORR., VII, p. 40, CORR., VIII, p. 34 and also a passage considered to be an unpublished fragment from the *Salon de 1767* published in the article "Another addition to the *Salon de 1767*" by Otis Fellows and Donal O'Gorman.

[57] CORR., VII, p. 95.

[58] *Ibid.*, p. 96. See also Part 1, Chap. II, p. 35 and CORR., IX, Annexe, p. 245.

[59] *Ibid.*, p. 96.

pointments. It seems that La Rivière's truculent behaviour and possibly the openly flaunted scandal of his private life incurred Catherine's indignation,[60] although she appears to have made up her mind about him before actually meeting him on her return from Moscow where she had inaugurated the legislative commission for the Code. Falconet too, took a strong dislike to his compatriot less than a month after his arrival. Informed of his protégé's scandalous behaviour by Falconet, Diderot reacted by being scandalized at the sculptor's accusations and passionately defending La Rivière's character, which he was personally prepared to vouch for.[61] Falconet countered by detailing the physiocrat's supposed misdemeanours, concluding acidly,

Tenez pour sûr que malgré vos lettres ici et vos sages conseils à Paris, l'apôtre de la liberté, sûreté et propriété s'est mal annoncé, s'est fait tout aussi mal précéder, et qu'il s'est fort mal conduit; tout cela dans la plus grande *évidence* possible.[62]

The correspondence between Diderot and Falconet for and against La Rivière continued until the September of that year as a counterpoint to their long-drawn-out argument for and against the importance of posterity.

Whom do we believe? Falconet was not the easiest of men to deal with and was subject to bouts of moodiness; his ungracious behaviour towards Diderot when he arrived in St. Petersburg is a notable instance. But by then he had fallen from Catherine's favour and was being persecuted by Betzki, so his attitude was more understandable if not excusable. In the case of La Rivière it seems likely that Falconet's reasons for disapproving of his behaviour were justified. This is substantiated by Catherine who found no reason to change her mind about him when she came to meet him. The conclusion that imposes itself is that Diderot with his customary undiscriminating generosity had deluded himself into ascribing to La Rivière a worthiness and nobility of character which he plainly did not possess. Admittedly, he claims that he had enjoyed his company for a period of months and had always separated from him "également satisfait de ses idées, de son ton, de ses moeurs, de ses lumières et de sa modestie;"[63] but then, Diderot was a close friend of Grimm's for many years before he

---

[60] See Correspondence between Catherine II and Falconet quoted by G. Roth in *Ibid.*, pp. 198, 219, 222 and CORR., VIII, p. 12.
[61] CORR., VIII, pp. 35-37.
[62] *Ibid.*, p. 80.
[63] *Ibid.*, p. 36.

realised that he had become "un des plus cachés, mais un des plus dangereux antiphilosophes." [64]

In the same way that Diderot's imagination led him to overestimate La Rivière as a man, it must also be held responsible for investing his ideas with a more revolutionary imprint than they in fact bore. It is once more the perceptive Falconet who points to the difference between La Rivière and Diderot's impression of him:

Pourquoi donner Mr de la Rivière comme un homme en quelque sorte exilé de son pays, puisqu'il n'a un congé que pour deux ans? Pourquoi faire entrevoir qu'il se ferme les portes de France, puisque cela n'en est pas? . . . Mr. de la Rivière ne dit point qu'il soit mécontent du ministère. Diderot a donné ses craintes pour des réalités.[65]

Although La Rivière's ideas are an advance on the traditional theory of divine right, the bold originality that Diderot sees in them is, in fact, a projection of the most audacious element in his own thinking. La Rivière is a thorough-going absolutist while Diderot believes in a monarchical system which is absolutist in structure but democratic in operation, where the monarch remains sovereign but is guided in his legislation by the enlightened general will of the nation. In this respect Diderot pushes La Rivière's theory of evidence, on which the latter founds his theory of legal despotism, much farther than its author is prepared to do. In La Rivière's system evidence impresses itself on the sovereign's conscience in some magical and undefined way, while in Diderot's it is transmitted by the will of the people, which in the most favourable circumstances is represented by the intelligent and enlightened members of the community.[66]

La Rivière was not a philosopher and did not appreciate all the implications of his ideas. Furthermore, he was an adherent of the physiocratic school which was looked upon with tolerance and a certain degree of benevolence by the authorities; so he could not but feel reasonably well disposed towards the régime. Diderot, with greater philosophical and political insight saw in La Rivière's system a doctrine fully assimilable with his own materialism and the remedy to the arbitrary despotism, which plagued not only his own country but the greater part of Europe. At this

---

[64] O.PH., p. 630., *Apologie de l'abbé Raynal.*
[65] Quoted by G. Roth in CORR., VIII, pp. 199-200.
[66] La Rivière does make a reference to individuals who are called upon by the monarch to aid him in his deliberations (*Op. cit.*, 2e Partie, Chap. xii, pp. 85-86). But this is in order to point out that they act in a consultative capacity only, otherwise they would infringe the sovereignty of the monarch. There is no suggestion that La Rivière sees them as representatives of the general will or the main channel by which evidence passes to the monarch's notice.

stage the democratic element in Diderot's thought, represented by his conception of the general will and its relation to evidence, is held in check by its subordination to the absolutist element. However, the latter is entirely dependent on his utopian dream of the private person of the sovereign, who is capable of interpreting the general will, of distinguishing evidence, and of enunciating the law. This utopianism is the product of two things: the transposition of the philosophical and moral ideal of the *sage* into political terms,[67] and his distrust of the common people.[68] In both the philosophical and moral, and the political spheres of his thought subsequent experience will lead Diderot to modify the character of his abstract speculation, thus gradually bringing about an inversion of the democratic and absolutist elements.

But before moving on to examine the nature of this transformation in Diderot's political thought and the circumstances which brought it about, we must take account of his odd but revealing encounter with Dom Deschamps, a specialist in speculative abstractions, whose peculiar metaphysical and political views briefly aroused his interest.

III. DOM DESCHAMPS AND THE *ÉTAT DE MOEURS*

It is difficult to gauge to what extent if any Dom Deschamps actually influenced the evolution of Diderot's political thought as the external evidence is slight. In the summer of 1769 the Benedictine made several unsuccessful attempts to persuade Diderot to read his four *Lettres sur l'esprit du siècle*, in which he defends religion against the attacks of the philosophes, considering it to be a temporary but necessary intermediary stage between ignorance and knowledge. Shortly afterwards Diderot did read the brochure that Deschamps had published anonymously. His reaction was to make a mock denunciation of the work, while unaware of its author's identity, in an open letter to Sartine intended for the *Correspondance littéraire*, but which Grimm did not publish:

Je n'en veux à l'auteur des *Lettres*, ni de sa bêtise, ni de sa férocité; mais je ne pardonne pas aux magistrats d'avoir permis la publicité d'un aussi sot ouvrage.[69]

But if Dom Deschamps' *Lettres* failed to arouse Diderot's interest, another work, his *Observations morales*, was far more successful. Diderot's response was typical of his reaction to any work containing ideas which

[67] See Part I, Chap. 1, pp. 26-27.
[68] See Introduction, pp. 12-13.
[69] CORR., IX, p. 108.

corroborated or coincided with his own: he received it with enthusiasm, remaining sublimely blind to all the other aspects of it which clashed with his beliefs. The ideal society which the author portrays, freed from the vitiating effects of laws, property and sexual taboos, liberated from the unnatural control of kings, priests and magistrates, moved Diderot to confess to a correspondent,

> Jugez combien cet ouvrage, tout mal écrit qu'il est, a dû me faire de plaisir, puisque je me suis retrouvé tout à coup dans le monde pour lequel j'étois né.
> De retour chez moi, je me suis mis à rêver aux principes et aux conséquences de mon gros bénédictin. . ., et je ne vis pas une ligne à effacer dans tous son ouvrage qui est rempli d'idées neuves et d'assertions hardies.[70]

Dom Deschamps had successed in striking a hidden chord in Diderot. He had aroused in him an anarchic trait which three years later would find its full expression in the *Supplément au Voyage de Bougainville*. As Herbert Dieckmann has argued, many of Diderot's ideas must be seen as *pensées contre* [71] or negative reactions to the restrictive conventions of contemporary society; and there is no doubt that his opinion of Deschamps' ideas can be placed in this category. But a second reference to Dom Deschamps in a letter to Sophie Volland implies another kind of response quite different from the one already mentioned. Diderot states that he was much amused by

> les efforts de notre apôtre du matérialisme pour trouver dans d'ordre éternel de la nature une sanction aux loix.[72]

Here it is not the anarchist but the political philosopher who is responding. Diderot has only perceived the materialist element in Dom Deschamps' metaphysics. The rather disconcerting fact that Deschamps was attempting to reconcile atheist materialism and deism into a higher synthesis, and that he considered an anarchic *état de moeurs* infinitely superior to an *état de lois* does not seem to have bothered Diderot unduly. His choice of vocabulary more than suggests that he saw in his fat Benedictine another La Rivière. Diderot, it would appear, has done little more than project his own ideas into the *Observations morales*, thereby deluding himself into thinking that Dom Deschamps was in complete agreement with him and with the author of *De l'ordre essentiel*.

On the little evidence that we have it would be dangerous to speculate

---

[70] *Ibid.*, p. 245.
[71] *Supplément au Voyage de Bougainville* ed. H. Dieckmann, *Introduction*.
[72] CORR., IX, p. 128.

at length on the extent to which Diderot reshaped Deschamps' ideas to conform with his own. However a short passage from another work written at the same time,[73] which brings together the main themes of the *Observations morales*, may give us some idea. Having argued that men must throw off the laws which hold their hearts and minds in bondage, and pass beyond the evils of the civilised state to the true *état de moeurs*, Deschamps continues,

C'est le seul concours des hommes cultivés qui peut faire passer les hommes de l'état de lois à l'état de moeurs et il ne s'agit pour les faire concourir tous ensemble à cet effet, que de les nécessiter à le faire, par la force de l'évidence qui les subjuguent (sic) nécessairement.[74]

The close similarity between Dom Deschamps' and Diderot's argument is too striking to require a detailed analysis. In order to find himself in complete agreement with the Benedictine Diderot only had to effect a mental transposition of terms, an operation which as likely as not he carried out quite unconsciously. Deschamps' *état de lois* becomes Diderot's arbitrary despotism, his anarchic *état de moeurs* Diderot's ideal political society also brought about by the force of evidence.

Diderot's contact with Dom Deschamps was shortlived. By the end of November 1769 their meetings had come to an end and Deschamps is subsequently mentioned nowhere in any of his writings or correspondence. If we are to believe Thibaut de Longecour Diderot took exception to his moral thought, which he considered to be

d'une impossibilité fondée sur la nature des choses et sur la nature de l'homme.[75]

He had not taken long to come to his senses and realise that Deschamps' peculiar philosophical concoction, which he called his *métaphysique*, was as hostile to atheist materialism as it was to Christianity. His disillusionment over Deschamps' philosophical and moral thought must have spread to his political thought as well. Diderot's periodic anarchic outbursts corresponded to the extreme points of his rejection of the existing social order. They satisfied the need, particularly on a sexual level, to escape into a world of dreams. But he always returned to a more profound faith in a politically ordered society. Dom Deschamps was a professional champion

[73] *La Voix de la raison contre la raison du Temps, et particulièrement contre celle de l'auteur du Système de la Nature, par demandes et réponses.*
[74] *Op. cit.*, XXXIV, quoted by F. Venturi and J. Thomas in *Le vrai système*, p. 204.
[75] Quoted by G. Roth in CORR., IX, p. 226.

of anarchy, the enemy of all authority and rule. Agreement between the two men on any plane could only be temporary, and then partly due to self-delusion on the part of Diderot.

In the period discussed in this chapter Diderot's political thought developed a coherent structure, thanks to the impressive example of Catherine on the one hand, and the dialogue with La Rivière and, to a lesser extent, Dom Deschamps on the other. These encounters, however, took place at a high level of abstraction, and bore little relationship to the hard, disquieting political realities which existed beyond the confines of Diderot's study. Only direct experience of these realities could purge him of his misconceptions. The gradual replacement of idealism by realism marks the next stage in the evolution of his political thought.

CHAPTER II

FIRST DOUBTS

Towards the end of July 1770 Diderot, the habitual stay-at-home, left Paris for Langres, and from there went on to Bourbonne, where Madame de Meaux, who had temporarily superceded Sophie in his affections, was awaiting him. Three years later, at the beginning of June 1773, Diderot once more packed his bags and set off, this time on a much longer journey to St. Petersburg, where Catherine II awaited him, this time in his capacity as a *philosophe*! Between these two departures dark clouds rolled up and lowered ominously on the political horizon. Over the past five years Diderot had developed into a political barometer, acutely sensitive to the changes taking place in France and Europe, so he could not fail to register with growing despondency the atmosphere of gloom and depression which characterised the years from 1770 to 1774. In the summer of 1770 the failure of the corn harvest led to considerable hardship and misery among the population of the countryside. The riots it sparked off indicated that the government's grain policy was far from satisfactory. The following year Maupeou, who had replaced the disgraced Choiseul, summarily dismissed the *parlements*: an act which convinced Diderot that legal government in France had degenerated into tyranny. In Prussia Frederick II was doing little to hide the face of a craven and ruthless despot behind the mask of an enlightened monarch. Whichever way he turned Diderot was faced with the depressing sight of the denial of all the hopes and aspirations he had formed for his fellow men: the decline of justice, the disappearance of legality in government, the rejection of the virtues of progress and enlightenment, the denial, in fact, of truth. Admittedly, there was England, a beacon of light and liberty in a darkening Europe, but Diderot's own prejudices blinded him to it.[1] True, there was Catherine, full of promise with her *Instruction*, but Russia was a long

---

[1] See previous chapter, pp. 106-107.

way off, and the pressing concerns of the moment left him little time to muse upon the hopes he had vested in the "Sémiramis du Nord."

But if Diderot's pessimism grew over the years between 1770 and 1774, so did his indignation at the way in which the "maîtres du monde," and in particular those of France, flouted justice and legality in order to further their own discreditable ends, to the increasing discomfort of the vast majority of the people. No longer did he allow pessimism to sour into despair as had happened after the completion of the *Encyclopédie*. Temporary discouragement there might be from time to time, but this was combated by an indignation which fired him with the courage and determination to battle for the truth, on which men's happiness depended.[2] Diderot's political apprenticeship was over. The time for simple theorizing had come to an end. He had built up a coherent body of ideas and now they must be put to the test. The philosopher must leave his cabinet, both in body and in spirit, and come face to face with the living issues of the day. This is not to say that Diderot abandoned his theoretical, speculative approach to political matters. Far from it! As regards politics he remained by preference and necessity a thinker and not a man of action. But his thought, as it evolves over these years, is increasingly imbued with a practical flavour, an empirical approach, as his attention is drawn to the economic, social and political problems of the day. Even the apparent flight from reality into the utopian Tahiti of the *Supplément* can be construed as a return to the sources of imagination and philosophical inspiration, which enabled him to refurbish and resharpen his insight into the turmoil of the real world.

When Diderot left Paris for Langres he carried with him in his intellectual baggage a political philosophy which had the virtue of being coherent. Its weakness lay in its utopianism; abstract notions unrelated to reality still predominated. When he left Paris for St. Petersburg he took with him a political philosophy, which if not yet entirely purged of its utopianism, nonetheless bore the unmistakable mark of contact with the unpleasant realities of the past three years.

I. GALIANI AND ECONOMIC EMPIRICISM

The great famine of 1770, the culmination of a series of poor harvests, provided Diderot with the opportunity to write his first major political work, the *Apologie de Galiani*. For the first time since the completion of the *Encyclopédie* he felt sufficiently well-equipped to enter into a de-

---

[2] *Pages contre un Tyran*, O.PO., p. 136.

bate of this nature. As with most first attempts the work has its weaknesses, but it is important in that it provides us with an introduction to Diderot's future approach to political and economic problems, and also constitutes a significant reorientation in his thinking.

The debate over governmental policy on the grain trade, which reached a climax between 1768 and 1770, has a history which reaches back to the royal declaration of the 31st August 1699. This set out to prevent the pernicious traffic in cereals which was considered to be the cause of famine and high prices. Reaction against this restrictive policy began in 1752 when Gournay, then *intendant de commerce*, and founder of a loosely organised school of *économistes*, pointed out to his chief, Trudaine, in a *mémoire* that

Les gênes que l'on met sur le commerce du blé (...) tendent à détourner les sujets du roi de la culture du blé.[3]

The opposition to restrictions gathered force as the physiocrats led by Quesnay began to influence public and governmental opinion. The outcome of the alliance of *économistes* and physiocrats was the promulgation of two edicts in 1763 and 1764 which abolished the previous restrictions on internal and external trade in cereals. Some export restrictions, however, remained. In a preamble to the 1764 edict the King declared,

Il nous a paru nécessaire de fixer un prix au grain au delà duquel toute exportation hors du royaume en serait interdite dès que le blé aurait monté à ce prix.[4]

This did not prevent the situation from deteriorating rapidly with two bad harvests in 1766 and 1767, together with the stocking of grain and the creating of monopolies which the new freedom had permitted.

The physiocrats had made economic matters a fashionable subject for discussion in the Paris *salons*. When, by 1770, it became apparent that the new legislation on the grain trade was responsible for the disaster, this subject moved once more to the centre of intellectual debate. It was a crucial issue, affecting the well-being of the nation as a whole. For a society which looked upon the search for happiness as the central article of its philosophical catechism, the issue could not fail to arouse passions. Until 1770 the physiocrats had had things very much their own way. Such opposition to them as there was, was sporadic or untalented. Even Diderot, who was attached to the school by his admiration for La Rivière, was

---

[3] Quoted by L. Biollay, *Le Pacte de Famine*, p. 86.
[4] *Ibid.*, p. 111.

quiescent. There was, however, one exception of remarkable talent, the Abbé Galiani, Italian diplomatist and economist *à ses heures*, who was to spearhead the revolt against the free trade policy on grain.

In November 1768 Diderot reported Galiani's opposition to the edicts:

Il prêcha beaucoup contre l'exportation des grains, et cela par une raison qui n'est pas commune. C'est qu'il faut laisser subsister les mauvaises loix partout où il n'y a pas dans le ministère des hommes d'assez de tête pour faire exécuter les bonnes, en pourvoyant aux inconvénients des innovations les plus avantageuses.[5]

Ten days later the full impact of Galiani's ideas came home to him. The terms he uses to describe his enthusiastic approval of them is strongly reminiscent of the manner in which he had earlier recorded his approval of La Rivière's views on reading *De l'ordre essentiel*.[6]

Enfin, l'abbé Galiani s'est expliqué net. Ou il n'y a rien de démontré en politique, ou il l'est que l'exportation est une folie. Je vous jure, mon amie, que personne jusqu'à présent n'a dit le premier mot de cette question. Je me suis prosterné devant lui pour qu'il publiât ses idées.[7]

The process of disassociation from physiocratic doctrine as represented by La Rivière had already begun. Diderot had entered into dialogue with an altogether subtler, more talented mind, a mind whose realistic appraisal of the economic situation in the *Dialogues sur les blés*, published under Diderot's auspices in 1769, contrasted favourably with the abstract theorizing of the physiocrats. La Rivière had helped Diderot clarify and systematize his political ideas, but he had reinforced their abstract, utopian qualities. Galiani was to enable him to break free from these intellectual restrictions by showing him the rich rewards that were to be gained from a study of the real conditions governing the economic and political life of the nation.

Galiani's *Dialogues* caused immediate alarm in the camp of the physiocrats. They realised that their position as economic theoreticians, enjoying public esteem and official favour, was under attack from a dangerous enemy. The battle was swiftly engaged with salvoes from the Abbé Baudeau [8] and the worthy La Rivière himself.[9] Galiani riposted effect-

---

[5] CORR., VIII, p. 216.
[6] See CORR., VII, p. 77.
[7] CORR., VIII, p. 233.
[8] *Lettres d'un Amateur* "à l'abbé Galiani."
[9] *L'Intérêt général de l'Etat* ou *La Liberté du Commerce des blés.*

ively and brilliantly.[10] The weakness of the physiocrats lay as much in the abysmally dreary prose style of their propaganda as in the arguments they put across. Galiani, however, was not only an economist and diplomat of the highest intelligence but a *littérateur* with a stylish command of French, who was able to convey his ideas with wit and polish. It is, therefore, all the more surprising that the physiocrats should choose for their second line of defence the Abbé Morellet, a professional polemicist whose style is so painfully ponderous and turgid that it is doubtful whether many contemporary readers would have bothered to wade right through his *Réfutation des Dialogues*, even if the authorities had permitted its publication.[11] Diderot, however, was one of the few who did accomplish the thankless task of reading Morellet's criticism of Galiani, and he found it "dur, sec, plein d'humeur, et pauvre d'idées.[12] Sartine, obviously pleased with Diderot's previous report on *De l'ordre essentiel*, had asked him to act as official censor for the *Réfutation*. Morellet's book, though it had little merit in its own right, performed a valuable service for Diderot; it impressed upon him even more clearly the greater quality of Galiani's thought compared to the ideas of the physiocrats. Morellet, following on the heels of Turgot, Baudeau, Dupont and La Rivière, had discovered that

> La lutte contre un homme de génie qui connaît le monde et les hommes, le coeur humain, la nature de la société, l'action et la réaction des ressorts opposés qui la composent, la force de l'intérêt, la pente des esprits, la violence des passions, les vices des différents gouvernements, l'influence des plus petites causes, et les contre-coups des moindres effets dans une grande machine est une lutte périlleuse.[13]

Diderot has put his finger upon the factor which separates Galiani from his antagonists and demonstrates his superiority: while their political and economic thought is the product of a rationally structured but closed system based on *a priori* principles, Galiani turns to the world of experiential realities in order to discover the truths pertaining to the problem of the corn trade, and to elaborate remedial formulae for it.

---

[10] *Récréations économiques* ou *Lettres de l'auteur des Représentants aux magistrats à M. le Chevalier Zanobi.*

[11] The work was technically published, but Sartine, who was opposed to the free trade policy, took advantage of the scandal that grew up around the *Réfutation* in order to confiscate it and send it to the Bastille. (See P. Vernière's Introduction to the *Apologie de Galiani*, O.PO., p. 64). Permission to publish was finally obtained in November 1775 when it was used to defend the position of Turgot against the onslaught of Necker who wished to replace him as minister of finance.

[12] CORR., X, p. 32.

[13] *Ibid.*, p. 33.

As far back as 1753, in the *Interprétation de la Nature*, Diderot had argued in favour of the experimental method in the physical sciences and against the sterility of the rationalist mathematical approach:

> Tant que les choses ne sont que dans notre entendement, ce sont nos opinions; ce sont des notions, qui peuvent être vraies ou fausses, accordées ou contredites. Elles ne prennent de la consistance qu'en se liant aux êtres extérieurs.[14]

Now Galiani had shown him that the same applies to economics. Morellot is "ni assez pourvu d'expérience, ni assez fort de raisons pour briser son adversaire comme il se l'est promis." [15] His non-empirical method has condemned him to failure in advance.

In the late summer of 1770 Diderot returned to Paris with first-hand experience of the ravages caused by the failure of the corn harvest in the provinces. Champagne had been one of the worst hit areas, and his personal preoccupations, an abortive attempt at a reconciliation with his brother and his pursuit of Madame de Meaux, had not prevented him from being deeply moved by the suffering and deprivation he witnessed:

> Croiriez-vous bien qu'au milieu de mes soucis, je n'ai pas cessé de souffrir de l'incertitude des récoltes? (...) Joignez à cette idée le spectacle présent de la misère. Je commence à me rassurer depuis que je vois la terre se dépouiller; et à en juger par le soulagement que j'éprouve, il falloit que la crainte de la disette pour mes semblables entrât considérablement dans mon malaise.[16]

But Diderot's reaction was not limited to one of sympathy for his fellowmen; Galiani had opened up new avenues of exploration for him. His journey to Langres and Bourbonne gave him the unique opportunity, as far as time and circumstances allowed, to carry out a field study on the most pressing problems of the day.[17] Armed with the detailed evidence he had acquired through personal observation and experience Diderot was ready to enter into the centre of the debate; by January 1771 his counterattack against Morellet's *Réfutation*, the *Apologie de Galiani*, was ready.[18]

---

[14] O.PH., p. 184.
[15] CORR., X, p. 32.
[16] *Ibid.*, p. 112.
[17] Diderot does not refer to the famine in his *Voyage à Bourbonne et à Langres*. These two short essays are intended as monographs on the towns in question, and are therefore not suited for the discussion of a topic of much wider interest.
[18] It was never published in his lifetime. On the 24th December 1770 Choiseul was dismissed. Terray immediately revoked the edict of 1764 and government control over the grain trade was re-established. Once the battle had been won, Diderot saw no point in pursuing the matter further.

The crux of the dispute between Galiani and Diderot on the one hand, and Morellet and the physiocrats on the other, which is highlighted in the *Apologie*, is the opposition between fact and theory. All the other issues thrown up by the controversy, the freedom of the corn trade, the sacrosanct nature of property, and so forth, are of secondary importance and in some respects dependent on which of the alternatives one opted for. In the first chapter of his *Réfutation* Morellet showed that he was aware that Galiani had adopted a factual approach to the problem:

Celui qui, pour prouver que le commerce des bleds doit être administré de telle et telle manière, ne s'appuieroit que sur des exemples d'Etats qui suivent cette forme d'administration et qui s'en trouvent bien, et d'Etats qui s'en écartent et qui s'en trouvent mal, fonderoit sa théorie uniquement sur des faits

and he rejects it out of hand:

. . . et sa doctrine ne mériteroit pas même le nom de théorie.[19]

Facts, claims Morellet, should only be used to confirm a theory "établie d'ailleurs," that is a theory which emerges from the consideration of agriculture in general, the nature of trade, the interest of the producers, buyers and sellers of a commodity, and the effects resulting from a prohibitive law or from freedom.[20] In other words the method of the physiocrats was to argue from principles to individual cases:

Il est bien clair que la marche la plus naturelle seroit d'abord de rechercher le principe général, celui qui s'applique au plus grand nombre de cas, sauf à reconnoître ensuite les exceptions si le principe en doit recevoir, et à rechercher les causes de ces exceptions.[21]

Diderot's reply confirms that he and Morellet are irreconcilably separated by fundamental differences of an ideological nature:

Je n'entends rien à cette logique. Quoi! il faut se faire dans sa tête un principe général, mais il me semble qu'il y a dans les sciences, dans les métiers, une méthode qui est précisément le rebours de la vôtre. On commence par des cas particuliers; à force de cas particuliers, examinés en eux-mêmes et comparés à d'autres, on aperçoit des ressemblances et des différences, et l'on se forme des notions plus ou moins générales, des théories plus ou moins étendues.[22]

---

[19] *Réfutation des Dialogues sur le Commerce des Bleds*, p. 28.
[20] *Ibid.*, pp. 28-29.
[21] *Ibid.*, p. 64.
[22] *Apologie*, O.PO., p. 87.

Observation and experiment, these are the keys to a fruitful study of economic questions! The implications of this discovery for Diderot's political thought are considerable and will soon become apparent, but for the time being he limits himself to the specific questions raised by the corn trade controversy.

Morellet's system, argues Diderot, is pernicious because it allows the deduction of a faulty doctrine, namely the freedom of the grain trade, from two axioms, one false and the other both false and dangerous, namely that a nation's wealth is entirely dependent on its natural resources, and that property must be treated as sacrosanct. In response to Morellet's claim that "la terre, le sol, la culture (sont) les seules sources des richesses existantes dans l'univers" and that the wealth of the manufacturing industries comes from the raw material they use,[23] Diderot demonstrates by a fine analysis of the economics of manufacture that "l'industrie a certainement un produit net, tout comme la terre." [24] But it is the second axiom which Diderot finds by far the more untenable and disreputable, and it is the one on which Morellet rests the bulk of his argument in favour of freedom. It is untenable because it flies in the face of reality:

> Est-ce qu'il y a quelque droit sacré quand il s'agit d'affaire publique, d'utilité générale, réelle ou simulée? On me fait prendre le mousquet, on m'ôte la liberté, on m'enferme sur un soupçon, on me coupe mon champ en deux, on renverse ma maison, on abandonne ma moisson aux animaux, on vide ma bourse par un impôt absurde, on expose ma vie, ma fortune, par une guerre folle...
> Quand je vous vois sauter lestement sur des observations dont la force m'est connue à moi par l'expérience, que diable voulez-vous que je pense de toutes vos généralités? [25]

It is disreputable because it places possessions before human life:

> Est-ce que le sentiment d'humanité n'est pas plus sacré que le droit de propriété...? [26]

The freedom of the corn trade, based on the principle that governmental interference would constitute an infringement of the right of property, leads to monopoly and speculation and the denial to thousands of their birthright, the right to live above starvation level. It is utterly utopian to assume, as Morellet does, that an unrestricted grain trade would maintain

[23] *Op. cit.*, pp. 184-185.
[24] O.PO., pp. 97-98.
[25] *Ibid.*, p. 118.
[26] *Ibid.*, p. 85.

a steady circulation of the commodity. Diderot had seen the effects of this policy with his own eyes; the speculative stocking it leads to creates untold hardship to the *petit peuple* in times of shortage.[27]

Diderot's attitude towards the proletarian section of the community at this point contrasts favourably with the patronising attitude shared by the physiocrats and Voltaire on the one hand and Rousseau's idealistic championship of the poor on the other. Unlike Morellet, who is surprised that Galiani "fasse sérieusement grand cas de l'opinion du peuple," [28] Diderot is realistic in his assessment of the dangerous potential of the downtrodden masses:

L'abbé Galiani craint le peuple; et quand il s'agit de pain, il n'y a qu'un homme ivre qui n'en ait pas peur. On voit que M. l'abbé Morellet vit à Paris, et qu'il ne l'a pas vu menacé de la disette dans nos provinces.[29]

Only a policy of control over the grain trade, which will ensure an adequate supply to all sections of the community, will free the nation from this constant menace to law and order. But Diderot's political realism goes hand in hand with a sincere feeling of compassion; the spectacle of the misery of the underprivileged wrings out of him a *cri du coeur* as poignant as anything Rousseau produced:

Vous tous, malheureux laboureurs, qui ne trouvez ni subsistances ni travail dans les pays ravagés et désséchés par les exactions de la finance, mourez où vous avez eu le malheur de naître; il n'est plus d'asyle pour vous que sous terre. Vous tous, artisans, ouvriers de toute espèce, que l'on vexe par les monopoles, à qui l'on refuse le droit de travailler librement, sans avoir acheté des maîtrises: vous que l'on tient courbés toute la vie dans un attelier pour enrichir un entrepreneur privilégié: vous qu'un deuil de cour laisse des mois entiers sans salaire et sans pain! n'espérez pas de vivre hors d'une patrie où des soldats et des gardes vous tiennent emprisonnés: errez dans l'abandon, et mourez de chagrin.[30]

Under the influence of Galiani Diderot underwent a profound revolution as a political thinker: the utopian was, in essence, replaced by the realist. However, he did not allow his political realism to degenerate into a shabby, cynical *raison d'état*. The philosopher and moralist in him were too strong to permit it. His political realism was constantly underpinned by the values which flowed from his moral thought, which had

---

[27] *Ibid.*, pp. 101-102.
[28] *Op. cit.*, p. 269.
[29] O.PO., p. 117.
[30] P.D., p. 94, HIST., IX, pp. 173-174.

equally undergone a considerable reorientation. Diderot had reached the conviction that the well-being of society can only be conceived of in terms of the ability of the individuals who make it up, to achieve liberation and self-fulfilment.[31] But this conviction will remain an inaccessible ideal so long as a vast section of the community does not have enough to eat. It is ridiculous to look for a moral improvement in society so long as this state of affairs continues to exist. Rameau may wish to attribute his moral depravity and failure to realise his artistic potential to hereditary flaws; the Philosophe may lay the blame at the door of a corrupt, artificial society; be this as it may, in the last resort it is his grinding poverty which must be held responsible. Human wretchedness dries up a man's potential at its source, hence Rameau is only the ghost of the artist he could have been:

Ah! monsieur le philosophe, la misère est une terrible chose. Je la vois accroupie, la bouche béante pour recevoir quelques gouttes de l'eau glacée qui s'échappe du tonneau des Danaïdes. Je ne sais si elle aiguise l'esprit du philosophe, mais elle refroidit diablement la tête du poète.[32]

Hunger robs a man of his moral integrity; he is ready to accept all kinds of self-abasement in order to fill his belly:

S'il est dans la nature d'avoir appétit (...) je trouve qu'il n'est pas de bon ordre de n'avoir pas toujours de quoi manger. Que diable d'économie! des hommes qui regorgent de tout tandis que d'autres, qui ont un estomac importun comme eux, une faim renaissante comme eux, et pas de quoi mettre sous la dent. Le pis c'est la posture contrainte où nous tient le besoin. L'homme nécessiteux ne marche pas comme un autre, il saute, il rampe, il se tortille, il se traîne, il passe sa vie à prendre et à exécuter des positions.[33]

Trade is a two-edged sword: it can be instrumental in the furtherance of man's well-being, or it can bring about his degradation. Unrelated to humanitarian considerations it leads to the moral and cultural impoverishment of society and the denial of basic human rights to the under-privileged. Even in a country like Switzerland, where material prosperity is more equitably spread throughout the community and the worst kinds of exploitation have been eliminated, an overriding concern for material comfort as an end in itself must necessarily sap the creative energy and moral vitality of the nation:

Tarissez la source des périls et vous tarissez en même temps celles des vertus, des forfaits, des historiens, des orateurs et des poètes.[34]

[31] See Part I, Chap. II, pp. 53-56.
[32] O.RO., p. 483.
[33] *Ibid.*, pp. 485-486.
[34] A.T., IV, p. 43.

In the last resort it opens the way to tyranny; herein lies Morellet's fatal flaw:

C'est un galant homme qui a cru servir ses concitoyens ... et qui n'a servi que le despotisme.[35]

When, on the other hand, trade is subjected to careful control, material prosperity will provide the conditions in which man may flourish and fulfil his destiny:

On n'élève des monuments éternels à l'honneur de l'esprit humain que quand on est bien pourvu de toutes les sortes de nécessaires; car ces monuments sont la plus grande superfluité de toutes les superfluités de ce monde.[36]

If trade and industry are made to serve the interests of society as a whole and not allowed to line the pockets of an unscrupulous minority, they will act as a bastion against the twin-headed monster of superstition and despotism:

L'aisance, dans laquelle on oublie le ciel, détruit la superstition, compagne et fille de la misère et du malheur; l'état qui vous émancipe, tel est celui du manufacturier qui s'en va avec ses deux bras et réduit le despotisme à rien.[37]

The *Apologie de Galiani* is not a great work; it is clumsy, untidy, and repetitive. As a contribution to the debate on the corn trade it cannot match Galiani's *Dialogues*. Its principal virtue resides in the fact that it embodies a significant realignment of Diderot's loyalties, and a profound reappraisal of the mode of his political thinking. Admittedly the *Apologie* does not constitute the complete eradication of utopianism from Diderot's political thought; the process is a gradual one: a step-by-step re-evaluation resulting from a succession of experiences. The episode from which the *Apologie* emerged, showed Diderot that ethical ideas, if they were to be anything more than ideals, must be related to a political doctrine which is constantly being renewed and reinvigorated by regular involvement in the realities of this world.

II. FREDERICK II AND THE BETRAYAL OF THE PHILOSOPHER-KING

Nowhere did the emergent empiricism of Diderot's political thought, represented by the *Apologie*, form a greater challenge to his utopianism

[35] O.PO., p. 80.
[36] A.T., IV, p. 46.
[37] O.PO., pp. 111-112.

than over the question of the philosopher king. Looking back from our present vantage point in history it may seem incredible that Diderot and so many of his contemporaries should have been deluded for so long by the fiction of an enlightened monarch whose wisdom, virtue and justice would make him the saviour of the nation. But if we place ourselves in the context of 18th-century France their mistaken enthusiasm becomes comprehensible.

It was an undeniable fact that political power in the nation was concentrated in the hands of an absolute monarch. But it was also true that the Church had established an insidious influence over the monarchy, and was using its privileged position to consolidate its interests and maintain its hold over the people. In contrast, the *philosophes* were denied any participation in the shaping of the nation's destiny. If they wished to see their enlightened principles become political realities, the only solution that presented itself was to support the monarch against the incursions of the Church on his sovereignty, and thereby win him over to their side.[38] It was in order to keep this hope alive – the only hope the *philosophes* could conceive of their ever becoming a political force in the nation – that the fiction of the philosopher king or the enlightened monarch was invented. Not that it seemed a fiction at the time. The firm belief that the powers of darkness could not hold out against the advancing tide of enlightenment gave it the stamp of a future reality. Furthermore, there was credible evidence that the hope was already in the process of becoming a reality, if not in France, then elsewhere in Europe, with the adoption of enlightened ideas by such forward-looking monarchs as Catherine II and Frederick II.

In Diderot's case, his concept of the enlightened monarch was an extension of his materialist philosophy and formed the unifying apex of his political doctrine. Despite continuous disillusionment at home the idealistic hope he shared with the philosophic clan, and in particular his privileged relationship with Catherine, had preserved this concept intact in all its utopian simplicity. However, two events following closely on one another forced him to re-examine his ideas, a re-examination which was ultimately to lead to a rejection of the notion of the enlightened monarch

---

[38] "In France the only possible agent of reform, the only party that the philosophes could support was the crown. 'The cause of the king is the cause of the philosophes' (a). And, if Louis XV could only be made to see it, the cause of the philosophes was the cause of the king: '. . . the philosophic spirit that has penetrated practically all classes of society except the masses has also done much to enhance the rights of the sovereigns' (b)." P. Gay, *Voltaire's politics*, p. 89.
(a) Letter to d'Alembert, 16 Oct. 1765, *Oeuv. comp.* XLIV, p. 88.
(b) *Siècle de Louis XIV, Oeuv. comp.* XIV, p. 538.

and the triumph of empiricism over utopianism. At the end of 1770 Diderot read Frederick II's *Examen* of d'Holbach's *Essai sur les préjugés*. Frederick's work had been published in Berlin in April of the same year. The following January, without prior warning, the new chancellor, Maupeou, dismissed the *parlements,* exiled their members to remote parts of France, and abolished their venal offices, replacing them by stipendiary posts. Frederick's book and Maupeou's action compelled Diderot to appreciate a political fact which his utopianism had previously prevented him from discerning, the fact that all absolute power contains within it the seeds of tyranny.

Unlike Voltaire and other *philosophes* Diderot had never entertained very cordial relationships with Frederick, despite various attempts of the latter to gain his confidence, such as obtaining his election to the Prussian Academy. Whether the young Diderot had at one time been attracted to the promising Crown Prince who had captured the imagination of liberal Europe with his *Anti-Machiavel* remains for lack of conclusive evidence a matter open to speculation. A passage first published in the 1770 edition of the *Histoire des deux Indes*, and later incorporated in the *Mélanges* manuscript of the Fonds Vandeul under the title *Au Roi de Prusse,*[39] does however give reason to believe that Diderot's attitude towards Frederick was, until 1770 at least, more ambivalent than has frequently been supposed. In this passage, in which Diderot addresses the Prussian King directly, he sadly recalls the great promise shown by Frederick in his youth, later compromised by his thirst for military glory and his machiavellian cynicism. In Diderot's eyes he has been guilty of the worst possible crime: a philosopher, he had betrayed the very cause of philosophy. To such a man one could not attribute the title of philosopher-king:

On ne l'accord pas aux princes qui, confondant les erreurs et les vérités, la justice et les préjugés, les sources du bien et du mal, envisagent les principes de la morale comme des hypothèses de la métaphysique, ne voient dans la raison qu'un orateur gagé par l'intérêt.[40]

Yet, despite his misgivings, Diderot is unwilling in this passage to dismiss Frederick as a lost cause. To do so would mean calling into question his faith in the possibility of creating an enlightened ruler by means of wise counsel, and this he cannot do without endangering the whole fabric of his political thought. So, putting on the cloak of the counsellor he exhorts Frederick to mend his ways and return to the noble and virtuous senti-

[40] MEL., p. 14. HIST., III, p. 82.

ments of his youth. In fact, so anxious is Diderot to replace him in a favourable light that he reinterprets his role in the Seven Years War. The conventional image of an aggressive military leader, who has ruthlessly pursued a policy of territorial aggrandizement in Silesia is replaced by a more flattering one of an enlightened protector of the freedom of small states against the aggression of Maria Theresa's Austria and Elizabeth's Russia. Diderot underlines his sentiment in characteristic fashion by suggesting that a conventional epitaph celebrating Frederick's military glory be replaced by a more instructive and noble one:

> Peuples, il brisa les chaînes qu'on vous préparoit. Princes de l'Empire Germanique, il ne sera pas toujours, songez à vous.[41]

However, Frederick's bitter attack on d'Holbach's *Essai sur les préjugés* confounded Diderot's pious hopes of redeeming him and restoring in him the lost virtue of his youth. On reading the *Examen* he could no longer avoid the fact that the so-called "philosophe de Sans-Souci" had compromised the high aspirations of philosophy in the pursuit of a ruthless *realpolitik,* founded on a doctrine of expediency and unrelated to moral considerations.

The opposition between d'Holbach and Frederick was total. They represented almost to a caricature the two poles of the dialectic which has characterised European culture since the Renaissance: d'Holbach, the rationalist progressive, championing a society in which the ruler, rejecting military glory and the prejudices of the nobility, draws his authority from an enlightened people; Frederick, the practical man of action, hardened and disillusioned by years of experience, viewing his fellowmen's weaknesses with cynical lucidity and aristocratic scorn, dubious of their ability to direct their own destinies, convinced of the necessity of the conservative values of obedience, order and tradition. The point on which their mutual antagonisms focussed most sharply, was d'Holbach's first premise, that truth is fundamental to men's happiness:

> Si la nature de l'homme l'oblige dans chaque instant de sa durée de tendre vers le bonheur, ou de chercher à rendre son existence agréable, il lui est avantageux d'en trouver les moyens et d'écarter les obstacles qui s'opposent à sa pente naturelle. Cela posé, la vérité est nécessaire à l'homme, et l'erreur ne peut jamais lui être que dangereuse.[42]

---

[41] MEL., p. 16, HIST., III, p. 85. Diderot was later to criticise his eulogy of Frederick, while prudently continuing to attribute it to Raynal: "Si j'avais quelque reproche à lui faire, c'est d'avoir un peu surfait le mérite d'une action dont l'éclat était obscurci par l'intérêt personnel," *Lettre apologétique de Raynal à Grimm*, O.PH., p. 636.

[42] *Essai sur les préjugés*, p. 2.

It was a short step from there to drawing the necessary political conclusions, and d'Holbach does not hesitate to take it: governments must renounce their shameful alliance with superstition, which has perpetuated ignorance and degradation among their peoples.[43] Only by rejecting falsehood and pursuing a policy of equity, enlightenment, tolerance and freedom of thought towards their subjects, will they achieve real power and security.[44] Frederick, indignant at such dangerous audacity, refuted d'Holbach's premise with more than a touch of cynicism:

(L'homme) est plus sensible que raisonnable. Voilà donc la plupart des opinions humaines fondées sur des préjugés, des fables, des erreurs et des impostures. Qu'en puis-je conclure autre chose, si ce n'est que l'homme est fait pour l'erreur, que tout l'univers est soumis à son empire, et que nous ne voyons guère plus clair que les taupes.[45]

Truth, for Frederick, is only one instrument among several which must be wielded adroitly in the business of governing a state:

Il faut dire la vérité avec discrétion, jamais mal à propos, et choisir le temps qui lui est le plus convenable.[46]

As Paul Vernière has pointed out,[47] Diderot, in writing the *Pages contre un tyran*, was as much concerned with defending his own ideas as those of d'Holbach, whose *Essai* had been strongly influenced by their conversations at Le Grandval. An unwavering respect for truth is a constant of Diderot's philosophical and political thought and he will spare no effort in defending it against its detractors. He had already taken up arms against the group of *philosophes*, headed by Mably, whose hostility to the concept of evidence he had interpreted as an attack on truth itself.[48] Now he finds himself once more called upon to come to its defence, this time against a king, a sovereign, and what is more, one who makes claims to be a philosopher, a child of the Enlightenment. Diderot's dismay at Frederick's betrayal, his distress at the realisation that the King of Prussia is a living denial of the central feature of his political thought, pours out in a stream of scorn and invective. With scathing logic he draws attention to Frederick's intellectual inconsistencies: the writer of the *Examen* is "le plus inconséquent des hommes ... le plus absurde des hommes ... c'est un

---

[43] *Ibid.*, pp. 10-11.
[44] *Ibid.*, pp. 22-23.
[45] *Examen de l'Essai sur les préjugés*, p. 133.
[46] *Ibid.*, p. 135.
[47] Introduction to *Pages contre un tyran*, O.PO., p. 132.
[48] See p. 105.

enfant qui balbutie . . . sublime raisonneur"; and there can be little doubt
that Diderot has his adversary very much in mind in his most virulent
and damaging criticism of aristocratic prejudice:

> Je n'en souffrirai pas plus patiemment un faquin titré qui m'insulte parce
> qu'il est le dernier de sa race, moi qui suis peut-être le premier de la mienne.[49]

In his final paragraph he brings the sustained tone of outrage and indignation to a climax with a devastating blow couched in heavy irony:

> Dieu nous préserve d'un souverain qui ressemble à cette sorte de philo-
> sophe-ci.[50]

Frederick has been finally and irrevocably dismissed from the ranks of the
philosopher kings, that special breed of men in whom lay for Diderot the
only saving hope of the nations.

Nevertheless, in the *Pages contre un tyran* themselves Diderot once
more appears to reaffirm his belief that if societies are to grow in truth and
virtue, then the transformation must be effected from the top by sovereigns who are themselves in love with these qualities:

C'est presque inutilement qu'on éclaire les conditions subalternes, si le ban-
deau reste sur les yeux de ces dix ou douze individus privilégiés qui disposent
du bonheur de la terre. Voilà ceux surtout qu'il importe de convertir.[51]

But suddenly this belief, so long held by Diderot has grown hesitant; the
introduction of a "presque" betrays a lack of certainty. And later on when
he develops his train of thought and asks,

> A qui appartient-il de concilier ces trois règles de notre conduite (la loi de
> nature, la loi civile et la loi religieuse), si ce n'est au chef de la société? à
> qui donc le philosophe s'adressera-t-il fortement, si ce n'est au souverain? [52]

the questions are not entirely rhetorical. Try as he may to reassert his
confidence in the enlightenment of the ruler as the only solution to the ills
of societies, Diderot is not happy. He cannot avoid the uneasy feeling that
the turncoat Frederick has called the whole matter into question. Diderot
may well ask,

> Si cette vérité se trouve jamais dans la tête d'un roi sage, que ne produira-
> t-elle point?[53]

[49] O.PO., p. 145.
[50] *Ibid.*, p. 148.
[51] *Ibid.*, p. 141-142.
[52] *Ibid.*, p. 142.
[53] *Ibid.*, p. 138.

but has not the Prussian king provided ample evidence that the advent of wise kings to the thrones of Europe is at best a contingent possibility, at worst an unattainable ideal divorced from reality?

The *Pages contre un tyran* are invested with a dialectic tension created by the conflict of irreconcilable concepts, and as such they are a characteristic expression of Diderot's thought as it reaches a turning point. An illuminating parallel may be drawn at this point between the *Pensées philosophiques* and the *Pages contre un tyran*. They both contain thought patterns which are striking in their similarity. In the *Pensées* Diderot defends a deistic conception of God as essential to the explanation of the function of the natural universe and as the necessary basis for morality. Yet, while rejecting atheism, he is nonetheless strongly tempted by it, as it constitutes a more honest and realistic intellectual attitude than deism, since the latter, in order to resolve basic philosophical problems, must resort to a premise, namely the existence of God, which itself is open to question. Similarly, in the *Pages contre un tyran* he continues to defend the concept of the enlightened ruler because it provides the only plausible formula for the establishment of a just and virtuous society based on truth. Yet, as atheism challenges the intellectual inadequacy of deism in the *Pensées*, so the condemnation of Frederick challenges the practical inadequacy of the concept of the enlightened ruler. In fact the process has gone further in the *Pages contre un tyran*, for not only does Diderot's disillusionment with the Prussian king challenge, it has already begun to undermine his faith in enlightened monarchism. The *Pages contre un tyran* announce the beginning of a short period of disarray in Diderot's political thought, where less and less able to accept his old utopian ideology, he has not evolved sufficiently to formulate a new one. But if the episode from which the *Pages contre un tyran* sprung was negative in its effect on Diderot's thought in that it tended to destroy without replacing what it destroyed, the Maupeou episode both hastened the destructive process and at the same time provided Diderot with the necessary elements for the elaboration of a new doctrine.

III. MAUPEOU AND THE DISMISSAL OF THE *PARLEMENTS*

Maupeou's summary dismissal of the *parlements* and their replacement by a salaried judiciary in January 1771 provoked a debate even more acrimonious than the one centring around the grain trade in the previous year. While Voltaire set himself up as the champion of Maupeou's reform, the *philosophes* in Paris, among them Diderot, lost no time in denouncing the new chancellor's move as an act of open tyranny. The opposing positions taken up by Voltaire and Diderot are symptomatic of a profound divergence of opinion on basic political issues.

Voltaire's support of Maupeou derived from his hatred of the *parlements* and his particular conception of the French monarchy. Were not the *parlements* the savage repressors of progressive ideas, the ruthless opponents of tolerance, the bloodthirsty judges of Calas and the Chevalier de la Barre? Did they not continually impede royal authority with their remonstrances? For Voltaire France's salvation lay in a centralising monarchy which would draw the anarchic forces of the nation into a harmonious unity. The patriarch of Ferney belonged to an older generation which had never overcome its admiration for Louis XIV, under whom, according to Voltaire, the French administration "atteignit son dernier degré de perfection." [54] For Voltaire "le gouvernement ne peut être bon s'il n'y a une puissance unique" [55] therefore Maupeou was justified in ending the *parlements'* usurpation of royal sovereignty.

According to René Pomeau, Voltaire's isolation from the Paris *philosophes* in the *Querelle des Parlements Maupeou* was a sign of his political insight:

> Il eut le mérite de ne point se laisser prendre à cette étonnante mystification politique du XVIIIe siècle: les anciens parlements, corps de privilégiés égoïstes, passant pour des défenseurs du peuple. [56]

But if there was a mystification concerning the political role of the *parlements* Diderot was not a party to it, and even less was he duped by it. In fact his reaction, to the dismissal of the *parlements* reveals, as we shall see, a more profound understanding of the political evolution of France than Voltaire was capable of.

In 1769 Diderot had written a review of Voltaire's *Histoire du Parlement de Paris*, intended for Grimm's *Correspondance littéraire* but never published. In it, he agrees with the author's contention that

> Nos parlements d'aujourd'hui n'ont rien de commun avec nos anciens parlements et nos Etats généraux, (...) ce ne sont que de simples cours de judicature salariées dont les prétendus privilèges ne sont que des espèces d'usurpations fondées sur des circonstances fortuites, quelquefois très frivoles. [57]

But not content to merely agree with Voltaire, he continues, "un plus

[54] *Siècle de Louis XIV*, Ch. 30 in *Oeuvres historiques,* I, p. 993.
[55] *La voix du sage et du peuple*, Oeuv. comp., XXIII, p. 466.
[56] *La Politique de Voltaire*, p. 26.
[57] CORR., IX, p. 64.

instruit auroit sans doute traité ce sujet important d'une manière plus profonde," and then proceeds to do just that, sketching a devastating picture of the *Parlement de Paris* as a fanatically violent and irreconcilable enemy of liberty, progress, philosophy and reason.[58] Four years later, when he turned his attention once more to the subject of the *Parlement*, his criticism had lost none of its bitterness:

> Jouissait-il de la considération publique? Non. Il n'en jouissait pas parce qu'il ne la méritait pas, et il ne la méritait pas, parce que toutes ses résistances aux volontés du souverain n'étaient que de la mômerie; que l'intérêt de la nation était toujours sacrifié et qu'il ne se battait bravement que pour le sien.[59]

Furthermore, the *Parlement de Paris* was more concerned with asserting its superiority over the provincial *parlements* than with wielding its political power effectively.[60] Consequently, Diderot cannot be deemed guilty of holding an unrealistic attitude towards the *parlements*, of seeing in them the defenders of the people.

However, unlike Voltaire, Diderot, fresh from writing the *Pages contre un tyran*, does not turn to absolutism. Instead his increasingly empirical approach to politics allows him to penetrate beneath the surface of the problem and examine the real issues that are at stake. The dissolution of the *parlements* is a sign that France has reached a turning point in its history:

> Nous touchons à une crise qui aboutira ou à l'esclavage ou à la liberté.[61]

Either the nation will transcend the crisis or it will succumb; in the latter case monarchy will degenerate into despotism. Progression or regression, the choice must be made. Until 1774, when Turgot became minister and the *parlements* were re-established Diderot remained convinced that the wrong choice had been made, and that naked tyranny had replaced legality.

Why is it that Diderot, so critical of the *parlements*, should nevertheless have taken such strong exception to Maupeou's action? For an explanation we must turn again to the *Mémoires pour Catherine II*. His observations on the *parlements* in the *Essai historique sur la police*, which opens the *Mémoires*, were written nearly three years after the event, but there

---

[58] *Ibid.*, pp. 64-66.
[59] *Mémoires pour Catherine II*, p. 16.
[60] *Ibid.*, p. 17.
[61] A.T., XVIII, p. 28.

can be little doubt that they reflect faithfully his feelings in 1771. Fully aware of the bankruptcy of the *parlements*, Diderot nevertheless saw in the institution the only safeguard, feeble though it was, against naked tyranny:

Il y avait entre la tête du despote et nos yeux une grande toile d'araignée sur laquelle la multitude adorait une image de la liberté.[62]

Even if this image of liberty was illusory, it performed a valuable service in preventing a servile mentality from pervading the nation. While it existed, there remained the possibility of reforming it so that it might properly fulfil the function the *parlementaires* had arrogated to themselves. But any such reform would require a radical reconstitution of the body's membership in order to replace the magistrates whose only concern was to protect and advance their own interests:

Si ce corps est bien composé, si les membres en sont de bons, honnêtes et braves citoyens, des patriotes zélés, des hommes justes et éclairés, la belle chose que ce corps! [63]

exclaims Diderot. Once reconstituted this body would act as a valuable check on the legislative activities of the sovereign through its prerogative of registered royal edicts:

Voici donc ce que l'enregistrement suppose: un souverain qui veut.
Un souverain qui notifie sa volonté à un corps de citoyens chargé d'examiner si cette volonté n'a rien de contraire aux constitutions fondamentales du royaume, au bien de son état et de sa personne et au légitime intérêt de ses sujets.[64]

The debate over the reform of the *parlements* thus affirms the superiority of Diderot's political insight over Voltaire's. Voltaire's support of Maupeou was a compound of anti-Christian sentiment, since the *parlements* were the foremost proponents of religious obscurantism, and a kind of political aestheticism which conceives of the absolute monarch as an artist harmonizing the forces of society into a beautiful unity.[65] Set against Voltaire's utopianism, Diderot's approach to the matter strikes us as a soberly realistic assessment of the changes slowly taking place in the political pattern of the nation. Admittedly, for both men the advancement

---

[62] *Mémoires*, p. 20.
[63] *Ibid.*, p. 15.
[64] *Ibid.*
[65] See R. Pomeau, *op. cit.*, p. 41.

of liberty is the centrepiece of their aspirations; in this they are children of their age. As Diderot puts it,

Chaque siècle a son esprit qui le caractérise. L'esprit du nôtre semble être celui de la liberté.[66]

But Voltaire fails to understand that the advancement of liberty will remain a doubtful affair if it is entrusted to an absolute monarch. Diderot, on the other hand, by an examination of the actual and potential roles of the *parlements*, discovers that the key to liberty lies in the movement of political power away from the monarch and towards a representative body of the nation's citizens.

So it is apparent that Diderot's political ideas have undergone a considerable evolution, not to say revolution, but one which is not yet complete. La Rivière had enabled Diderot to elaborate an absolutist doctrine whose unity reflected the unity of his philosophical and moral thought, but which was at the same time anti-despotic. The guarantee of unity lay in the concept of sovereignty vested exclusively in the person of the ruler; the guarantee against despotism lay in the concept of the wisdom of the ruler who legislates in consultation with his citizen-advisors and according to the dictates of evidence.[67] But this unity was by its very nature artificial as it consisted of the reconciliation of two irreconcilable elements: the principle of absolutism, represented by the sovereign ruler, and the principle of democracy, represented by the citizen-advisors. Only the predominance of a utopianism as strong as Voltaire's could prevent this monolithic structure from bursting asunder. Diderot's participation in the debate over the *parlements* finally destroyed this precarious equilibrium, which had already been disturbed by his disillusionment over Frederick. From now on the artificial synthesis of absolutism and democracy is replaced by an open conflict between the two ideologies in Diderot's mind, a conflict which is sustained by the clash between the waning utopianism and the increasing empiricism governing his political thought.

IV. THE FAILURE OF ABSOLUTISM

This rift in the unity of Diderot's political thought is analogous to the partial disintegration of the previously unified structure of his philosophical and moral thought. The destructive agent in both cases is the experimental method. In both cases the disintegrating process brings about the

[66] CORR., XI, p. 20.
[67] See p. 106.

separation of hostile elements which had earlier been held together in a forced harmony. The *Neveu de Rameau, Jacques le Fataliste*, and the *contes* have demonstrated the incompatibility of a rigidly deterministic view of man with the irreducible and essential values of human personality.[68] Similarly a methodical evaluation of political realities has shown Diderot that monarchical absolutism is incompatible with the right of the nation to see that legislation is carried out in accordance with the public interest.

But not only are these two developments analogous, they are also closely related: both tackle at different levels the problem of alienation and the means of overcoming it. A crude determinism, whether biological as in the *Neveu* or metaphysical as in *Jacques*, implies the inevitability of alienation since it condemns as sterile those desires and impulses in man which appear to run counter to it. When Rameau exclaims,

Le point important est que vous et moi nous soyons, et que nous soyons vous et moi. Que tout aille d'ailleurs comme il pourra,[69]

and when Jacques announces,

J'ai pris le parti d'être comme je suis,[70]

both are in effect rejecting the inevitability of their alienation. This rejection denotes not only the possibility but the desirability of overcoming the conditions of alienation, the need to formulate a philosophical and moral vision which eliminates the alienating factors inherent in a rigid determinism. This discovery has its reverberations in the realm of Diderot's political thought: monarchical absolutism, although ideally realising the *morale universelle* in society and so ending man's political alienation,[71] in reality perpetuates it by preventing the implementation of the wishes of society. Consequently political alienation will only be overcome if the will of the people, whether it appears good, bad, or indifferent, is allowed to realise itself. Diderot makes this point categorically in the *Fragments Echappés*:

On dit quelquefois que le gouvernement le plus heureux serait celui d'un despote juste et éclairé: c'est une assertion très-téméraire. Il pourrait aisément arriver que la volonté de ce maître absolu fût en contradiction avec la volonté de ses sujets. Alors, malgré sa justice et ses lumières, il aurait tort de

---

[68] See Part I, Chap. II, pp. 49-56.
[69] O.RO., p. 405.
[70] *Ibid.*, p. 574.
[71] See Part I, Chap. I, pp. 26-27.

les dépouiller de leurs droits, même pour leur avantage (...) Il n'est jamais permis à un homme, quel qu'il soit, de traiter ses commettants comme un troupeau de bêtes (...) S'ils disent: Nous sommes bien ici; s'ils disent, même d'accord: Nous y sommes mal mais nous y voulons rester, il faut tâcher de les éclairer, de les détromper, de les amener à des vues saines par la voix de la persuasion, mais jamais par celle de la force.[72]

It is clear then, that a radical change has taken place in Diderot's thought. No longer is the ruler, even if he is ideally just and enlightened, in a position to act as the interpreter of the general will of the nation. Real as opposed to theoretical sovereignty, in the sense of the inalienable right to self-determination, lies in the hands of the people. Any attempt to infringe this right, even if it were carried out with the best of intentions, constitutes a denial of their humanity: "Il n'est jamais permis à un homme, quel qu'il soit, de traiter ses commettants comme un troupeau de bêtes." In effect, though not formally, Diderot has reduced the ruler to the role of executive, the servant of the legislative body. He exceeds his mandate if he acts "sans consulter la volonté générale, sans recueillir, pour ainsi dire, la pluralité des suffrages dans l'opinion publique." [73] If he does so, he is guilty of causing political alienation which in turn leads to moral alienation:

C'est aliéner les coeurs et les esprits, tout décréditer, même le bon et l'honnête.[74]

Experience has shown Diderot that absolutism, whether metaphysical or political, denies man the right to choose his own destiny. The parallel developments in his philosophical and political thought that we have been tracing, point towards the same conclusion: the elimination of the barriers which separate man from his true nature, and the creation of emancipating conditions favourable to his self-fulfilment.

But if effective sovereignty is to be transferred from the ruler to the people, does this mean that the *sage*, whose political function was to provide the ruler with enlightened counsel, has now become redundant? The answer to this question is provided in an article Diderot wrote for the *Correspondance littéraire*:

Avec (le) temps cet homme de lettres s'est ligué tantôt avec le chef contre les (pe)uples, et il a chanté la tyrannie, tantôt avec le peuple contre le tyran,

[72] A.T., VI, p. 448.
[73] P.D., p. 108, HIST., X, p. 138.
[74] *Ibid.*

(et) il a chanté la liberté; et dans l'un et l'autre cas il est devenu un ci(toy)en important.[75]

It had never been Diderot's intention to preach tyranny, but from this observation he appears to have the guilty feeling that this is what he has been doing, albeit inadvertently. Having realised his mistake he sees that the political future of the *sage* lies with the people: only if they exercise power can the day of freedom dawn. So it is to the new sovereign, to the people that he must turn; but his role remains the same, that of indispensable counsellor and guide. Yet how could he fulfil his new function without calling down upon himself the wrath of the authorities? Diderot had no taste for martyrdom, his short stay at Vincennes has convinced him of that. Besides, long experience editing the *Encyclopédie* had taught him that heroic gestures were futile; the only effective way of achieving one's ends was to be devious. Raynal's *Histoire des deux Indes* was the perfect solution. While enjoying the protective cover of anonymity – Raynal was prepared to take responsibility for all the contributions to the work – he could once more reach a large and important public, as he had done with the *Encyclopédie*. Diderot's contribution to the *Histoire* doubled from the 1770 to the 1774 editions, then doubled again from the 1774 to the 1780 editions.[76] By the early 1770's the *Histoire* had become his real "moyen d'expression publique," [77] the major vehicle by which he could proffer his counsel to his new masters, the people.

He may vacillate later on, it is true; he may be half tempted to see in Louis XVI or in Catherine the real possibility of an enlightened absolute monarch; but these will be only temporary aberrations. The die has been cast; whatever proclamations he may later make in his correspondence or in other works open to the public gaze, his true opinions and intentions can now be clearly seen in his contributions to the *Histoire des deux Indes*. Without a shadow of doubt he has crossed decisively into the other camp:

Tout écrivain de génie est magistrat né de sa patrie (...) Son tribunal, c'est la nation entière; son juge est le public, non le despote qui ne l'entend pas, ou le ministre qui ne veut pas l'écouter.[78]

But one despot at least, it appeared, was prepared to listen to Diderot. A long-standing invitation to visit Catherine could no longer be postponed.

---

[75] H. Dieckmann, "Les contributions de Diderot à la 'Correspondance littéraire et à l'Histoire des deux Indes'," (*Sur la Russie*). p. 426.
[76] See M. Duchet, "Diderot Collaborateur de Raynal," p. 541.
[77] M. Duchet, *op. cit.*, p. 546.
[78] P.D., p. 101, HIST., X, p. 139.

A deep sense of personal gratitude and the strong attraction of her power-ful personality, if nothing else, would have been sufficient to draw him to St. Petersburg. But there were other more profound reasons which may have ultimately decided him to undertake the perilous journey to his "Sémiramis du Nord."

CHAPTER III

FADING HOPES

On the 11th June 1773 after many fond farewells Diderot finally took leave of friends and family and set out somewhat reluctantly from Paris on his long delayed journey to St. Petersburg. France by this time, had all the appearances of an arbitrary tyranny. Although historians have since emphasised the more positive reforming aspects of the Maupeou government, at the time the ruthlessness and total disregard for popular opinion with which Maupeou and his associates set about consolidating royal authority earned them the hatred and contempt of almost all sections of society. With the abolition of the *parlements*, it seemed, all pretence at constitutional government had been dispensed with. The last barrier had been removed between the people and the whims and fancies of a vicious tyrant who would deal swiftly and mercilessly through his lackeys with anyone who dared gainsay him. An exaggeration, no doubt; but this was the situation as many saw it, not least Diderot whose highly critical account of the Maupeou administration, contained in the *Essai historique sur la police* [1] was written during the journey to St. Petersburg, and whose distaste is expressed in a curt rhetorical passage elsewhere in the *Mémoires*:

> ... qu'est-ce qu'il y a de commun entre notre ministère et la nation? Le ministère a son esprit qui, certes, n'est pas le nôtre. [2]

All hope for the dawn of a new age of justice, freedom, virtue and happiness in which the nation could control and forge its own destiny had been lost. With all power securely and unrestrictedly vested in the monarch, any prospect of an evolution towards popular sovereignty was purely academic.

But if in France the outlook was singularly unpromising, Holland and Russia, the two countries which Diderot was to visit, presented a fairer

---

[1] In *Mémoires pour Catherine II*.
[2] *Ibid.*, p. 278.

aspect. Holland was one of the few countries in a mainly monarchical Europe living under a republican régime; if freedom and popular sovereignty were to be found anywhere; then surely it was here in this small trading nation. Russia was blessed with a great and wise monarch who had revealed to the world her intention of divesting herself of her autocratic power and placing it in the hands of the nation. In fact, as we shall see in this chapter and the next, Diderot was destined in both cases to experience varying degrees of disappointment. But this does not detract from the considerable importance of this period for the shaping of his political thought, for during this short time he had the opportunity of broadening and diversifying his direct experience and understanding of political, social and economic matters in an unprecedented fashion. In both Holland and Russia, but particularly in the latter, he was able to examine the political machine with a freedom unknown in France to a person in his position. In Holland, thanks to wide contacts, many provided by his host Prince Galitzin, Diderot was able to carry out during the course of his two stays a detailed survey of numerous aspects of Dutch life and commit them to paper in the *Voyage de Hollande*. In Russia, thanks to the remarkable privileges accorded him by Catherine, he had direct access to the centre of power and could discover at first hand the manner in which the reins of government were manipulated. The results of his Russian experience are contained in the *Mémoires pour Catherine II*, written for the most part between Diderot's interviews with Catherine,[3] and the *Observations sur le Nakaz*, a commentary on Catherine's *Instruction* [4] written during his second stay at The Hague. Such direct and abundant experience of political realities, coming at a time when, as we have seen, the empirical method had all but ousted his earlier utopian idealism, provided him with a unique opportunity for testing the validity of his doctrine and developing its implications.

I. HOLLAND: THE MYTH

With the evidence available it is difficult to establish with absolute certainty what knowledge of the country and its political situation in particular, Diderot managed to acquire in the course of his first stay in Holland. In his first letter, written to the Volland sisters three days after his arrival, he shows some concern over the apparently large programme of visits that his zealous host, Galitzin, had drawn up for him:

---

[3] See MEM., Introduction, pp. xxiii-xiv.
[4] *Instruction de S.M.I. pour la commission chargée de dresser le projet d'un nouveau code de lois.*

Nous avons des projets de toute couleur. Si nous les remplissons, je verrai beaucoup, je ne manquerai pas d'amusement. Je résiderai peu et je ne travaillerai guère. Je voudrais pourtant bien travailler.[5]

But it appears that he only left The Hague on three occasions: once to visit the University of Leyden, where he met a number of academics and notables;[6] once on a short sightseeing trip to Amsterdam and nearby Zaandam;[7] and once to meet Galitzin's wife at Utrecht on her return from Berlin.[8] Otherwise Galitzin's programme seems to have remained largely unfulfilled. In his next letter to the Volland sisters Diderot writes in marked contrast to the first,

C'est ici qu'on emploie bien son tems. Point d'importuns qui viennent vous prendre toutes vous matinées (...) Notre vie est tranquille, sobre et très retirée...

and a little further,

Je ne sors guères; et quand je sors, je vais toujours sur le bord de la mer.[9]

No doubt his desire to work prevailed over his host's plans for him; indeed, this seems the only plausible explanation for his finding time during those two months to annotate Helvétius' *De l'Homme* and Hemsterhuis' *Lettre sur l'homme et ses rapports,* to compose a work which was later to become the *Paradoxe sur le comédien,* to write the *Première satyre,* and to produce two or three months worth of copy for the *Correspondance littéraire.*[10]

But if Diderot did not travel far afield during his first stay at The Hague, and does not appear to have spent much time or effort researching into the Dutch, he was sufficiently serious about Holland to compile "des notes assez intéressantes sur les habitants."[11] These notes were eventually to form part of the *Voyage de Hollande* which was more or less completed during his second stay. Unfortunately lack of critical work on the text prevents us from distinguishing with any certainty the parts written during the first stay at The Hague from those written afterwards. While this is of little consequence for much of the text which consists of a

[5] CORR., XIII, pp. 15-16.
[6] *Ibid.*
[7] See *Ibid.*, pp. 22-23.
[8] See *Ibid.*, p. 23.
[9] *Ibid.*, pp. 32-33.
[10] See *Ibid.*, pp. 46-47.
[11] *Ibid.*, p. 46.

conglomeration of factual information, it does pose a problem for the assessment of his reaction to the Dutch political situation as it appears in the comments and criticisms which intersperse the factual report. However, if we refer back to Diderot's correspondence during his first stay, we can draw some tentative conclusions as to the kind of passages in the *Voyage* which reflect his opinion in 1773. Admittedly, Diderot in his letters is not very forthcoming about Holland, preferring to keep his impressions until he can recount them to his friends "au coin du foyer." This dearth of comment in itself suggests that he had not as yet penetrated beneath the surface of facts and appearances. In the only two short passages in his correspondence in which he does comment on political matters he gives the impression that his understanding of the situation in Holland was conventional and uninformed, in fact representative of a belief fairly widespread in Europe of the Enlightenment that the United Provinces were an oasis of republican virtue in a desert of monarchical and aristocratic vice. The two passages appear in a letter to Madame d'Epinay, and with slight variations in a letter to Sophie and her sister of the same date. In the first passage Diderot notes that the people are "bien possédé du démon républicain," and illustrates his observation with a remark made by a saddler,

Il faut que je retire ma fille de ce couvent de Bruxelles où l'on me l'infecterait de cette bassesse monarchique qui doit régner là.[12]

In the second he describes his encounter with the Bentincks and compares their bearing with that of the founders of the two great Roman patrician families:

A leur air grave, à leur ton sentencieux et sévère, on se croiroit entre Fabius et Regulus. Rien ne rappelle les vieux romains (sic) comme ces deux respectables vieillards.[13]

The evidence, such as it is, points to the conclusion that during his first stay Diderot remained victim of an illusion; he did not see through the republican façade that Holland presented to the world, to the economic and moral decline, the corruption and retreat from republican values which had begun after the War of the Spanish Succession, and which Montesquieu had so clearly diagnosed.[14] If we accept this conclusion, it does much to explain the ambivalences regarding the Dutch political si-

---

[12] *Ibid.*, p. 35.
[13] *Ibid.*, pp. 36-37.
[14] "Voyage de Gratz à La Haye," *Oeuvres complètes*, pp. 863-864, 872, 873-874.

tuation which appear in the *Voyage de Hollande*. It suggests that the passages in which Diderot extols the republican virtues and liberalism of Holland date from 1773, and that those in which he criticises the Dutch for allowing these qualities to decline date from his second stay in 1774 when he had had time to inform himself further on the subject, although some lines may have been added as late as 1780 when Diderot revised the work before its publication by Meister in the *Correspondance littéraire*.[15]

It is not difficult to understand Diderot's failure to detect the difference between the outward appearance of Dutch politics and the less edifying inner reality. Apart from the fact that he does not appear to have applied himself to the subject with much vigour, there can be no doubt that after Maupeou's France, Holland, although the country had fallen away from its past republican glories, afforded Diderot a sense of release and satisfaction which encouraged him to look upon the political system in the most favourable light. This is strikingly apparent in his description of the assembly of the States General, the ruling body of the seven provinces; after explaining the seating arrangement of the deputies, he continues in a vibrant oratorical tone:

> Tel est l'ordre d'une des plus solennelles et des plus augustes assemblées qu'il y ait au monde. C'est là que sont agitées les affaires de la république et du monde. C'est là qu'on voit des commerçants, des bourgeois prendre le ton imposant et l'air majestueux des rois.[16]

Nothing could have been calculated to arouse Diderot's enthusiasm more; here was a nation in which the citizens were sovereign, and, what is more, behaved as though they were.[17] And one must remember that citizen for Diderot meant the property-owning and merchant middle-classes, for "il n'y a point de patrie pour celui qui n'a rien ou qui peut emporter tout ce qu'il a." [18] However, the truth of the situation reveals how wrong Diderot was in thinking that the doctrine in which his philosophical, moral and political thought, the doctrine of popular sovereignty, was a reality in Holland. The members of the States General, together with those of the provincial States and the town councils, far from representing the middle-class citizenry, belonged to the regent class, a closed caste of upper middle-

---

[15] See *Textes politiques*, ed. Y. Benot. Introduction, p. 54, n. 2.
[16] A.T., XVII, p. 383.
[17] In *La Hollande et les Hollandais au 17e et au 18e siècles vus par les Francais*, pp. 233-235, R. Murris draws an interesting if somewhat vague comparison between Diderot's attitude to the States General and that of more disabused Frenchmen who had preceded him. The comparison underlines the readiness with which Diderot was prepared to accept Dutch institutions at their face value.
[18] A.T., XVII, p. 386.

class burghers, whose nepotism had made their offices more or less hereditary. In addition, as a result of inter-marriage practically all difference between these bourgeois patricians and the nobility had disappeared. Consequently during the 18th century the regent oligarchy had become increasingly differentiated from the ordinary burgher; as G. J. Renier has written: "The bourgeoisie no longer looked upon the hereditary administrators as its own representatives. The middling classes, a fortiori, felt they had nothing in common with these men who despised them and who had begun to affect a mode of dressing which distinguished them from all other citizens." [19]

Seen in this light some other observations made by Diderot in the *Voyage de Hollande* and almost certainly written in 1773 also strike one as naive and ill-informed. Let us take some representative passages to demonstrate the extent to which he took the appearance to be the reality. In one he describes what he calls the "democratic" and "aristocratic" sides of the nation:

Chaque province, chaque ville, est une république particulière qui s'administre par ses lois, ses usages, ses coutumes, à la pluralité des voix, sans aucune distinction des personnes, voilà le côté démocratique; la noblesse veille à la sûreté du pays, voilà le côté aristocratique.[20]

We have already seen how far from the truth is the first part of this statement; the second part betrays a similar ignorance since the nobility had all but lost its separate identity through amalgamation with the regent class. Diderot's innocent adherence to the democratic-republican myth is further illustrated by the following remark:

...une des choses dont on est continuellement et délicieusement touché dans toute la Hollande, c'est de n'y rencontrer nulle part, ni la vue de la misère, ni le spectacle de la tyrannie.[21]

and by a passage on civil liberty:

Ici chacun est maître chez soi; la liberté civile y met tous les habitants de niveau; les petits ne peuvent être opprimés par les grands, ni les pauvres par les riches. En maintenant les privilèges des citoyens, le magistrat défend les siens. C'est un crime que de faire la moindre violence à un particulier dans sa maison. La liberté de penser, de parler et d'écrire est presque illimitée.[22]

[19] *The Dutch Nation*, p. 230.
[20] A.T., XVII, p. 382.
[21] *Ibid.*, p. 378.
[22] *Ibid.*, p. 402.

The state of affairs described may have been true in the earlier days of the Dutch Republic, but by the latter half of the 18th century things had changed for the worse. To quote Renier again: "On the one side there were the masters, who indeed consisted of a small minority. On the other side there were those who had no power or authority. They were united neither by common interests nor by common aspiration. But a growing hatred of the masters animated them. At the bottom of the social ladder poverty was spreading. There was much misery about 1740, but some twenty years later the situation had grown even worse." [23] Admittedly the Dutch still enjoyed a freedom of speech, thought, and of the press which was the envy of continental Europe, and no doubt they were safe in their own homes: but to conclude from this and a superficial perusal of the political system that they enjoyed political liberty in the fullest sense is a sad misinterpretation of the facts. The constitution may have been a wise one as Diderot claims,[24] but it had been manipulated by the regent class to serve their own ends. It required more than two short months to get the true measure of the Dutch government. An anonymous Englishman, long resident in the country, showed far more perception when he wrote as far back as 1740: "Their government is aristocratical: so that the so much boasted liberty of the Dutch is not to be understood in the general and absolute sense, but *cum grano salis.*" [25]

We have already put forward some explanation for Diderot's failure to discover the aristocratic reality hidden behind the democratic-republican façade of the Dutch political system: his relative seclusion at The Hague, his preoccupation with literary and philosophical projects, his understandable predisposition to believe in the full and effective existence of Dutch republicanism. But another reason of a more positive nature suggests itself, though again through lack of sufficient evidence, we can only present it as a speculative theory. Although, as we have seen, Diderot did not travel very much during his first stay in Holland, on two occasions at least, at Leyden and Utrecht, he had the opportunity of meeting intelligent and knowledgeable men with whom he no doubt discussed, among a variety of subjects, the political situation in Holland. We do not know precisely whom he met at Leyden, in his letter he refers casually to "des princes et des sçavants," [26] but it is likely that some of them belonged

---

[23] *Op. cit.*, p. 230.
[24] See A.T., XVII, p. 386.
[25] *A description of Holland: or the present state of the United Provinces*, p. 73. Quoted by C. R. Boxer in *The Dutch Seaborne Empire 1600-1800*, p. 42. Neither to his credit was Voltaire deceived by the appearance of democracy in Holland. See J. Vercruysse, "Voltaire et la Hollande," pp. 173-174.
[26] CORR., XIII, p. 15.

to the new generation of young Dutch intellectuals, imbued with the ideas of the Enlightenment, which had arisen by 1770. Rijkloff Michael van Goens, the brilliant young academic whom Diderot met at Utrecht was one of the leading lights of the new generation. His defence and promotion of the new ideas coming from England and France earned him a reputation as a controversial figure; indeed, he came to be the *bête noire* of all those who thought that the new ideas where threatening the very foundations of religious orthodoxy.[27] Of these young intellectuals Renier has written: "(They) revived old Netherlandish notions of local liberty and national sovereignty, and *developed a disconcerting tendency to take the professions of republican faith made by the regents of the States party at their face value.*" [28] It is, then, feasible that Diderot was encouraged in his misguided belief in the republican virtues of the ruling oligarchy by young men like van Goens [29] who were equally prone to take their desires for realities.

"L'esprit d'observation est rare;" wrote Diderot in the preface to the *Voyage de Hollande*, "quand on l'a reçu de la nature, il est encore facile de se tromper par précipitation." [30] In general his study of Holland, its people's life and manners, escapes the kind of errors which result from the drawing of hasty conclusions. It is in the main a sober and objective account in which the few observations that he does make flow rationally and dispassionately from the factual information that fills most of the pages. To the extent that his failure to detect the advanced decline of republicanism and democratic processes in Holland can be ascribed to his own naive enthusiasm which prevented him from maintaining the degree of objectivity he prescribes in his preface, he can be blamed for undue precipitation in drawing conclusions. But in as much as he reflected the false assumptions prevalent among progressive Dutch intellectuals at the time, he cannot be justly held to account for presenting a false picture of the situation. Whether he was blinded to the truth by his own preconceptions or those of others does not detract from the fact that his first stay in Holland consolidated his belief that if justice and liberty are

---

[27] See H. L. Brugmans: "Autour de Diderot en Hollande," p. 17 *et passim*. Brugmans misdates the two letters from Diderot to van Goens. Their dating has been correctly identified in CORR., XIII, (see p. 22, p. 13).

[28] *Op. cit.*, p. 231. Our italics.

[29] His opponents' accusation of heterodoxy forced him to resign his chair in 1776. Through influential contacts he became a regent of the Utrecht town council. In the subsequent conflict between the democratic patriot and Orangist parties he became a front rank propagandist for the Orangist cause. This retreat from progressive views and their political consequences was doubtless brought about by the influence of family tradition and his sympathy for William V.

[30] A.T., XVII, p. 366.

to flourish in a state then sovereignty must be vested in the citizens, that is the property-owning middle classes who have a vested interest in the nation's welfare. It was then, a short but significant period of consolidation through direct experience.

Diderot did not seek to elaborate a doctrine of popular sovereignty in the light of his newly acquired experience and knowledge. As it stood the Dutch constitution was a model of political wisdom and uniquely suited to the country for which it had been fashioned. But when it came to applying the lesson learnt from it to nations with very different characteristics, particularly economic and geographical ones, prudence was advisable:

Mais peut-elle (cette constitution) convenir à un grand empire? C'est une question à examiner.[31]

While Diderot showed little inclination to share Montesquieu's view that climatic conditions affect the choice of political régimes open to a nation, physical size and the related economic factors must be taken into account. Holland was a small country unable to support its inhabitants adequately from the land and dependent on trade for its wealth. France was a vast, predominantly agricultural nation for whom trade would remain in the foreseeable future only a secondary source of wealth. Holland could only offer the confirmation of a principle; [32] paradoxically the vast and backward Russian Empire, ruled by a despotic monarch, was to provide the conditions in which Diderot could elaborate his doctrine in practical terms.

II. DIDEROT AND CATHERINE II: AN ATTEMPT AT CONVERSION

The encounter between Diderot and Catherine II was one of the most fascinating, paradoxical and telling events in the intellectual and political life of the 18th century. Its uniqueness has, however, been largely underestimated by scholars of the Enlightenment who have tended to ascribe a uniform character to the various contacts between members of the philosophic movement and the sovereigns of Northern Europe. The *philosophes* have generally been presented as supporting and encouraging monarchs who claimed to use their autocratic powers for the furtherance and implementation of progressive principles within their own coun-

---

[31] *Ibid.*, p. 386.
[32] Generally speaking this is true, though on the particular problem of the responsibilities of deputies to their constituents Diderot does show himself to be influenced in his subsequent thinking by Dutch practice. See below p. 166.

tries. Albert Lortholary is representative of this view when he writes, "On peut soutenir que la plupart des 'philosophes,' de 1760 à 1785, penchent plus ou moins, *dans la pratique*, vers le despotisme éclairé." [33] This opinion is underlined by Paul Hazard who, noting the *philosophes'* attitude to the Northern monarchs, remarks, "Le despotisme changeait de sens, pourvu qu'on lui ajoutât seulement un adjectif et qu'on l'appelât despotisme éclairé." [34] This generally accepted view has recently been challenged by R. Derathé [35] who argues that the term "despotisme éclairé" is an invention of nineteenth century historians.[36] He then goes on to attack the falsity of the concept embodied in this term, arguing that the *philosophes* did not favour absolutism, and that what they admired in Frederick II and Catherine II in particular was not the extent of their power or its absolute or despotic nature, but the fact that this power was used in the service of the State and national welfare, that it had freed itself from the domination of fanaticism and superstition, and that it had placed itself under the patronage of enlightened philosophers.[37] Leaning heavily on Voltaire to support his case, Derathé contends that the *philosophes'* main concern was to break the alliance of throne and altar and replace it by an alliance of enlightenment and monarchy.[38] But if we take Voltaire as the most consistent representative of the philosophic movement's attitude towards monarchy, and there seems little reason not to, then it is clear that Derathé's strictures over the use of the term "enlightened despotism" to describe this attitude are not valid. For as Theodore Bestermann has reminded us, Voltaire's resolute opposition to rule by committee and firm belief that great things are only achieved through the wisdom of an individual led him to "the conviction that the only possible system of government for France was an absolute monarchy." [39] But although he insisted that the monarch should be the sole source of political power, it was "only on condition that this power was exercised with wisdom and toleration." [40] In short Voltaire was, unlike some of his contemporaries who also claimed to share the same political philosophy, an unswerving proponent for most of his life of enlightened despotism.

---

[33] *Le mirage russe en France*, p. 145.
[34] *La pensée européenne au XVIIIe siècle, de Montesquieu à Lessing*, t. II, p. 76.
[35] "Les philosophes et le despotisme" in *Utopie et Institutions au XVIIIe siècle*, pp. 57-75.
[36] Diderot, however, refers specifically to "un despotisme juste et éclairé," MEM., p. 118.
[37] *Ibid.*, p. 68.
[38] *Ibid.*, p. 70.
[39] "Voltaire, absolute monarchy and the enlightened monarch" in *Studies on Voltaire*, Vol. XXXII, p. 17.
[40] *Ibid.*, p. 19.

Derathé's thesis would be little more than a quibble about words, which would do little to affect prevailing views on the subject, were it not for an important footnote which presents quotations on the theme of absolutism by d'Holbach, Helvétius and Diderot. This footnote, whatever it does for the first two, presents Diderot in an entirely false political light. D'Holbach and Helvétius, who declare their support for enlightened despotism, are seen by Derathé as untypical of the main body of *philosophes,* whereas Diderot's devastating reply to Helvétius' remark in *De l'Homme*: "Rien de meilleur que le gouvernement arbitraire sous des princes justes, humains et vertueux," in which Diderot argues that this sort of government is the most pernicious of all as it accustoms the people to accept successors who may be evil and stupid, is taken as representative of the general view. So not only does Derathé confuse the issue over enlightened despotism, but he also does Diderot the disservice of denying the original and progressive character of his political thought in the context of the French Enlightenment. D'Holbach and Helvétius are *not* untypical in their favourable comments on enlightened despotism; there is nothing to distinguish the attitudes they express in the passages selected by Derathé from Voltaire's own opinion. It is Diderot, realistically pointing to the hidden dangers of this form of government, who is the odd man out.

Voltaire's royalism, as René Pomeau has noted,[41] stems in large part from a pragmatic realism: if he ignores the tyranny of the so-called enlightened despots of the North, it is because they use their power to hold the clergy in check; if he believes in absolute monarchy for France it is because it is the only workable political system at the present time and within the foreseeable future. Diderot in his approach to the Russian political and economic system is equally realistic, but his realism is of a very different kind from Voltaire's and leads him to radically different conclusions. In general terms Voltaire's pragmatic realism is sustained by a fundamentally static view of society, a feature of the absolutist ethos of the first half of the 18th century, whereas Diderot's realism is determined by a predominantly dynamic conception of social evolution which corresponds to his own materialistic view of nature in flux, and is also representative of the mobile quality of the later Enlightenment. It is a realism which is progressive and empirical rather than pragmatic and rational, and it directs and controls both his investigation into the Russian reality and his assessment of Catherine's programme for reform and, at a later stage, the more real and, to Diderot, less encouraging directions that her

[41] *Politique de Voltaire,* p. 40.

policies were taking. The acuteness of Diderot's insight into the political situation in Russia and the radical and progressive political doctrine which it reveals is simply and forcefully illustrated in a manuscript in the Fonds Vandeul entitled *Sur la Russie* which has been published by Herbert Dieckmann.[42] In this text, written in 1772, more than a year before he went to Russia, Diderot uncovers the basic error of approach in Catherine's projected plan to reform and thereby bring a greater degree of civilisation to Russian society. In Diderot's eyes Catherine's attempt to restructure the country over which she rules is doomed to failure because "(elle) a commencé son édifice par le faîte, en appelant auprès d'elle des hommes de génie de toutes les contrées," [43] whereas she should begin at the bottom and establish a firm material and social basis for modern civilisation by stimulating technology and encouraging the development of the manufacturing potential of the masses. This would create a prosperous new class which would cultivate the arts and develop a feeling for liberty.[44] Diderot's realistic appraisal of the socio-economic structure of Russian society and his understanding of the mechanics of social evolution enables him to smell out the hidden contradiction in Catherine's reform policy and more generally in the theory of enlightened despotism itself; as Georges Dulac has remarked: "Le directeur de l'*Encyclopédie* voit une contradiction radicale entre les méthodes despotiques et les intentions civilisatrices." [45]

The programme of reform and accompanying critique of enlightened despotism contained in embryo in *Sur la Russie* are worked out in detail in the *Mémoires pour Catherine II* and the *Observations sur le Nakaz*. Both reform and critique have a dual foundation: the realism we have already mentioned, but also an ideological view of the individual's relation to society formulated in the *Réfutation d'Helvétius* and the *Commentaire de*

---

[42] *Les contributions de Diderot à la "Correspondance littéraire" et à l'Histoire des deux Indes."*

[43] *Ibid.*, p. 424. Cf. Rousseau's criticism of the reforms of Peter the Great: "Il a vu que son peuple était barbare, il n'a point vu qu'il n'était pas mûr pour la police; il l'a voulu civiliser quand il ne fallait que l'agguerrir. Il a d'abord voulu faire des Allemands, des Anglais, quand il fallait commencer par faire des Russes; il a empêché ses sujets de jamais devenir ce qu'ils pourraient être, en leur persuadant qu'ils étaient ce qu'ils ne sont pas." (*Contrat social*, II, 8, p. 103). Rousseau is more conscious than Diderot of the need to start by giving a people a national character, without which economic, social, and political development is doomed to failure.

[44] The only unrealistic feature of Diderot's formula for the civilisation of Russia is the proposal to import a colony from the West to act as a leaven, which will inculcate the slave people with a sentiment of freedom. Diderot does not appear to realise that this sentiment would develop naturally from the changes he prescribes; though it is possible that he suggested this piece of unlikely social engineering as a means of stimulating what is a natural but a painfully slow process.

[45] Review of Diderot, *Mémoires pour Catherine II*, édition de Vernière, p. 66.

Hemsterhuis.[46] The question immediately poses itself as to whether realism and ideology can coexist in any meaningful way in the world of political practice, and it is a question which is central to the understanding of the relation of Diderot's later political thought to his time. Because if Diderot so confuses ideology and reality that his politics take on the air of a purely ideal or utopian construction then we are perhaps justified in lumping him together with the other *philosophes* as does Sergio Cotta who sees in him a typical representative of the rationalist-universalist school which has totally ignored Montesquieu's introduction of historical and social relativism into the realm of political thinking.[47] Cotta's fundamental criticism of Diderot's political thought is resumed in the following sentence from his article:

La politique n'admet pour Diderot ni éléments naturels ni constantes historiques, mais se résout totalement dans l'application de la vérité rationnelle.[48]

There are many statements in the *Mémoires* alone which appear to justify this opinion and discredit any claims the work might have to be an exercise in political realism; statements so uncompromisingly absolute in tone and implication that taken in isolation it is indeed difficult to see how a political doctrine based upon them could be anything other than idealist or utopian, or at the very least hardly capable of impinging upon the huge variety of economic, social and historical realities the world has to offer. However, when replaced in their context these apparently rigid statements of principle take on a rather different complexion. Let us take as a typical example Diderot's frequently expressed belief that man's sole duty is to ensure his own happiness. This constant of his philosophical and moral credo reappears in the *Mémoires* suitably adapted to the political context:

Il n'y a qu'un devoir, c'est d'être heureux. Puisque ma pente naturelle, invincible, inaliénable, est d'être heureux, c'est la source et la source unique de mes vrais devoirs, et la seule base de toute bonne législation.[49]

Now we have already seen in the *Réfutation d'Helvétius* and the *Commentaire de Hemsterhuis* [50] that this principle, far from being a statement of purely rational doctrine and therefore idealist in its assumptions and

[46] See Part I, Chap. III, pp. 59-73.
[47] "L'illuminisme et la science politique: Montesquieu, Diderot et Catherine II."
[48] *Ibid.*, p. 286.
[49] MEM., p. 235.
[50] Part I, Chap. III.

utopian in its implications, stems from an understanding of the individual's relation to society which itself is based upon a scientific theory of consciousness and which was preceded at an earlier stage by an investigation into happiness and the individual in Diderot's fiction.[51] Admittedly, it may be argued that his theory of consciousness and the conclusions he reaches concerning human nature in his fiction are false because his data is insufficient: in the first case biological science was not well enough advanced to sustain such a theory; in the second his "case histories" are too narrowly selected. But this kind of criticism can still be levelled at most conclusions reached in the field of the social sciences, such is the nature of the discipline. It does not, however, detract from the fact that Diderot employed a substantially empirical method to reach the conclusions on which he bases his political doctrine, which finds its broadest expression in the passage on the individual's duty quoted above. It should also be noted that recent research by psychologists and anthropologists has tended to confirm the theory that in man the biological and the social exist in a dialectical relationship, that there is a complete synthesis of nature and culture in the individual.[52] Diderot naturally, was unable to conceive of the process in such a sophisticated manner, but his understanding of the interrelation of the processes of individuation and socialisation which flows from his theory of consciousness, in as far as it broke down the brutal opposition between the biological and the social, was a movement in the right direction. It therefore cannot be properly argued that Diderot is the proponent of an ideology, in the sense usually given to this term when applied to the doctrines of the political theoreticians of the 18th century in contrast to the empiricism of Montesquieu. That is to say, he is not an idealist, who rejects facts in favour of scientifically unverifiable theories as a means of proposing and justifying a new social order. On the contrary, his political doctrine, which has at its centre the concept of popular sovereignty, takes as its starting point the conclusions drawn from a scientific investigation into the biological and psycho-sociological factors affecting human personality. Admittedly Diderot did not, like Montesquieu, try to understand the infinite diversity of human institutions at all times and in all places, but he can nevertheless make claims with Montesquieu to have attained to a scientific understanding of certain aspects of human society; for if Montesquieu was the first to discover the laws underlying every type of society, Diderot was the first to discover, in an albeit primitive form, the laws governing the relationship of the

---

[51] See Part I, Chap. II.
[52] See G. Besse, "Observations sur la *Réfutation d'Helvétius* par Diderot," pp. 35-38.

individual to society. In this respect their discoveries are complementary.

It does remain true, however, that in certain respects Diderot did not succeed in emancipating himself from certain outmoded forms of rationalist conceptualisation which clashed with the fundamental reorientation of his political thought along empirical lines. Sergio Cotta has pointed to his inability to raise himself to an historical vision of mankind as evidenced by his failure in the *Essai historique sur la police* to understand the positive values of feudal society,[53] and he highlights the gulf separating Diderot from Montesquieu by quoting the following passages from the *Essai*:

> Montesquieu dit que c'est un grand et sublime spectacle que celui du gouvernement féodal. Je n'entends pas cela. Le plan s'en exposerait en dix pages et les maux ne s'en exposeraient pas en mille.[54]

Diderot's anti-historicism in the *Mémoires* is paralleled by an equal rejection of geographical relativism in the *Observations*, also noted by Cotta.[55] In reply to Catherine's assertion that Russia is a European power Diderot retorts that it is of little importance whether the country is Asian or European, and he continues:

> Les moeurs sont partout des conséquences de la législation et du gouvernement; elles ne sont ni africaines ni asiatiques ni européennes, elles sont bonnes ou mauvaises. On est esclave sous le pôle où il fait très froid. On est esclave à Constantinople où il fait très chaud: il faut que partout un peuple soit instruit, libre et vertueux. Ce que Pierre Ier apporta en Russie, s'il était bon en Europe, était bon partout.[56]

The tendency to slip back into bald generalisation of this kind is an undoubted weakness in Diderot's political thought and accounts for much of the naivety of which Catherine subsequently accused him.[57] But Diderot himself was lucid and honest enough to admit there was a gap, an immense distance, to use his own words, between "un philosophe systématique, qui arrange le bonheur d'une société sur son oreiller" and "une grande souveraine qui, du matin jusqu'au soir, rencontre au moindre bien qu'elle projete des obstacles de toutes les couleurs que l'expérience seule des choses apprend à connaître et que le pauvre philosophe n'a point fait entrer en calcul." [58] But we should not allow Diderot to con-

---

[53] *Op. cit.*, p. 283.
[54] MEM., p. 11.
[55] *Op. cit.*, p. 286.
[56] O.PO., pp. 349-350.
[57] *Diderot et Catherine II*, pp. 519-520.
[58] MEM., pp. 109-110.

demn himself out of his own mouth: he may from time to time make statements and criticisms and suggest reforms which appear to mark him off as an old-fashioned rationalist out of contact with reality, but this does not invalidate the empirical basis of his doctrine nor the thoroughly empirical manner in which he diagnoses the ills of Russian society and proposes the necessary cures. He may fail to understand the positive values of feudal society and be thus justly accused of anti-historicism, he may wrongfully ignore the influence of climate and geography on manners; but there is no doubt that had he been able to escape the rationalist forms by which his thought still tends to be constricted, he would have had no difficulty in adapting his theory of the relationship of the individual to society to any kind of society at any time.

Sergio Cotta's error is to have taken certain residual rationalist characteristics of Diderot's political thought in the *Mémoires* and the *Observations* and present them as central features. As a result Diderot is placed together with the other *philosophes* as a proponent of a rationalist ideology in politics which stands in complete opposition to the empirical science of the lone Montesquieu. This, as we have seen, is a considerable oversimplification which neglects the original formation of Diderot's political doctrine and his manifest attempt to apply it in the case of Russia only in the light of a profound and detailed analysis of Russian society based on information which he sought constantly from all sources available, not least Catherine herself. Having made this important rectification, we can now go on to examine in greater detail Diderot's political thought as it evolved through his experience in Russia.

"Je suis forcé de m'avouer à moi même," wrote Diderot on his return from St. Petersburg, "que j'avois l'âme d'un esclave dans le païs qu'on appelle des hommes libres, et que je me suis trouvé l'âme d'un homme libre dans le païs qu'on appelle des esclaves." [59] His feeling of physical and psychological distance from his own country, an inevitable sense of separation from the alien Russian world in which he was living, and the remarkable informality of his relations with Catherine, all combined to give Diderot a sense of freedom, independence and, not least, objectivity in his day to day life, but more particularly as regards politics, the like of which he had not experienced before. With regard to France, the sense of release, of disinvolvement was not immediate, as is borne out by the impassioned outbursts in the *Essai historique sur la police*, composed in part on the journey between The Hague and St. Petersburg. But Diderot's

[59] CORR., XIV, p. 12.

growing detachment is already detectable in his second paper, *Ma Rê-verie à moi Denis le philosophe*, in which he fulfils a diplomatic mission imposed upon him by the French ambassador, Durand de Distroff, with extraordinary frankness. And by the time he comes to list the economic and social reforms he would wish to see undertaken in France in *Du Luxe*, he has reached a degree of dispassionate argument and objectivity which he had found impossible at home. A detached, objective assessment of political realities is then the starting point for the dual task that Diderot set himself in the *Mémoires*, namely the reform of France and Russia. But Diderot had also set himself a third and in some respects far more difficult task, a task in which he was ultimately to have no success, that of persuading Catherine of the necessity and viability of his proposals for the reform of the Russian constitution and the structure of Russian society. This third task, in that it forced Diderot into using somewhat devious means in his attempts to persuade Catherine, had the effect of weakening the force of some of his proposals.

Nowhere is Diderot's caution more apparent in the *Mémoires* than when he touches upon the delicate subject of Catherine's commission. For on the successful establishment of the body envisaged by Diderot in the radically new role of national legislature, hang all his other proposals for reform. He is well aware that his conversations with Catherine provide him with a unique opportunity for persuading her of the desirability of investing a measure of political power in a representative body of the nation, but he is equally alive to the need for extreme prudence in tackling Catherine on the subject. After a bout of advance publicity in Western Europe provided through the good offices of Voltaire in the summer of 1767 Catherine had called together the States General of the Russian Empire for the express purpose of establishing a code of laws. The legislative commission, whose political education or rather lack of it ill-prepared it for such a mission, held 203 sessions in an atmosphere of mounting confusion and was suspended *sine die* at the request of the members themselves on the outbreak of the Russo-Turkish War in December 1768. As her *Instruction* to the commission makes abundantly clear, Catherine had no intention of sharing her power with anyone; on the contrary, both commission and code were intended to consolidate and formalise support for her imperial authority. Diderot's and Catherine's conceptions of the role of the commission could not have been farther apart. Diderot knew this; it was imperative, therefore to exercise extreme care in his handling of the subject. To reveal his hand completely would be self-defeating: if he were to argue that the commission should become the effective representative of popular sovereignty he knew perfectly well what the consequences would be. Catherine would dismiss the suggestion instantly and no doubt the intimacy and confidence which existed between them would be lost, as would the opportunity, unparalleled then or since, for a mere philosopher to bring about a radical revolution in a vast nation through the agency of its ruler. Diderot's failure lay in his naive belief that such a change lay within the bounds of possibility, not in his lack of prudence. On the contrary, he exercised great care not to offend or alienate his imperial host by going too far.

He prepares the ground by stating his case obliquely in the *Essai historique*: in a rapid and somewhat fanciful survey of the French constitution from the earliest days up to the present time Diderot describes the gradual decline of the idea whereby the king was no more than the depositary for the nation's laws, up to its final disappearance with the dissolution of the *parlements*, the only remaining counterweight to the power of the monarchy. The slow crumbling away of the power of the people over the centuries with the parallel building up of the power of the sovereign has reached its logical and sombre conclusion in the transformation of monarchy into despotism: "Il y avait dans le commencement un roi, des seigneurs et des serfs," writes Diderot, "Il n'y a aujourd'hui qu'un maître et des serfs sous toutes sortes de noms." [60] At strategic points in the course of his narrative and with the gay unconcern for historicism that we have already discussed, Diderot draws particular attention to moments in the history of the constitution where, in his opinion, a wise and disinterested monarch might have checked and indeed reversed the process of decline. His intention in mounting this panorama of French constitutional history is to insinuate into Catherine's mind an object lesson in the nature of despotism and its dangers, and the desirability of the monarchy's alienating at least some part of its power to the people for the sake of both parties. And in order the more certainly to win Catherine over to his views, Diderot frequently draws an adroit comparison and flattering parallel between the situation in France, past and present, and what he hopes, through his cajolery, coaxing and persuasion, Catherine will achieve in Russia. In the course of this clever propagandistic exploitation of history, which would be masterful were it not for his anti-historicism Diderot exposes each of the main principles of his doctrine and their practical application to the Russian situation which he will dwell on at greater length in subsequent *mémoires*. But as we have already noted, he is careful not

[60] MEM., p. 13.

to dogmatise; each point he makes is presented in the form of a self-evident conclusion readily acceptable to a person like Catherine who is open to persuasion by rational argument.

The survey opens with a short analysis of the fate of the laws promulgated by the kings and their councils under the first two French dynasties. At the end of each dynasty the legal system disintegrated; the wise Charlemagne resuscitated the laws in the second dynasty but he was unable to ensure their permanence after his death. Diderot loses no time in outlining the main points of his doctrine in the light of this analysis, and at the same time draws Catherine in the role of reforming monarch into the argument:

Sa Majesté Impériale concevra combien la législation mise sous la sauvegarde d'un seul homme est vacillante et de peu de durée. C'est la nation même qui doit en être la conservatrice d'âge en âge, condition qui suppose des lois simples, un code qui puisse être entre les mains des sujets dès la plus tendre enfance. Les prêtres ont été bien plus adroits que les rois. Mais peut-être que Catherine II est la première souveraine qui ait sincèrement désirée que ses sujets fussent instruits.[61]

In order that the nation should not be the victim of the whims and vagaries of a succession of rulers of unequal worth, the wise ruler will permanently alienate from himself that part of his authority pertaining to the preservation of laws. But so that this might be carried out effectively the huge complex muddle of customary law must be replaced by a simple code. Turning to the problem as it applies to Russia, Diderot uses a mixture of reason and appeals to Catherine's vanity to try and persuade her of the need to set up the commission on a permanent basis, with each representative freely chosen and liable to confirmation or recall by his province.[62] Such a step would be essential if she proposed to "éterniser ses lois," an aim close to her heart, and "élever contre le despotisme à venir une autorité insurmontable,"[63] a task which she does not appear to have had so close to her heart. Diderot, aware that he might receive less than full consensus on this latter point from Catherine, makes an all-out bid to win her over by appealing to the virtues which she prizes most highly in a ruler:

Il est bien grand, bien courageux, bien humain dans une souveraine de former elle-même une digue à la souveraineté.[64]

[61] *Ibid.*, p. 2.
[62] *Ibid.*, pp. 8-9.
[63] *Ibid.*, p. 9.
[64] *Ibid.*

So convinced is Diderot that the salvation of Europe is ultimately dependent on Catherine's readiness to take this final step that at times a note of anguish betrays a fear that the hope he has vested in her may come to nothing, a fear that the commission, suspended at the outbreak of the Russo-Turkish War, may never reassemble. The men and the money lost can be made up . . .

. . . mais qui rendra à ses peuples les années qui s'écoulent? Voilà la vraie perte, la perte irréparable, la perte qui fait gémir tous les penseurs honnêtes de l'Europe qui soupirent après le résultat de ses premières opérations.[65]

But Diderot cannot allow himself to flounder in the slough of despond for long, for to lose faith in Catherine would be to give in to irremediable defeat and despair. And so to escape a reality too unpalatable to be endured he returns once more to his fond illusions:

Mais heureusement Sa Majesté Impériale peut tout, et, plus heureusement encore, elle ne veut que le bien. Aussi qu'elle est grande! Combien son nom est révéré chez toutes les nations! Et qu'elle doit être heureuse! [66]

No longer did monarchical absolutism form the centre-piece of Diderot's political thought. A growing awareness of political realities at home and his hostility towards Frederick had brought about a radical change in his attitude to the ruler. Experience had shown him that, however just and enlightened a monarch might be, absolutism was in the long run unrealistic and contrary to the interests of the nation. Yet in so much as he lays upon the unsuspecting Catherine the final responsibility for bringing about the radical changes in the political constitution that he longs for, it is apparent that he has not entirely overcome his tendency to idealise the figure of the wise ruler. France, Russia, indeed the whole of Europe could only begin their march towards freedom, justice and prosperity if real sovereignty were transferred from the rulers to their peoples, but paradoxically it was a ruler who must inaugurate the change. Beneath the obvious flattery and desire to persuade there lies an undoubted admiration and affection for Catherine, emotions so strong that they held Diderot victim of a last illusion. Only when it had been shattered would he be free to expound a political doctrine which was truly empirical, both in formation and practical outworking. But as yet he was unable to take the step which would finally free him from the idealism which he had all but succeeded in shaking off; he was too strongly infatuated with Cathe-

[65] *Ibid.*, p. 10.
[66] *Ibid.*, p. 11.

rine. She alone, by setting an example within her own country was able to rescue European nations from the arbitrary changes which had governed their destinies through the ages:

> ...ce mouvement obscur et sourd qui nous tiraille, qui nous tourmente et nous fait tourner et retourner, jusqu'à ce que nous ayons trouvé une position moins incommode, mouvement qui agite un empire mal policé, comme il agite un malade.[67]

In Catherine and Russia lay the only hope; in England the parliamentary system was utterly corrupt, and Diderot saw in its corruption the possibility of worse horrors.[68] Prussia with its present ruler was a naked dictatorship; and France had become a nation of slaves insensible even to the discomforts of their enslavement.[69] In France too, the haphazard accumulation of a vast mass of contradictory laws and institutions over the centuries had led to a state of legal incoherence, with the result that legality had been stifled:

> On ne prononce plus selon la loi. On prononce selon les personnes; c'est-à-dire qu'il n'y plus de lois, quoiqu'on les cite plus que jamais.[70]

Russia, on the other hand, was a relatively primitive and formless society, a convenient *tabula rasa* for a radically new experiment in civilisation. For the first time man would be able to free himself from "l'impulsion fortuite des circonstances" and develop his social environment according to a "plan réglé." [71] For the director of the *Encyclopédie* who had devoted so many years of his life to the rationalisation, propagation and advancement of science and technology, the arms in the endless fight against nature, this was to be the supreme step in man's progress towards the mastery of his destiny. Once taken, the sense of alienation would be at an end and men's personalities and talents would be able to unfold and flourish; they would discover and fulfil potentialities within themselves that they had hardly dreamed of, living as they had done in an atmosphere of oppression and constraint. In a moment of visionary euphoria in the aptly titled *Rêverie* Diderot calls upon his compatriots to imagine the changes that would occur if Catherine were on the throne of France:

---

[67] *Ibid.*, p. 13.
[68] "Il n'y a en Angleterre que la voie de la corruption; peut-être ici faut-il y ajouter la voie de la terreur," *Ibid.*, p. 9.
[69] "Mais nous avons perdu jusqu'à cette inquiétude automate. Nous ne nous sentons plus," *Ibid.*, p. 13.
[70] *Ibid.*, p. 35.
[71] *Ibid.*, p. 34.

Quel empire! Quel terrible empire elle en ferait, et en combien peu de temps! Et vous, quels hommes vous seriez, car je vous déclare à tous que vous ignorez ce que la nature vous a donné. Vous êtes des ressorts que le poids d'une mauvaise administration tient courbés, et cela depuis que vous êtes nés, et qu'elle tiendra courbés tant que vous durerez.[72]

But convinced that France will not be the site of the New Jerusalem he bids his compatriots come and sample life in St. Petersburg:

Venez seulement passer un mois à Pétersburg. Venez vous soulager d'une longue contrainte qui vous a dégradés; c'est alors que vous sentirez quels hommes vous êtes.[73]

They, like Diderot, would gain a foretaste of the individual emancipation and fulfilment that would be the immediate outcome of Catherine's reforms, once she had put them into practice with the encouragement and counsel of her *philosophe*.

Having sketched the broad outlines of his political programme Diderot passes on to a more detailed examination of its various aspects, the most important being discussed in a number of key *mémoires*. In these he exposes at length his proposals for the future of the commission (IX, XV, XXIV), his views on education in Russia (XVI, XVII, XVIII, XXX, XXXI, XLIII), and his suggestions for economic reform in France (XXVI). There is also a short but important *mémoire* (XLIX) on the formation of a Third Estate in Russia. If we accept with Paul Vernière [74] that the table of contents of the *Mémoires* corresponds roughly to the order of composition and presentation of the individual papers, it is clear from the numbering of those referred to that Diderot's discussions with Catherine followed no particular plan. There is no apparent reason for this, but we can presume that the informal nature of the conversations accounts in large part for their desultoriness. But it is also highly likely, bearing in mind Diderot's awareness of the need for caution in his dealings with Catherine, particularly with regard to matters she might consider to be contentious, that he consciously contrived to avoid offending her by spreading such delicate subjects over a number of discussions and accompanying papers, separated from one another by less controversial items. A disagreeable medicine administered in small doses at calculated intervals is less likely to be spat out than a large single dose.

This is particularly true of the subject which was for Diderot indisput-

[72] *Ibid.*, p. 43.
[73] *Ibid.*
[74] *Ibid., Introduction*, p. xxiv.

ably the most urgent and at the same time the least likely to be readily received by Catherine: his proposals for the re-establishment of her commission in a radically new role. In the *Essai historique sur la police*, as we have seen, he approaches the subject obliquely, and is only explicit with regard to the French situation where he examines the possibility of converting the *parlements* into a representative body of the nation with absolute right of veto over legislative proposals made by the monarch. Where he refers to the commission itself, he confines himself to suggesting fleetingly and somewhat hesitatingly that it would be desirable for Catherine to set it up on a permanent basis. For the rest he restricts himself to statements of a general nature on the need for the ruler to confide to the nation responsibility for the preservation of the laws. After the *Essai historique* Diderot takes care to allow some time to elapse before making any further references to the commission that might be too obtrusive, though at the same time he realises that it would be unwise to let the subject lie entirely dormant. Hence in a short *mémoire* (V) in which he touches briefly upon the delicate problem of the succession to the Imperial throne, a source of constant trouble to the nation as the form of succession had never been properly constituted, he suggests that the commission should be allowed to give a constitutional ruling on the matter. Warming to his subject Diderot goes on to advise that in the case where the ruling dynasty dies out the nation should itself through its representatives in the commission decide to whom the crown should be entrusted. There is, however, nothing very audacious or original about this recommendation, indeed Diderot had made exactly the same point years ago in the article *Autorité politique*.[75] But now he is no longer satisfied with this position; it is only a staging point on a long and difficult journey whose final destination is the conversion of his host to the radically new conception of the commission that he has in mind. For a moment it looks as though he has decided to change his tactics and go all the way: "Il y aurait," he continues, "un conclave de commissaires . . .," but then his courage fails him: "Mais pourquoi suivre un rêve? Je n'en ai pas le courage. J'aurai bien assez souvent rêvé sans m'en douter, sans rêver en m'en doutant." [76] Frightened by his own temerity, Diderot draws back from the brink, dissimulating the utter seriousness of his intentions beneath the mantle of "un rêve." But as we know from the *Rêve de d'Alembert*, fantasy is often a means of making the truth more palatable.

---

[75] O.PO., p. 20.
[76] MEM., p. 51.

Three *mémoires* later Diderot for the first time in his conversations with Catherine tackles the subject directly in the paper which has as its title *De la commission formée pour la confection des lois*. But he restricts himself mainly to a relatively anodine aspect of the subject by formulating tentative questions as to its composition and the responsibilities of its members in relation to the provinces they represent. It is, however, interesting to note at this point that Diderot works into his suggestions on the role and function of the representatives belonging to the commission a feature which he noted with satisfaction in the Dutch constitution, and which set it higher in his estimation than the only other important system based on representation, namely the British constitution. This was the rule which made the Dutch representatives subject to instant recall by their provinces, thus preventing them from enjoying the unlimited powers of British members of Parliament, powers which had led to bribery, corruption and coercion, and consequently to the international disrepute that the British parliamentary system had fallen into in the second half of the century. Obviously, given the vast distances in the Russian Empire, instant recall was not practicable, so Diderot devises an arrangement whereby the permanent representative may be overruled by another delegate sent by his province to pronounce on a specific issue, thereby guaranteeing that the province's interests are never neglected or replaced by the permanent representative's own private interests. Although Diderot could not as yet tackle the question of the commission itself, his evident desire to see the insertion of this important feature of the Dutch constitution into the Russian system of representation is particularly significant. For behind it lies the wish to encourage the setting up of machinery which permits as full and sustained an expression of the national will as is compatible with practical realities.

Diderot's realistic attempt to translate popular sovereignty in a large state into practical terms through a representative system bears comparison with a similar exercise carried out by Rousseau in his *Considérations sur le Gouvernement de Pologne*. Rousseau knew full well that the principles of the *Contrat social*, in which he insists on the direct participation of the people in the legislative process, could not be applied directly to a state the size of Poland; but he was also alive to the danger that representation presented of diluting not to say entirely destroying the real sovereignty of the people. He avoids it by requiring that the representatives should be renewed at frequent intervals and that they should be constrained to follow closely precise and detailed instructions drawn up by the electoral colleges, so that they are, in fact no more than the spokesmen of the people who elect them.[77] R. Derathé believes that Rousseau, in making this stipulation was like Diderot inspired by the example of Holland.[78] There is no doubt an element of coincidence in this, but it does underline the fact that Diderot's and Rousseau's political doctrines were now converging, or rather than Diderot's political thought which had for so long trailed several years behind Rousseau's was now catching up. The *Considérations* were written in 1772, the ninth *mémoire, De la Commission*, was drafted towards the end of 1773. The two men had travelled along very different roads to reach a similar destination: Rousseau had chosen the wide, open road of reverie and idealism, born of a detestation of a society to which he had been unable and then refused outright to accommodate himself; Diderot after a false start had elected to follow a less easily negotiable route, full of sinuosities and obstacles which had to be mastered, this was the road of reality.

Diderot rounds off his tentative remarks in the ninth *mémoire* with a conclusion which holds the key to his projected reforms of the Russian political system and society:

> Il y a deux idées auxquelles j'avoue que je tiens beaucoup: le *concours* qui assure au mérite sa récompense, et la *commission* qui assure aux lois et aux institutions, toute la durée qu'elles peuvent avoir.
> Ces deux idées, au défaut desquelles les nations ont vu de siècle en siècle empirer le désordre, sont tout à fait analogues à celles d'après lesquelles vos institutions ont été formées.[79]

Reward based upon merit and achieved through competition (both in education and in later life) and the commission seen as guarantor of the permanence of the laws and institutions of the nation are the essential dual foundation on which Russia, and by extension all nations, must rest if a society which is stable, ordered and just is to come about. It is no coincidence that Diderot in the *Mémoires* and in his later writings on Russia returns to these two subjects more frequently than to any others. Let us, however, set aside for the moment his views on educational reform, a vast subject which would require a detailed study of its own to do it justice, and follow his thoughts further as he pursues the difficult task of persuading Catherine into accepting his reform of the commission's function.

Obedient to his strategy of caution Diderot delays further reference to the subject until the fifteenth *mémoire, De la Commission, des lois, du concours . . .*, when he returns to the attack. But this time, having sum-

---

[77] P.W., II, p. 450.
[78] *Rousseau et la science politique de son temps*, p. 278, n. 1.
[79] MEM., p. 60.

moned up the courage which had previously eluded him, it is with a vengeance. No more does Diderot pretend he is dreaming, no longer does he couch his thoughts in the form of hesitant questions or vague conjecture, this time he announces his colours straight away:

Jusqu'à présent, dans tous les papiers que j'ai osé écrire et lire à Votre Majesté Impériale, c'est moi qui lui ai parlé. C'est moi qui lui parlerai dans tous ceux qui suivront, et moi seul.
Mais ici, je ne suis que l'organe passif de la raison.[80]

Diderot is conscious that what he is about to put forward for Catherine's consideration is not a result of speculation or a subject for surmise; it is an unalterable and objective statement of fact, borne in on his mind by a lengthy and dispassionate examination of all the relevant details. This statement of fact is a simple one: Catherine must "conserver ses créations et les conserver sans atteinte," [81] and of all the wise institutions she has created it is, of course, the commission which Diderot singles out as being in greatest need of being rendered immutable and immovable. If it is not, then it will inevitably fall into an irremediable decline, either immediately or after her disappearance. This is the burden of the *mémoire*.

It may seem surprising that Diderot goes no further; he does not appear to deal with the function of the commission, nor does he tackle the thorny problem of the transfer of sovereignty to it. Furthermore, what he says is not new: he has insisted on the need to give the commission a permanent status on several previous occasions. These points can be explained quite simply. Firstly, as has been demonstrated, Diderot is stating the case as an observable fact and no longer as a speculative opinion. Secondly, once the case for a permanent commission has been made, it leads on inevitably to the acceptance of a number of other constitutional changes which are implicitly contained within it. Again, the fact that Diderot was not prepared to spell these out immediately in the same paper in so many words is understandable on the grounds of caution. But for a woman of the intelligence of Catherine they should have been quite obvious. Whether they were or not Diderot takes no chances, and after again allowing a suitable amount of time to elapse, he returns to the subject one last time in the *mémoire* entitled *De la Commission et des avantages de sa permanence* (XXIV) in order to draw out the implications of the previous *mémoire*.

Before launching into the subject Diderot takes some precautionary measures:

---

[80] *Ibid.*, p. 78. Our italics.
[81] *Ibid.*, p. 79.

Je ne sais ce qui me manque pour traiter de cet objet dignement, peut-être la tête de Montesquieu ou la vôtre. Je ne me sens pas la force de former un plan. Il faut que je m'en tienne à des vues générales, moi qui sais que les vues générales sont le produit des hommes ordinaires, et qui ne fais cas que des vues particulières, les seules qui touchent à la chose et au fond de la chose.[82]

No doubt this opening paragraph expresses some unease on the part of Diderot at his lack of knowledge of the intricacies of the imperial administration, but the main reason for these self-deprecatory remarks can only be that he was unwilling to go into too much detail regarding the Russian situation for fear of offending and alienating Catherine. But as we shall see Diderot soon threw his initial precautions to the wind, setting all his hopes, it seems, on winning over his listener with a mixture of reasoning and impassioned oratory.

In the prefatory remarks Diderot's reference to Montesquieu appears at first sight to express a certain feeling of diffidence at the task that lies before him. But as we read on into the second paragraph it becomes clear that he intends to use Catherine's confessed master in a piece of casuistry calculated to disarm her in advance of the audacious remarks he is to make on the role of the commission:

Celle qui a fait son bréviaire de l'*Esprit des Lois*, où le despote est comparé au sauvage qui coupe l'arbre pour en cueillir le fruit plus commodément, entendra patiemment ce que j'oserai lui dire; ma hardiesse sera certainement la marque la plus forte d'admiration que je puisse lui donner.[83]

Diderot's intention is to place himself under the protective sign of Montesquieu and annex his own thoughts to the teachings of the President. This consciously calculated act is further illustrated by the apostrophe to Montesquieu which rounds off the main section of the *mémoire*:

O Montesquieu, que n'es-tu à ma place! Comme tu parlerais! Comme on te répondrait! Comme tu écouterais! Comme tu serais écouté! [84]

It is questionable whether this move was a very wise one; Diderot should have realised that a woman as intelligent and perceptive as Catherine would not have been duped by this attempt to present his proposals and the doctrine on which they are based as a logical continuation of Montesquieu's condemnation of despotism. Unfortunately it seems that this naivety grew in proportion to his enthusiasm, leading him to the fatal mis-

[82] *Ibid.*, p. 117.
[83] *Ibid.*
[84] *Ibid.*, p. 127.

take of all teachers who become absorbed in their subject to the extent of failing to ascertain whether their pupils agree with them or even follow them. This is borne out by a remark made by Catherine at a much later date to the French ambassador, the Comte de Ségur, who reported it in his *Mémoires:*

Comme je l'écoutais plus que je ne parlais, un témoin qui serait survenu nous aurait pris tous deux, lui pour un sévère pédagogue et moi pour son humble écolière. Probablement il le crut lui-même, car au bout de quelque temps, voyant qu'il ne s'opérait dans mon gouvernement aucune des grandes innovations qu'il m'avait conseillées, il m'en montra sa surprise avec une sorte de fierté mécontente.[85]

The pupil, less taken by the subject, showed a greater insight into the teaching relationship than her master.

Be this as it may, Diderot, confident in the illusion that he had prevented any possibility of Catherine's disaffection from his views, dispensed with further circumlocution and moved straight on to a total demolition of the doctrine of enlightened despotism which we must quote at length:

Tout gouvernement arbitraire est mauvais; je n'en excepte pas le gouvernement arbitraire d'un maître, bon, ferme, juste et éclairé.
Ce maître accoutume à respecter et à chérir un maître, quel qu'il soit.
Il enlève à la nation le droit de délibérer, de vouloir ou de ne pas vouloir, de s'opposer, de s'opposer même au bien.
Le droit d'opposition me semble, dans une société d'hommes, un droit naturel, inaliénable et sacré.
Un despote, fût-il le meilleur des hommes, en gouvernant selon son bon plaisir, commet un forfait: c'est un bon pâtre qui réduit ses sujets à la condition des animaux; en leur faisant oublier le sentiment de la liberté, sentiment si difficile à recouvrer quand on l'a perdu, il leur procure un bonheur de dix ans qu'ils payeront de vingt siècles de misère.[86]

The similarity between this passage and the one from the *Fragments Echappés*, quoted and discussed in the previous chapter and written almost two years earlier, is striking. Identical ideas are repeated, couched in the same phraseology, and in the case of the herdsman and his animals the same metaphor. Diderot has taken the plunge and revealed to Catherine undisguised his commitment to the principle of popular sovereignty which he had previously only been prepared to make public under the cover of anonymity through the *Histoire des deux Indes*. However, in so doing he

[85] *Mémoires* du Comte L.P. de Ségur, III, p. 47. Quoted by B. Guy, "The Prince de Ligne and Diderot," p. 263.
[86] MEM., pp. 117-118.

steps back slightly from the position taken up in the *Pensées Détachées* where he stated that the only proper judge of the writer of genius was the public and not "le despote qui ne l'entend pas, ou le ministre qui ne veut pas l'écouter." [87] The reason is obvious, in Russia there was no such public, but there was, or so he thought, a despot who would indeed listen to him.

Filled with the certainty that he has Catherine's ear he goes on, after arguing the impossibility of ensuring a continuity of sovereigns who are all good, enlightened and effective, to deal in detail with the problem in the Russian context, thereby neglecting his original intention to keep to "des vues générales." It is not enough, argues Diderot, to have abdicated the legislative authority to the commission; it is essential, if this generous act is to continue in its effectiveness, that the laws passed by that body be made immune against all attempts to nullify or reverse them by outside influences, in particular any of Catherine's successors. In order that this may be achieved the commission itself, the maker and depository of the laws, must be constituted on a permanent basis, for

Les lois formées, écrites, publiées, connues, observées ne sont pourtant que des mots qui ne peuvent subsister sans un être physique, constant, immuable permanent, éternel, s'il en est auquel ces mots soient attachés, que cet être physique doit agir et parler, et que par conséquent ce n'est pas le marbre qui résiste peu et qui est muet.[88]

However, by claiming that Catherine had abdicated the legislative authority Diderot was very much begging the question, since a reading of her *Instruction* will reveal that one of the main purposes of the code to be drafted by the commission was the reinforcement of autocratic rule, as the very size of Russia in Catherine's view made this the only possible form of government. Diderot must have read the *Instruction* by this time, and it can only be concluded that this is a conscious piece of misinterpretation by him subtly aimed at persuading Catherine to see her convocation of the commission in this new light without her being aware of it. The fact that the commission had been suspended, however, did not allow Diderot to exploit similar ambiguities regarding its permance. Permanent it definitely was not, and not until it was made so could there be any meaningful transfer of sovereignty. For as long as its existence was menaced by events as comparatively negligible as the Russo-Turkish War, power ultimately and inevitably remained with the ruler.

[87] P.D., p. 101, HIST., X, p. 139.
[88] MEM., p. 119.

Diderot, it should be noted, never uses the words sovereign or sovereignty in reference to the commission; in fact throughout the *mémoire* the terms are exclusively applied to Catherine.[89] It seems as though he is exercising something little short of a confidence trick upon her by maintaining that in the situation he describes she would retain ultimate sovereignty, whereas in fact she would lose most if not all of it. This lack of candour is apparent at several points in the *mémoire* where Diderot tries to reassure Catherine that she will be able to maintain her power despite the constitutional change. He argues, for example, that "par la position des Etats de Sa Majesté Impériale son corps de représentants ne sera jamais dangereux," [90] and elsewhere that "l'avancement des enfants lui donnera toujours assez et trop d'autorité sur les pères qui formeront la commission," [91] but he has great difficulty in penning in his real thoughts, and they continually escape and expose the tenuous nature of his reassurances. For instance, the first remark quoted above is followed by the rider that "s'il le devenait, par des combinaisons d'événements impossibles à prévoir (modern communications, in the event!), ce ne serait presque jamais au détriment de l'empire." [92] But it is when Diderot identifies himself so strongly with Catherine in envisaging the reforms to be undertaken as to slip into the first person – "C'est ce corps rendu permanent que j'opposerais à la ruine à venir de mes lois et de mes institutions, etc." [93] – that he most completely gives himself away. After arguing that the intervention of the commission would enable the general good to be accomplished and thus obviate the dangers menacing the person of the ruler as has been so often the case in the past and moreover still was,[94] he goes on to proclaim,

'Quel merveilleux moyen de lever les obstacles! Qu'il est sur! C'est le concours et l'opposition des volontés générales aux volontés particulières, l'avantage de la démocratie sur toutes les autres espèces de gouvernement.[95]

Without a doubt Diderot is here envisaging the commission as the ex-

---

[89] Diderot does not spell his conception of sovereignty out in so many words until the *Observations,* where in reply to Catherine's "Le souverain est la source de tout pouvoir politique et civil" he writes, "Je n'entends pas cela. Il me semble que c'est le consentement de la nation représentée par des députés ou assemblée en corps, qui est la source de tout pouvoir politique et civil," T.P., p. 75.

[90] MEM., p. 122.

[91] *Ibid.*, p. 125.

[92] *Ibid.*, p. 122.

[93] *Ibid.*, p. 119 et seq.

[94] Vernière suggests that Diderot must have known of the plot mounted against Catherine by the Tsarevitch Paul a few months before his marriage. (See MEM., p. 298, n. 196).

[95] MEM., p. 121.

pression of popular sovereignty based on the democratic principles of
representation. What is particularly remarkable is the juxtaposition of the
terms "volontés générales" and "démocratie." In employing the first
term Diderot shows the influence of Rousseau, but its plural form marks
an important divergence between the two men in the conception. Like
Rousseau Diderot makes a cardinal distinction between the general will
of the nation seen as a corporate being and the sum of the individual wills
of its members concerned with their own interests, which do not necessarily coincide with those of the State. In the latter case the idea is expressed
by Rousseau in the formula "la volonté de tous," while with Diderot it
only remains implicit. Like Rousseau too, Diderot considers that the will
of the people must take precedence over the will of the individual. However, whereas for Rousseau the citizens who make up the general will are
indistinguishable from one another and form one group, namely the nation as a whole, for Diderot this is not the case. For him the sovereignty of
the people is manifested in a number of isolated general wills which belongs to a number of separate groups corresponding to the class divisions
of society. He may have been influenced by the actual composition of
Catherine's commission which was made up of deputies summoned from
the nobility, city inhabitants, free rural population and prelates selected
by the Synod. Diderot, therefore, while formulating a principle of general
will which resembles Rousseau's is nonetheless more prepared to compromise with the actual situation to which it is to be applied. This compromise inevitably leads to a further weakening of the principle as originally enunciated by Rousseau, since in addition to representation which
itself dilutes the general will but which, as we have seen, is admitted as a
practical necessity by Jean-Jacques himself, it accepts the idea of party
politics. In neither of the cases where Rousseau was offered the task of
reforming existing political structures was he prepared to go this far in
accommodating different party interests in his recommendations. In both
the *Projet de constitution pour la Corse* and the *Considérations sur le
gouvernement de Pologne* he insists that there should only be one class
participating in the legislative process either as representatives or electors,
the citizen class.[96]

A further divergence of views between Diderot and Rousseau on the
question of the franchise arise from the different emphasis that they
place on property. In his critique of absolution in *De la commission* Diderot states:

---

[96] P.W., II, pp. 325 and 444.

Où il n'y a point de propriété il n'y a point de sujets; (. . .) où il n'y a point de sujets l'empire est pauvre, et (. . .) où la puissance souveraine est illimitée il n'y a point de propriété.[97]

Property, in his view, is an essential prerequisite for a citizen to be a citizen, for without it he can have no vested interest in his nation. One of the chief failings of absolutism is that it constantly subjects all property to the arbitrary whim of the ruler so that in effect it can never be a legal or a psychological reality for the individual. Diderot thus implies, although he does not state it here openly, that only those who are property-owners should be allowed to participate in the legislative process. Rousseau, on the contrary, establishes no such requirement in the *Projet pour la Corse* or the *Gouvernement de Pologne*; indeed in the *Projet* he tends to the opposite view from Diderot:

Loin de vouloir que l'état soit pauvre je voudrais qu'il eut tout et que chacun n'eut sa part au bien commun qu'en proportion de ses services. . . Ma pensée (. . .) n'est pas de détruire absolument la propriété particulière parce que cela est impossible mais de la renfermer dans les plus étroites bornes, de lui donner une mesure, une règle, un frein qui la contienne, qui la dirige, qui la subjugue et le tienne toujours subordonnée au bien public. Je veux en un mot que la propriété de l'état soit aussi grande, aussi forte et celle des citoyens aussi petite, aussi foible qu'il est possible.[98]

Diderot would no doubt have looked upon Rousseau's opinions on the issues of the application of the principle of the general will and the apportionment of property as the impracticable not to say dangerous musings of an incorrigible idealist. How could one possibly abolish overnight class divisions which had existed for centuries and replace them by a single homogenous class of citizens? What could Rousseau's view on property lead to other than the replacement of an odious monarchical absolutism by an equally pernicious state absolutism? Diderot has the merit of avoiding the implications which arise from Rousseau's conception of state ownership, but he is not as alive as Jean-Jacques to the dangers of the exploitation of man by man as soon as inordinate differences in wealth are allowed to occur. He also shows a greater readiness to come to terms with the practical exigencies of a real political situation, though in the longer term he shows less vision. Rousseau, by minimising personal property as a qualifying factor for citizenship, looks forward to the age of the urban industrial society; Diderot, who will develop the theme of the interrelation of liberty and property in the *Observations sur le Nakaz*, in

[97] MEM., p. 123.
[98] P.W., II, p. 337.

taking the opposite stand, shows himself to be far more restricted by the considerations imposed upon him by an agricultural society.

However, Diderot was no more satisfied than Rousseau with a transfer of authority to the nation's assembly and then leave it at that. He, like Jean-Jacques, was anxious to see the elevation to citizenship of those masses who as yet toiled under a burden of ignorance and servitude and were incapable of taking on the responsibilities that full membership of the sovereign would involve. The two men's solutions to this problem as they are set out in the *Mémoires* and the *Gouvernement de Pologne* differ somewhat, although Russia and Poland presented broadly a similar situation, each country containing a vast and grossly underprivileged population of serfs and a much smaller urban population which though relatively affluent was with some exceptions deprived of any political power. Rousseau's solution was to bring about the gradual enfranchisement of peasant and town-dweller by establishing a merit roll of individuals who would accede to citizenship; the second stage would be to enfranchise whole villages and towns.[99] Diderot's approach is less methodical and more modest than Rousseau's, but it shows greater imagination and in certain respects a more practical grasp of some of the social and educational changes that might be necessary if such a reform were to be brought about. In the short but highly pertinent article *Du Jeu du Souverain et d'un Tiers Etat* (XLIX) he puts forward the daring proposal that an élite should be drawn from the masses by a system of scholarships and competitions. This in turn would require the establishment of compulsory elementary education throughout the land.[100] Rousseau in his suggestions for educational reform in Poland is rather less adventurous in that, although he proposes state education for the poor, he restricts access to the nobility.[101] It is not at all clear under Rousseau's system by what means the underprivileged would gain the necessary qualities which would admit them to the citizens class, whereas under Diderot's the groundwork is laid for the formation of an increasingly strong and viable Third Estate.

Diderot also makes two further suggestions for the development of a Third Estate in two other articles in the *Mémoires: De la ville de Saint-Pétersbourg* (VII) and *Idée systématique sur la manière d'amener un peuple au sentiment de la liberté et à l'état policé* (XXXVIII). In the first he proposes that serfs should be freed and sent to the capital to become skilled workers. In the second he develops a point briefly touched upon

[99] P.W., II, p. 499.
[100] MEM., p. 242.
[101] P.W., II, p. 439.

in the first, and proposes that colonies of free peoples such as the Swiss should be implanted in Russia. They in due course would be joined by members of the indigenous population, thus over a period of time spreading the leaven of liberty throughout the nation. The latter suggestion is too utopian to merit serious consideration, and Diderot himself is doubtful about it value:

Si ces idées sont justes, j'en ai dit assez; trop, si elles sont chimériques.[102]

As for the first suggestion, while it does not bear comparison with his proposals for educational reform it does show a remarkable intuition about the Russian situation in its implication that the movement towards the enfranchisement of the masses could only take place once the process of urbanisation had begun.

Although Diderot shows close affinities with Rousseau in his conception of the general will and his desire to place the sovereign power in the hands of the people, in the division that he proposes between the executive and legislative powers the influence of Montesquieu appears to preponderate. In Diderot's view the portion of Catherine's authority to be confided to the commission must be most rigorously determined. The body would not be called upon to tackle any matter foreign to its purpose for fear that it might be tempted to encroach on areas of decision-making outside its own:

Il ne se mêlerait ni de guerre, ni de politique, ni de finances.
Son district, et son district entier, se réduirait à la conservation des lois faites et à l'examen des lois soit à faire, soit à abroger, des institutions, etc.[103]

Yet, ultimately Diderot's belief in the necessity of the division of powers within the state lacks conviction, for in the last resort he is more concerned that the legislative assembly should guard its authority intact, even if

---

[102] MEM., p. 199.
[103] *Ibid.*, p. 121. D'Holbach in his *Système social* (Book II, Chap. V) also argues for a monarchy in which a portion of the sovereign authority is in the hands of a representative body elected by property-owning citizens. He is vague as to the exact constitutional function of this body, and only declares that the citizens chosen to represent the nation will be "intéressés à sa conservation (de l'Etat) ainsi qu'au maintien de la liberté" (p. 50). Pierre Naville in *Paul Thiry d'Holbach et la philosophie scientifique au XVIIIe siècle* remarks, "(Une monarchie limitée par un pouvoir représentatif) est celle où le peuple conserve la portion du pouvoir que la nation se réserve originellement dans les lois fondamentales et originelles de l'Etat" (p. 388). Although Meister claimed that Diderot gave d'Holbach some help with the *Système social* (*Correspondance littéraire*, March 1789), it would be idle to speculate from which of the two men the theory of the limitation of monarchy by representation originated. Whatever the answer d'Holbach is far more cautious than Diderot as is shown by his outright rejection of democracy (*Op. cit.*, Book II, p. 31).

this leads to an encroachment on the executive authority of the monarch:

> Si l'on avait l'un de ces deux choix à faire, ou d'un souverain trop fort contre sa nation, ou d'une nation policée trop forte contre son souverain, le dernier de ces deux inconvénients serait le moindre.[104]

But to Diderot's dismay it was the former state of affairs that persisted. All his attempts to convince Catherine of the need to abdicate her authority to a permanent commission failed. His other suggestion for educational, social, economic and administrative reform equally fell on a deaf ear. Catherine in a remark to Diderot, reported by the Comte de Ségur, gave her explanation for not being able to put his reforms into operation:

> Vous oubliez, Monsieur Diderot, dans tous vos plans de réforme, la différence de nos deux positions: vous, vous ne travaillez que sur le papier qui souffre tout ... tandis que moi, pauvre impératrice, je travaille sur la peau humaine qui est bien autrement irritable et chatouilleuse.[105]

An eloquent image and an elegant piece of self-defence, which no doubt contains a certain amount of truth. Diderot could not expect to have mastered the vast complexity of the Russian situation during his short stay, and consequently a good number of his proposals might be criticised as unrealistic. However, the fact that Catherine would not even countenance their spirit let alone their detail indicates that she rejected them for reasons other than those of impracticality. To discover these reasons one has to look no further than the *Instruction* which Diderot had studied during his stay at St. Petersburg. When he left the capital for the journey homeward he took with him a copy of the text. In the peace and quiet of Galitizin's home at The Hague he settled down, pen in hand, to a close study of the *Instruction*; the result was the *Observations sur le Nakaz*, a commentary on the work which combined an exposure and refutation of the basic principles of Catherine's political doctrine and a direct and uninhibited restatement and development of the themes broached with circumspection in the *Mémoires*.

---

[104] *Ibid.*, p. 123.
[105] Quoted by P. Vernière, O.PO., p. 219.

CHAPTER IV

THE END OF AN ILLUSION

I. POPULAR SOVEREIGNTY VERSUS ENLIGHTENED DESPOTISM

During the return journey from St. Petersburg, Diderot's confidence in Catherine's readiness to bring about radical reform seemed to hold firm. From a posting stage at Hamburg he wrote to Sophie:

Si elle règne jusqu'à quatre vingt ans, comme elle me l'a promis, soyez sûre qu'elle changera la face de son empire.[1]

And it is the same sentiment which concludes the *Observations* themselves.[2] However, another letter written to an anonymous friend on his arrival at The Hague, in which he gives an account of his stay and return journey, reveals his deeper feelings. A phrase slipped almost casually into the enthusiastic narrative betrays the underlying sense of frustration and disillusionment which he had brought back from his stay in Russia: Catherine, despite her greatness and wisdom was "la souveraine la plus despote qu'il y ait en Europe." [3] In its immediate context this remark could be taken as the statement of a simple political fact: unlike any other European monarch, Catherine was constitutionally not tethered by any kind of laws which could effectively limit her power. But the wider context of Diderot's conversations with her and his reading of the *Instruction* lend it a significance which transcends that of a bald statement of fact. It becomes a comment on and a criticism of Catherine's true aspirations and intentions as embodied by the reform, which despite their appearance of enlightenment were, as Diderot had come to realise, designed to take

[1] CORR., XIII, p. 210.
[2] T.P., p. 176, Given the chronological nature of this study we prefer Y. Benot's edition of the first manuscript (B.N. n.a.fr. 13.766) to P. Vernière's edition of the last manuscript (B.N. n.a.fr. 24.939) which includes additions taken from the *Histoire des deux Indes* and inserted into the original text by Diderot's son-in-law Vandeul after 1780. (For a study of the manuscripts see Vernière's Introduction *to Observations sur le Nakaz* in O.PO., pp. 336-339.
[3] CORR., XIII, p. 226.

Russia along a political path diametrically opposed to the one he had envisaged.

The term "despote" and "despotisme" recur with such frequency in the *Observations* that they become an obsessive theme, almost a leitmotif of despair which runs right through the work, yet one which is continually tempered by a real affection for Catherine as a person and a lingering, forlorn hope that even yet she will turn her steps to the path, so painstakingly mapped out by Diderot, which will lead to the freedom and happiness of her peoples. Unfortunately the *Instruction* provides him with little or no evidence on which to base his hope, for it is the expression of a political philosophy which is totally alien to his own. Superficially, it might appear, Catherine's conception of the purpose of government does not differ from Diderot's. When she asks herself the question "What is the object of an absolute government?," she replies:

> Ce n'est certainement point de priver les hommes de leur liberté naturelle, mais de diriger leurs actions vers le plus grand de tous les biens.[4]

In his commentary Diderot provisionally accepts that during the reign of a just, enlightened and firm monarch everything would be directed towards this end. But he then goes on to point to the essential weakness of her argument:

> Ce pouvoir absolu qui, placé dans la main d'un bon maître, faisait tant de bien, le dernier de ces bons maîtres le transmettrait à un méchant, et le lui transmettrait scellé par le temps et par l'usage: et tout serait perdu.[5]

Rooted in the realities of life, Diderot's frequently reiterated exposure of the dangers inherent in enlightened absolutism is a powerful weapon which he uses with devastating effect throughout the *Observations*, as well as in the *Réfutation d'Helvétius*, and in his later contributions to the *Histoire des deux Indes*. But his attack on enlightened despotism goes beyond this fairly evident criticism into a searching analysis of the motivations of the enlightened despot himself. When Catherine once more returning to the subject of the purpose of government, states:

> L'objet et la fin des gouvernements monarchiques est la gloire des citoyens, de l'Etat et du souverain,[6]

Diderot immediately corrects her:

---

[4] Article 13 of the *Instruction*, quoted by Y. Benot, T.P., p. 71 n. (a). Hereinafter, all references to passages in the *Instruction* will refer directly to articles quoted in the footnotes of the *Textes politiques*.

[5] T.P., pp. 71-72.

L'objet, la fin de tout gouvernement doit être le bonheur des citoyens, la force et la splendeur de l'Etat et la gloire du souverain.[7]

The differences in the two versions are telling, as are the criticisms implied in Diderot's alteration of the wording. Whereas the *philosophe* carefully differentiates the aims of government according to the separate elements which compose the nation, the empress does not. For her there is only aim – glory – to be bestowed upon citizens, State and sovereign alike. Thus Catherine betrays the true motives behind her championship of monarchical absolutism: in a nation in which all the reins of power are held in the hands of a single person all glory must inevitably be his. Government instead of serving the interests of the state and its citizens becomes a means to self-glorification. The nation is simply an extension of the personality of the ruler, to be used by him for his own self-fulfilment. Catherine's intended reforms do nothing to change this state of affairs, unless it is to give her decisions a façade of legality:

Je ne vois que quelque forme de différence entre le despotisme et la monarchie pure; le despote fait tout ce qu'il veut, sans aucune forme; le monarque est assujetti à des formes qu'il néglige quand il lui plaît, et qui ne font que suspendre ses volontés sans les changer, quand il les respecte.[8]

Either way government remains the pure and unadulterated expression of the monarch's will. This is the political philosophy to which Catherine unswervingly subscribed, a fact of which Diderot in studying the *Instruction* had become painfully aware:

C'est l'esprit de la monarchie pure qui a dicté l'instruction de Catherine II.[9]

Thus Diderot implicitly admits that Catherine no longer qualified for the title of *sage*, that she is as prone to the corrupting effect of unlimited power as any other ruler. It is the very nature of things that power feeds the passions and no ruler however enlightened can escape this rigorous law. Reason or evidence is an ineffectual counterforce:

L'évidence n'empêche ni le jeu de l'intérêt ni celui des passions; un commerçant déréglé voit évidemment qu'il se ruine, et ne se ruine pas moins. Un souverain sentira qu'il tyrannise ou par lui-même ou par ses ministres, et n'en tyrannisera pas moins.[10]

[6] *Ibid.*, p. 73, n. (a).
[7] *Ibid.*, p. 73.
[8] *Ibid.*
[9] *Ibid.*
[10] *Ibid.*, p. 80.

In Catherine's case, the proper aims of government are subordinated to the satisfaction of her will to dominate and control.

So Diderot finally adopts the view that not only is absolutism wrong because it provides no guarantee against the accession of a ruler who lacks the necessary qualities which make for enlightened government, but it is wrong because the concept of the enlightened monarch is itself a myth with no possible foundation in the reality of human nature. This opinion had already been articulated by Rousseau seven years earlier in a letter to the Marquis de Mirabeau:

On prouve que le plus véritable intérêt du despote est de gouverner légalement: cela est reconnu de tous les temps. Mais qui est-ce qui se conduit sur ses plus vrais intérêts? Le sage seul, s'il existe. Vous faites donc, messieurs, de vos despotes autant de sages. Presque tous les hommes connaissent leurs vrais intérêts, et ne les suivent pas mieux pour cela. Le prodigue qui mange ses capitaux sait parfaitement qu'il se ruine, et n'en vas pas moins son train: de quoi sert que la raison nous éclaire, quand la passion nous conduit?
Video meliora proboque,
Deteriora sequor: –
Voilà ce que fera votre despote, ambitieux, prodigue, avare, amoureux, vindicatif, jaloux, faible; car c'est ainsi qu'ils font tous, et que nous faisons tous. Messieurs, permettez-moi de vous le dire, vous donnez trop de force à vos calculs, et pas assez aux penchants du coeur humain et au jeu des passions. Votre système est très bon pour les gens de l'Utopie; il ne vaut rien pour les enfants de l'Adam.[11]

This passage indicates how closely Diderot's thought has followed Rousseau's, even to the point of using the same example of the dissolute merchant. There is no evidence to prove the direct influence of Rousseau, but there can be little doubt that Diderot here again is indebted to the man whom in so many other respects he affected to despise.

But apart from the reasons already discussed Diderot has further grounds for rejecting the form of absolutism which Catherine elaborates in the *Instruction*. We have seen that Diderot provisionally accepts her claim, set out in Article 13, that the aim of monarchical government is to direct man's actions towards natural liberty, with the added proviso that the ruler must be enlightened, just and firm. When, however, Catherine returns to the question of the relationship which should exist between the governed and those who govern, in Articles 250 and 251, it becomes apparent that their views on natural liberty and its preservation are as dissimilar as the views they hold on every other major aspect of political doctrine. In Catherine's view

---

[11] P.W., II, p. 160.

Il faut dans la société civile, comme en toute autre chose, un certain ordre; il faut que les uns gouvernent et que les autres obéissent. Telle est l'origine de toute espèce de dépendance, qui est plus ou moins grande, selon la condition de ceux qui obéissent.[12]

She holds that it is in the nature of things that society should consist of those who govern and those who obey, consequently absolutism is the type of government which most fully conforms with the requirements of nature. But obedience is not incompatible with that other requirement of nature, liberty; indeed it is by their very obedience to the dictates of the ruler that the ruled attain fully that most precious part of their natural heritage. Inadequately endowed to attain it by their own efforts they need a guide who can "diriger leurs actions vers le plus grand de tous les biens." [13]

Catherine's absolutist theory differs little from Diderot's own doctrinal position while under the influence of La Rivière's *De l'ordre essentiel,* a position long since rejected. It is hardly surprising therefore that he finds unacceptable Catherine's opinion that natural liberty can only be achieved and preserved for most men by obedience to their rulers. In his somewhat disjointed commentary on the Articles 250 and 251 he dismisses her theory that society originated from the need of the weak to depend upon the strong:

C'est la nécessité de lutter contre l'ennemi commun toujours subsistant, la nature, qui a rassemblé les hommes.[14]

The men who became leaders in primitive societies naturally merited their positions of power and authority because of their superior physical strength which was directed towards the protection of their fellows. It was only subsequently that authority was abused by being directed away from its original purpose of preserving society towards the satisfaction of the private interests of the ruler. But society can only flourish and create happiness if it is a free association of individuals who co-operate by placing their differing talents in the common pool. The model of this free association exists in the natural state among the animals and no doubt existed at the dawn of society:

Les chiens sauvages s'associent et chassent de compagnie; les renards s'associent et chassent de compagnie. L'homme isolé n'aurait pu veiller dans la cabane, préparer les aliments, chasser, combattre les bêtes, garder ses troupeaux, etc. . . . Cinq hommes font et font bien toutes ces choses.[15]

[12] T.P., p. 119, n. (a).
[13] *Ibid.,* p. 71, n. (a).
[14] *Ibid.,* p. 120.

Translated into contemporary terms this principle of nature declares that the happiness of society will only be ensured

> . . . si la liberté et la propriété sont assurées; si le commerce est sans gêne; si tous les ordres de citoyens sont également soumis aux lois; si l'impôt est supporté en raison des forces ou bien réparti; s'il n'excède pas les besoins de l'Etat; et si la vertu et les talents y ont une récompense assurée.[16]

It follows that within these bounds a man should be free to act as he wishes. Any attempt to restrict or direct his actions further in the name of an abstract and illusory ideal can only succeed in diminishing the one real happiness that does exist; that of the individual. Diderot demonstrates this argument by taking as an example the fundamental dictum of the *économistes* that the well-being of society would be ensured if all efforts were directed towards the exploitation of the earth's riches. If man was only made to plough, gather, eat and sell, admits Diderot, all well and good;

> . . . mais il me semble qu'un être qui sent est fait pour être heureux par toutes ses pensées.[17]

That kind of philosophy, he continues, is a total denial of man's nature, as it maintains him in a state of brutishness and imposes restrictions on his happiness and enjoyment of life.[18] As we have shown elsewhere [19] Diderot's conception of happiness at this stage is developed out of a fairly sophisticated materialist interpretation of human consciousness: the individual can only achieve self-fulfilment through self-creation by the continuous and unimpeded interiorisation of the external realities which he perceives. This can only take place within the context of a positive and dynamic relationship between the individual and the society in which he lives: individuation and socialisation are indissolubly linked. However, this double process, by its very nature, requires an atmosphere of freedom in which to operate; any move coming from outside to direct, control or otherwise restrict it must necessarily vitiate it. It follows, then, that all ideologies which are imposed on individuals through legislation with the hope of bringing about some abstract concept of social happiness are bound to fail. Such legislation continually forces the citizen to sacrifice his

---

[15] *Ibid.*, p. 122.
[16] *Ibid.*
[17] *Ibid.*, p. 122-123.
[18] *Ibid.*, p. 123.
[19] Part I, Chap. III.
[20] T.P., p. 123.

own tastes and happiness to the good of society,[20] an aim which, conceived of in these terms, is and can only be a myth, for as Diderot argues:

Je veux que la société soit heureuse; mais je veux l'être aussi; et il y a autant de manières d'être heureux qu'il y a d'individus. Notre propre bonheur est à la base de tous nos vrais devoirs.[21]

The general happiness of society is no more than the sum total of the happiness of all the individuals who go to make up that society.

Diderot chose to attack the doctrine of the *économistes,* but his criticisms are equally applicable to Catherine's philosophy of absolutism. Like the *économistes* she has made the fatal mistake of assuming that men's freedom and happiness can be dictated to them according to a preconceived set of principles. They all failed to recognise that such attempts are by the very nature of things self-defeating; that it is the individual himself who is alone capable of appreciating the conditions necessary for his own happiness, and that consequently he alone is capable of knowing and maintaining the degree of freedom essential to this end.

But by insisting so vehemently on the individual's right to the kind of happiness that suits him and which will differ from his neighbour's to the extent that they are different people with different needs, is Diderot contradicting the other pillar of his moral and political philosophy, the happiness of society as a whole, as Yves Benot claims? [22] It should be apparent by now that this is not so. Benot, a Marxist scholar, evidently believes with the *économistes* and Catherine that the composition of human nature and society are such that man's felicity on earth can only be gained if he is forced by law to comply with the principles and precepts which emanate from an oracular fountainhead designated, according to conviction, by God, Reason, or History. Such a belief is irreconcilably hostile to the view that there are as many ways of being happy as there are individuals, and that our own happiness is the basis of all our real duties. For Diderot, however, the two concepts are not implacably opposed, on the contrary they are integrally related. Only in a pluralist society in which individuals can freely satisfy their own tastes will the well-being of that society be properly served.

This principle is illustrated in a passage towards the end of the *Observations* in which he once more takes to task the narrow utilitarianism of the *économistes* and for good measure Rousseau's gloomy attribution of the corruption of civilised society to the progress made in the arts and

[21] *Ibid.,* p. 123.
[22] *Ibid.,* p. 123, n. 1.

sciences. To reject the bulk of civilised man's aesthetic, intellectual and
scientific accomplishments either because they are superfluous to his material needs or because they are harmful to his moral welfare is a sure sign
of faulty logic and intellectual parochialism.[23] The *économistes* are
guilty of economic puritanism, Rousseau of moral puritanism, both of
which seek to rob men of their individuality by reducing them to an ideological stereotype:

> Ces visions suivies jusqu'où une bonne logique pourrait les conduire, ont
> mis l'homme de Rousseau à quatre pattes, et celui des Economistes à la queue
> d'un charrue.[24]

Diderot rejects the implied *dirigisme* of both doctrines for a more flexible
system which is secured only by fundamental laws and where individuality can otherwise freely flower:

> Ordonnez bien trois ou quatre points importants et abandonnez le reste à
> l'intérêt et au goût des particuliers.[25]

Dirigisme, contrary to the belief of its exponents, cannot create a healthy
and flourishing society, it only succeeds in impoverishing human life by
denying society the benefits which accrue when each member pursues his
own personal tastes and interests. The *économistes*, for example, in requiring that all excess wealth should be reinvested in production, would rob
society of the great architectural and artistic creations to which men have
devoted their opulence in order to satisfy their tastes. These creations not
only provide cultural benefit, they are economic and moral investments
as well, since they draw visitors from other countries and promote virtue
and talent. "Le beau," concludes Diderot, "ne se sépare point de l'utile," [26]
and by useful he means what is of both economic and moral utility.

By focusing the debate between *dirigisme* and the doctrine of an open
society on the question of personal taste Diderot underlines the fundamental differences which separate the two, and which make the latter,
in his opinion, infinitely more desirable. The greatest accomplishments
of the civilised world, those which have done most to improve the life of
the community, have been the result of individuals free to devote their
talents, wealth and energies to the satisfaction of the inner penchants of
their personalities. They have achieved fulfilment through the successful

[23] *Ibid.*, pp. 161-163.
[24] *Ibid.*, p. 163.
[25] *Ibid.*
[26] *Ibid.*

creative pursuit of their interests in every field of artistic and intellectual endeavour. Taste, then, is at one and the same time the purest expression of a man's individuality and the means by which he can most fully contribute to the happiness of the society in which he lives.

But we have seen that for Diderot liberty is only one of two conditions necessary for citizenship, the other being property. Indeed it is property which in the first place guarantees liberty by delimiting the ruler's authority over his subjects and by acting as the instrument whereby the subject lays claim to that liberty and exercises it.[27] For property is the source of wealth which allows the citizen to enlighten himself and cultivate his tastes. "Qui se déclare ennemi de l'or, sans restriction," writes Diderot in the *Réfutation d'Helvétius*, "se déclare, ou je me trompe fort, protecteur de l'ignorance." [28] If one adds to this the view that only property gives the individual a vested interest in the nation, it follows that only the property-owner can rightfully make claims to citizenship. It is not surprising, therefore, that Diderot considers that the body in whom the legislative authority should be vested in Russia should be composed of "les grands propriétaires." [29]

Yet, although he holds that opulence is essential to the maintenance of freedom and the pursuit of happiness Diderot rejects the conception of luxury that most contemporary thinkers after Melon, with the exception of Rousseau and the physiocrats, saw as one of the most important and desirable sources of opulence. One critic has correctly remarked that Diderot was "l'apologiste le plus convaincu du luxe," [30] and has then incorrectly assumed that he was defending the same thing as Voltaire and the other *philosophes*. In this matter, as in so many others, Diderot showed greater perspicacity. In both the *Mémoires* and the *Observations* [31] he makes a careful distinction between the luxury of a society in which money is a god and talent and virtue count for nothing, and luxury in a society which has an excellent administration, freedom of commerce, a protected agriculture and an equitable tax system. In the former luxury is "(le) signe de la richesse d'un petit nombre, masque de la pauvreté du grand nombre et source de la corruption de tous;" [32] in the latter it is "(le) signe de

---

[27] "La souveraineté et la liberté ne consistent pas à faire tout ce que l'on veut; la souveraineté et la liberté sont limitées l'une et l'autre par la même barrière: le respect de la propriété de la part du souverain, et son usage de la part du sujet," T.P., p. 84.
[28] A.T., II, p. 420.
[29] T.P., p. 86.
[30] M. R. de Labriolle-Rutherford, "L'Evolution de la notion de luxe depuis Mandeville jusqu'à la Révolution," p. 1030.
[31] MÉM., XXVI, *Du Luxe*; T.P., pp. 128-129.
[32] T.P., p. 129.

la richesse et de l'aisance dans toutes les conditions." [33] Voltaire's *Le Mondain*, in which he sings the praises of luxury, is a charming piece but nevertheless "l'apologie de la fièvre d'un agonisant, fièvre que je ne prendrai jamais pour une bonne chose." [34] Diderot, unlike Voltaire, cannot accept a form of luxury which requires the permanent division of society into the rich and the poor. He is totally opposed to the view, drawn from Mandeville and which enjoyed considerable popularity, that a nation's prosperity is dependent on an economically depressed labour force and that high wages would make workers indolent and lazy. Diderot dismisses it as being untenable on psychological but also on humanitarian and political grounds. In answer to a provincial Intendant who had claimed that the peasant's lot was so hard that only extreme poverty and the fear of starving to death held him there, he retorts,

Aucun péril, (...) aucun travail n'effraye l'homme, lorsqu'il est compensé par le produit ... on est toujours pressé d'entrer où l'on est sûr de trouver l'aisance et la fortune, et (...) quelque dure que soit la journée de l'agriculteur, l'agriculture trouvera d'autant plus de bras que la récompense de ses peines sera plus sûre et abondante.[35]

But as long as the peasants are inhumanly excluded from the class of property-owners and are reduced to digging other people's land, agriculture will never flourish. Only property can give a man that sense of involvement and self-respect which will draw the best from him in his work and thus eventually contribute to the increased prosperity of the society in which he lives. "Autant vaut l'homme, autant vaut la terre. La première propriété est personnelle," [36] writes Diderot in the *Observations* in support of Catherine's suggestion that the serfs be allowed to own property. In the final analysis he sees property as a necessary extension of the individual's personality, the means by which he can exploit his talents and satisfy his inner needs, and without which his psychological and moral growth remains stunted.

To resume, Diderot's theory of property is a difficult one to grasp in its totality, involving as it does a complex mixture of psychological and political principles, which must be pieced together from a variety of scattered remarks. It is, however, an integral part of his political thought; property alone opens the door to the cultivation of one's intelligence, talents and tastes, which in turn provide the qualifications necessary for

[34] MEM., p. 145.
[35] *Ibid.*, p. 409.
[36] T.P., p. 124.

citizenship. It follows that all things in the State should be oriented both towards its protection and the free exploitation of the wealth that accrues from it. Property requires an atmosphere of political freedom in order that its benefits may be realised; conversely property contributes to and sustains this selfsame atmosphere of freedom. Liberty and property are in Diderot's thought two sides of the same coin, the fixed point to which all the multiplicity of laws, regulations and ordinances should refer if they are to form a unified pattern.[37]

As a piece of political psychology Diderot's theory of property cannot be faulted. Within the social and economic context of the age, it appears to constitute a credible means of stimulating social progress and creating an enlightened and committed citizenry which was necessary if rule by the people were to replace rule by an absolute monarch. Unfortunately as a purely economic concept it reckoned without the intractable nature of the forces which were already beginning to evolve as a result of developments in technology and the means of production, and which in the following century were to lead to the stark choice between free enterprise capitalism and state socialism. Diderot, with his restricted knowledge of economic matters could not be expected to understand that this advocacy of property for all with its vision of a nation made up of small businessmen, tradesmen, and independent peasants was doomed before it could ever be translated into reality.

Finally, in our examination of the *Observations*, let us consider Diderot's conception of law as it relates to freedom and property.

If freedom and property are together the cornerstone on which a just and healthy society is built, how can the mentality that favours them be nurtured and preserved? For, as Diderot warns us,

A mesure qu'un peuple perd le sentiment de la liberté et de la propriété, il se corrompt, il s'avilit, il penche vers la servitude." [38]

Personal interest, when it is freed by education from the shackles of ignorance and the dangers of seduction by the prospect of short term gains, can help foster right attitudes. But he realises that it is idealistic to expect too much from education alone.[39] He is aware that although one Frenchman in twenty is extremely enlightened, it is to no effect.[40] Ultimately it is not personal interest and education but legislation which fashions a

[37] *Ibid.*, p. 114.
[38] *Ibid.*, pp. 156-157.
[39] *Ibid.*, p. 81.
[40] *Ibid.*, p. 80.

nation's spirit.[41] The laws must first create the right political conditions before the educated individual can effectively pursue his own interests, and these right political conditions are the foundation and preservation of liberty and property.[42]

Since all laws must be defined in relation to liberty and property, which are absolute requirements of human nature,[43] it is evident that Diderot is firmly set within the natural law tradition. Yet had he not stated in the *Fragments Echappés* that the people have an inalienable right to say, if they wish, "Nous sommes mal ici mais nous voulons y rester" [44] a statement which implies that the general will can override or replace natural law? It is tempting to see here once more a certain parallel with Rousseau who, while he does not reject natural law, is so close to identifying it with the general will that as Alfred Cobban stated, "in so far as this identification is assumed" the idea "ceases to be capable of playing its former role in the state as a moderating influence over political power." [45] There is admittedly a certain vacillation in Diderot's thought here, but it would be wrong to assume that he concedes to the general will the same unqualified power that Rousseau unwittingly did. In the last resort Diderot believes that since the general will is expressed by an enlightened body of citizens it will comply with the dictates of natural law. Unlike Jean-Jacques he is not prepared to commit himself to the acknowledgment of the human origin of laws; for although "Il ne peut y avoir de vrai législateur que le peuple," [46] nevertheless "La nature a fait toutes les bonnes lois, c'est le législateur qui les publie." [47] Elsewhere, while accepting that a positive law that is good and useful in one circumstance may be harmful and bad in another, he nevertheless holds to the belief that positive laws are only corollaries of natural laws and are therefore like them eternal and common.[48] In this important respect then Diderot does not follow Rousseau. His visit to Russia had reinforced him in the belief that popular sovereignty and the unimpeded expression of the general will were the only satisfactory means of ensuring the happiness of society and its separate members, but his attachment to the concept of natural law pre-

[41] *Ibid.*, p. 88.
[42] Cf. "Quelle que soit la multiplicité des lois, des règlements. des ordonnances. il est impossible qu'ils se contredisent si on les rapporte tous à un point fixe: et ce point fixe est donné, c'est la liberté et la propriété," *Ibid.*, p. 114.
[43] Cf. "Un peuple libre ne diffère d'un peuple esclave que par l'inamovibilité de certains privilèges appartenant à l'homme comme homme" *Ibid.*, pp. 74-75.
[44] A.T., VI. p. 448.
[45] *Rousseau and the Modern State.* p. 169.
[46] T.P., p. 61.
[47] *Ibid.*, p. 88.
[48] *Ibid.*, p. 68.

vented him from stepping outside the ambit of the liberal, individualistic, rationalist tradition. In this conceptual sense Diderot's political thought, unlike Rousseau's, could not then or in the later stages of its evolution be called revolutionary.

II. HOLLAND: THE REALITY

Diderot arrived at The Hague on the morning of the 5th April 1774 and remained there once more as the guest of Prince Galitzin until the middle of October when he set off on the final stage of the protracted return journey to Paris. This second stay was to be less satisfying and settled than the first. Exhausted by the journey the sexagenarian was slow to recuperate; by mid-June he was still sleeping an unaccustomed eight to nine hours a night, and had not yet found the courage to start working.[49] The French edition of the *Plans et Statuts*,[50] which Catherine had asked him to publish in Holland and which was the main reason for his prolonged stay, was a constant source of annoyance because of the dilatoriness of the Dutch publishers whom Diderot found quite intolerable.[51] He had been separated from family and friends for almost a year now, and there was only one thing he wanted to do – return to Paris as soon as possible and never leave home again. Beside the fatigue, the frustration and the longing for home, there was also the realisation, despite the continued enthusiasm for Catherine displayed in his letters, that his mission to St. Petersburg had been at the deepest level a failure. But if Diderot had every reason to be dejected, he was temperamentally incapable of remaining dispirited for long. Tasks large and small awaited him: the *Réfutation d'Helvétius* and the *Voyage de Hollande* started on the outward journey had not been finished, Catherine's *Instruction* begged to be annotated, and in the longer term a new edition of the *Encyclopédie* suggested by Catherine required consideration. Of the projects mentioned only the new edition of the *Encyclopédie* was not to see the light of day. The others were completed at The Hague or soon after his return to Paris. Among them the *Voyage de Hollande* once more attracts our attention, in which as we argued in the previous chapter, we believe it is possible to discern the change that took place in Diderot's attitude towards the political situation in Holland from the first to the second stay at The Hague.

---

[49] CORR., XIV, p. 15.
[50] *Plans et Statuts des différents établissements ordonnés par Sa Majesté Impériale Catherine II pour l'Education de la Jeunesse et l'Utilité générale de son Empire*, écrits en langue russe par M. Betzki et traduits en langue française d'après les originaux, par M. Clerc. Amsterdam, 1775.
[51] "Leurs boutiques sont des nids à rats; leurs imprimeries, d'infâmes barraques; ils

Three passages in particular, because of the more perceptive and critical attitude that they contain, can be taken with some certainty to have been written during Diderot's second stay. The first two consist of the last paragraph of the section entitled *Du Stadthoudérat* and the section which immediately follows it, *Politique*, and which deals with essentially the same subject. The third is to be found in the chapter entitled *L'Habitant du Pays ou Des Moeurs* and consists of a paragraph in which Diderot notes the progress of corruption in the country.[52]

In the first part of *Du Stadthoudérat* Diderot seems fairly certain that the strong republican spirit manifest in the institutions of Holland and in the Dutch themselves was more than adequate as a counterforce to any attempts of the hereditary Stadtholder to extend his authority beyond that constitutionally arrogated to him as chief of staff of the land and naval forces of the United Provinces. He cites an attempt, made by the Stadtholder in 1772, to block the nomination of a strongly republican secretary by the cities of Rotterdam and Amsterdam who successfully fought off his unconstitutional infringement of their privileges.[53] He quotes the retort of a wine merchant when the States of one of the provinces were deliberating in the following years whether to send a delegation to enquire about the health of the Stadtholder's wife who had just given birth:

Envoyez qui vous voudrez; pour moi je n'y vais pas: je suis roi." [54]

However, in the last paragraph the tone changes sharply. Diderot is now less confident that the republicanism of the Dutch is a sufficiently strong barrier against the encroachments of the Stadtholder on the liberties of the people. The danger lies not so much in the post itself as in the fact that it has been made hereditary. Since the qualities required of a great general are not necessarily innate, the Dutch, by fixing the post in one family in perpetuity, have guaranteed themselves a long succession of inept military leaders. In a well-ordered society posts should only be filled by those who have the necessary talents to carry out their duties competently. But over and above the problem of incompetence and ineptitude the conversion of the Stadtholdership to a hereditary office raises a far more serious issue of a political nature which Diderot examines in *Politique*.

To illustrate the harmful political effects of placing the Stadtholdership on a hereditary basis Diderot points to the influence it is having upon

sont rustres, paresseux, avares, ignorants; il ne tendent qu'à leur intérêt qu'ils entendent mal," CORR., XIV, p. 64.
    [52] A.T., XVII, p. 416.
    [53] *Ibid.*, p. 388.
    [54] *Ibid.*

trade, the life-blood of the Dutch nation. A trading nation, he argues, can only flourish if it is allowed the greatest freedom in its commercial transactions; democracy is the form of government which suits it best. For it is self-evident that no one knows how to run a business better than the business man himself. Once his efficiency and expertise are impeded by an external authority which attempts to run his affairs for him either by influence or legislation, then all is lost. Since the Stadtholdership has been made hereditary it has extended its authority beyond the bounds of its military prerogative and has increasingly interfered with the free functioning of trade by introducing a series of regulations, inspections and other controls. The result has been the development of an administration "diamétralement opposée à l'esprit et au bonheur général" [55] of the Dutch nation. The Stadtholder's incursion into the freedom of the merchant is another instance of the *dirigisme* which Diderot had so strongly attacked in his *Observations* on Catherine's *Instruction*. In the sphere of commerce as in the general life of the nation, the well-being of society is best served when the individual is free to observe the dictates of nature by following his own interests:

Il ne faut pas de législation où la nature a constitué un despote attentif, juste, ferme, éclairé, qui récompense et qui punit toujours avec poids et mesure; l'intérêt, sans cesse favorable à ceux qui le consultent sagement, n'est jamais cruel que pour ceux qui l'entendent mal.[56]

But Diderot is not optimistic; the fatal effects of this *dirigiste* form of government are already beginning to be felt, and as the authority of the Stadtholder increases so will they, leading in the extreme to slavery and misery.

Diderot's experience with Catherine had taught him that authority vested in a single hereditary ruler inevitably leads to *dirigisme* and the suppression of individual initiative. This lesson he now applies on his return from St. Petersburg to the Dutch political situation, and as a consequence his naive enthusiasm for the virtuous republicanism of the Dutch is replaced by a truer assessment of the decline that nation had undergone since the zenith of its power and freedom in the 17th century. Political decline had been accompanied by moral corruption, and of this too Diderot had become aware since his return from Russia. The link between moral corruption and false luxury in France which he had analysed in the *Mémoires* and the *Observations* he now discerns in Holland:

[55] A.T., XVII, p. 391.
[56] *Ibid.*

La corruption des moeurs fait des progrès; elle marche d'un même pas avec le luxe et la richesse . . .; La beauté, les talents, l'éducation, la sagesse d'une fille, ne lui servent de rien, c'est l'argent qui répare le manque de ces qualités. Les vertus qui recommenderaient un jeune homme ne lui seraient guère plus utiles. Voulez-vous attacher les regards, soyez encore plus riche." [57]

For lack of external evidence our dating of the different passages of the *Voyage de Hollande* that we have examined in this chapter is obviously only tentative. But we believe we have set forth sufficient arguments to demonstrate that a noticeable evolution of Diderot's understanding of the Dutch political system and consequently of his attitude towards it during his two stays at The Hague can be deduced from the *Voyage*. Disillusionment over Catherine gained him a new insight into failing Dutch republicanism and the increasing authority of the Stadtholder. His first stay in Holland had provided him with confirmation of the rightness of principles of popular sovereignty, his second stay furnished him with the confirmation of the wrongness of the absolutist principle.[58] Armed with these convictions he returned home to a new and fluid political situation.

III. LOUIS XVI: NEW HOPE AT HOME

After a long agony Louis XV died on the 10th May 1774 to be succeeded on the throne of France by the young and inexperienced yet serious-minded Louis XVI. Diderot's reaction to the news in a letter to Sophie Volland was cautious:

---

[57] A.T., XVII, p. 416.

[58] A passage in a chapter of the *Pensées Détachées* entitled *Colonies hollandaises* (p. 370) condemns the corruption of republicanism in Holland. This passage first appeared in the 1770 edition of the *Histoire des deux Indes* and would therefore seem to contradict our opinion that Diderot was ignorant of the true state of affairs in the United Provinces during his first stay at The Hague. However the corresponding passage in the *Fragments Imprimés* (pp. 362-364) does not include this condemnation and is followed by a manuscript page in which the United Provinces are praised in the following terms:

Nous n'en voyons aucune (nation), dont l'objet étant le commerce et la liberté qui s'appellent, s'attirent et se soutiennent, se soit mieux conduite pour conserver l'un et l'autre (*sic*). (Quoted by H. Wolpe, *op. cit.*, p. 207).

Since the *Fragments Imprimés,* which consist of pages cut from the third edition of the *Histoire des deux Indes,* were in all probability selected by Diderot himself as his own contributions to Raynal's work (see M. Duchet, "Diderot Collaborateur de Raynal: A Propos des Fragments Imprimés du Fonds Vandeul"), the likely explanation for the anomalous passage is that it was written by Raynal and not by Diderot, the latter including it in the *Pensées Détachées* because it provided a suitable introduction to his own condemnation of the decline of Dutch republicanism which follows it, and which was originally a contribution to the third edition of the *Histoire des deux Indes.* This explanation gains substance from the fact that Raynal had written an *Histoire du Stadthoudérat*, a vituperative anti-Orangist manifesto, as early as 1747.

Il est arrivé sur votre horizon un grand événement qui sera sans doute suivi de beaucoup d'autres. Quelquefois je désire d'en être témoin; quelquefois aussi, je me félicite d'être où je suis.[59]

That changes would come with the new reign was clear. The two main factions at court, the Choiseulists, a group of aristocratic coteries comprising nobles of the sword and the robe who had labelled themselves the "patriot" party, and the *dévots*, were both for different reasons longing to see the dismissal of Terray and the Chancellor, Maupeou, and assert their own influence over the government. Beyond the Court there lay a third interest, hardly a party – that of the physiocrats and the *philosophes* whose political doctrines lacked complete homogeneity but who were nonetheless initiators and products of the progressive and reforming movement of the Enlightenment. There was an outside chance that this last group might gain power in competition with the two influential court factions. It is this, no doubt, that accounts for the cautious note in Diderot's remark. Perhaps in Louis XVI destiny had at last served France with that enlightened ruler who would draw to himself men of wisdom as a first stage in the transference of authority to the nation, that monarchical Messiah of whom Diderot had written in a fervid moment of faith:

Il paraîtra, il paraîtra un jour, parce que le temps amène tout ce qui est possible, et il est possible, l'homme juste, éclairé, et puissant que vous attendez.[60]

However the man who was to effect this unexpected change and bring the men of progress into key positions of power was not so much the hesitant and dilatory young Louis but the scheming and cynical old courtier, Maurepas, called back from exile by the new king who was utterly confounded by the morass of problems which faced him on his accession.

On the 19th July Turgot, a disciple of the physiocratic school, was elevated from the office of Intendant of Limoges to the Marine. A little over a month later, on the 24th August, he was further promoted, this time to the post of Controller-General of Finances, the most important office in the government of Louis XVI, who was not prepared to place his powers at the disposal of a chief minister. On the same day, Maupeou and Terray were dismissed, and Sartine, Diderot's old school friend, replaced Turgot at the Marine. Further nominations to governmental posts of men with particularly strong sympathies for the *philosophes* seemed to consolidate what the conservatives, with considerable anxiety, called "le

[59] CORR., XIV, p. 34.
[60] *Réfutation d'Helvétius*, A.T., II, p. 446.

triomphe des Encyclopédistes." By December of that year the *parlements* had been recalled from exile.

In the short space of five months the unhoped for had occurred: enlightened men were in the seats of power and with the return of the *parlements* liberty was once more guaranteed.[61] Diderot's wildest dreams were not far from being realised. He had left France in 1773 despairing of his country's ever rising out of the tyranny in which he believed Maupeou had caused her to founder. He had travelled east to Holland and thence to Russia in search of solace and with the belief that in these countries he might find justice and humanity either flourishing or about to burst forth. In 1774 the situation had been almost completely reversed: discouragement from Catherine had been followed by disappointment in Holland; now it was France which offered, if not a new dawn in the age of man, at least a strong intimation that the nation was moving resolutely towards the day when it would take its destiny fully into its own hands.

Although Turgot had been a contributor to the *Encyclopédie*, Diderot had little regard for his economic theories, a sentiment that was cordially reciprocated. Yet this did not prevent Diderot from holding the Controller-General in high esteem as an honest and worthy public servant. While at St. Petersburg Diderot had mused on the radical changes that would come about if ever Turgot were to enter the government:

> J'en pousserai un cri de joie, car il faut que l'esprit de notre ministère soit tout à fait changé, et que l'état des choses s'amende d'une manière presque miraculeuse.[62]

But he had been convinced that Turgot would never leave Limoges. Now that the impossible had happened his comment to Catherine on the event is more nuanced but no less positive:

> Il est arrivé bien des révolutions dans notre ministère; ce sont les économistes, les disciples de La Rivière qui tiennent le timon de nos finances. Votre Majesté Impériale n'en aura pas meilleure opinion, mais nous nous sommes si mal trouvés des maltôtiers et des robins, que je défie les gens d'esprit de faire pis. Au moins ceux-ci sont justes, instruits et désintéressés, et l'expérience des choses les défera peut-être de la morgue de l'école et de la folie du système. L'économiste est en administration ce qu'est le stoïcien en morale. Ils ne sont supportables que dans le moment du malheur.[63]

---

[61] "Le rétablissement de l'ancienne magistrature a ramené le temps de la liberté," (*Réfutation d'Helvétius*, A.T., II, p. 275).
[62] MEM., p. 160.
[63] CORR., XIV, pp. 121-122.

If Turgot and his team remained in office for ten years, he writes in the *Réfutation*,[64] then all France's misfortunes will be set right.

The advent of Turgot, with a reforming plan which, if it had been implemented, would have in effect brought about a revolution in the political life of France,[65] temporarily halted in Diderot the maturation of an idea which in one sense was to take him beyond even Rousseau as a political thinker opposed to the existing order: this was the acceptance of violence as one of the possible and legitimate means of overthrowing an oppressive régime. The only individual before the Revolution to surpass Diderot in this respect was the obscure Abbé Meslier, one of whose sanguinary recipes for the treatment of priests and kings Diderot had incorporated without great seriousness in his *Eleuthéromanes*, composed on Twelfth Night, 1772, when for the third year in succession he had been crowned *Roi de la Fève*.[66] The indications that Diderot had begun to think in terms of violent revolutionary action are few, but none the less important for their paucity. It seems that this new departure in his thinking was stimulated by his reflections on the structure of different societies, but in particular that of the monarchical state, while at St. Petersburg:

La monarchie est une haute pyramide dont les différents Etats forment les plans. Le peuple est à la base, écrasé du fardeau des autres plans . . .
Dans l'état monarchique, malheur à la monarchie si les boules de la base viennent à s'agiter! Le pyramide se renverse et il ne reste qu'un amas de ruines.[67]

Here revolution in a monarchical society is seen solely through the eyes of the political scientist as a spontaneous phenomenon that would occur given certain circumstances. But Diderot has only thought about revolution in academic terms, as is clear from a short passage in the *Réfutation*:

---

[64] A.T., II, p. 275.

[65] It included freedom of trade, the suppression of government intervention in the means of production and exchange, the suppression of the corporation, a complete overhaul of the tax system, religious tolerance, freedom of expression, and a project for a parliamentary constitution. For an analysis of the events leading up to Turgot's nomination as Controller-General see D. Dakin, *Turgot and the Ancien Régime*, Chap. IX.

[66] Compare *Les Eleuthéromanes* where Diderot, describing man as obedient to the voice of nature and driven by anger, continues:
Et ses mains ourdiraient les entrailles du prêtre
Au défaut d'un cordon pour étrangler les rois (A.T., IX, p. 16)
with Meslier in his *Testament* who hopes that the people will take advantage of the wish "que faisoit autrefois un homme qui n'avoit ni science ni étude, mais qui selon les apparences ne manquoit pas de bon sens," to wit, "que tous les grands de la terre et que tous les nobles fussent pendus et étranglés avec les boiaux des prêtres," (*Le Testament* . . . I, pp. 18-19).

[67] MEM., p. 176. The same image of the pyramid of balls is found in the *Observations*, T.P., p. 97.

On demandait un jour comment on rendait les moeurs à un peuple cor-
rompu. Je répondis: *Comme Médée rendait la jeunesse à son père, en le
dépeçant et le faisant bouillir.*[68]

Here the destruction of a social system wrought by conscious political
action – the passage refers specifically to French society – is accepted as a
possible means of curing a society of its ills and bringing about its rejuvenation. In other words Diderot has become aware that violent revolutionary action can be effective in replacing a corrupt and oppressive régime by a humane and just one. But in the French context the recent
events lead him to qualify his remark:

Alors, cette réponse n'aurait pas été très-déplacée.[69]

The tyranny of Louis XV might have justified revolutionary action, but
with the political situation radically altered since the accession of Louis
XVI such an extreme position is no longer necessary. In his constant os-
cillation between Socratic courage and Aristippean caution Diderot once
more reverts to the latter. Elsewhere in the *Réfutation* he remarks that one
of the questions facing the man of sagacity and insight is:

Faut-il sacrifier aux hasards d'une révolution le bonheur de la génération
présente pour le bonheur de la génération à venir ...? [70]

This question which Diderot had increasingly felt required an affirmative
answer, he now replies to in the negative.

In one sense it would be wrong to place too great an emphasis on the
emergence of this new element in Diderot's political thought, for inas-
much as it refers to a concrete situation, namely the political climate of
France at the latter end of Louis XV's reign, it amounts to little more than
rhetorical bravado. The nexus of circumstances which set off the events
of 1789 did not exist, in particular, the aristocratic revolt which was taken
over by the Third Estate and is now considered by most historians to be
the essential contributory factor to the Revolution, was nowhere to be
seen, despite the dissolution of the *parlements*. In another sense, however, as we shall see in the following chapter, this new idea was no mere
passing fancy in Diderot's mind. Admittedly, hardly had it seen the light
of day than it seemed to fade away. The "triomphe des Encyclopédistes"
had made it look irrelevant, but it had not vanished entirely; it was to lie
dormant, to be revived with new vigour when the halcyon days of Turgot's

[68] A.T., II, p. 276.
[69] *Ibid.*
[70] A.T., II, p. 346.

ministry were little more than a memory and a sentiment of gloom and foreboding had once more reasserted itself in the minds of the enlightened and forward-looking men of France.

It has been argued in the course of this chapter that Diderot had over the period of his journey to Russia irrevocably declared himself a champion of popular sovereignty and a resolute opponent of monarchical absolutism. It must, however, be made clear in concluding that he remained firmly convinced that even under a new order a nation's political health was ultimately dependent on the present and active participation in the processes of government of a small number of men, distinguished by the excellence of their moral integrity and their ability to grasp and solve complex issues, which constantly confront every type of society. This view, which Diderot retained essentially unchanged from his abandoned absolutist doctrine is expressed once more in a pastiche of Sallust, which forms one of the *Principes de Politique des Souverains*:

> Salluste a fait l'histoire de toutes les nations dans le peu de lignes qui suivent: "J'ai beaucoup lu, j'ai beaucoup entendu, j'ai beaucoup médité sur ce que la république avait achevé de grand dans la paix et dans la guerre; je me suis interrogé moi-même sur les moyens qui avaient conduit à une heureuse fin tant d'entreprises étonnantes, et il m'a été démontré que cette énorme besogne n'avait été l'ouvrage que d'un très petit nombre de grands hommes.[71]

These men, without whom no government can successfully undertake to serve the needs of the nation are epitomised in the figure of the *philosophe,* whose portrait as a servant of the people Diderot painted in a moment of vision in the *Mémoires*:

> Le philosophe attend le cinquantième bon roi qui profitera de ses travaux. En attendant, il éclaire les hommes sur leurs droits inaliénables. Il tempère le fanatisme religieux. Il dit aux peuples qu'ils sont les plus forts et que, s'ils vont à la boucherie, c'est qu'ils s'y laissent mener. Il prépare aux révolutions qui surviennent toujours à l'extrémité du malheur des suites qui compensent le sang répandu.[72]

In spite of encroaching old age and increasing infirmity Diderot devoted himself in the last ten years of his life to the fulfilment of the role he had described.

[71] O.PO., p. 205.
[72] MEM., p. 235.

CHAPTER V

TOWARDS REVOLUTION

The last ten years of Diderot's life were marked by two events which crystallised his political thought in its final form and which together marked a major turning point in the destiny of modern France and Europe. They were the fall of Turgot and the American Revolution. In Turgot, the most radical minister of finance France had ever seen, the Ancien Régime had been given its last chance to reform; by ignominiously rejecting him and thus bowing to the pressures of the serried ranks of privilege it finally sealed its own fate. But by one of those constant paradoxes of history, accounted for by the short-sighted self-interest of the rulers of nations, France, while closing the door to progressive reform at home, was vigorously pursuing the opposite course in her foreign policy. By supporting the revolt of the British colonies in North America against their mother country she was unwittingly acting as a midwife to the birth of a nation founded on alien notions of liberty, justice and equality. Among the *philosophes* support for the uprising in America was fairly general, though for many it appears to have been as much an excuse to release their latent anglophobia as an opportunity to express their commitment to the principles it embodied. As for Turgot, the reaction to his fall was not unanimously disapproving; disagreement, even downright hostility in some quarters, at his economic policies, divided the camp. On both issues Diderot showed a greater depth of understanding, not only as to the way they affected the present, but as to the implications they held for the future.

I. DIDEROT BETWEEN TURGOT AND NECKER

Documentary evidence of Diderot's opinion of the Turgot administration after the first flush of enthusiasm recorded in letters written from The Hague and in the first months after his return to Paris [1] is hard to

---

[1] See previous chapter.

come by. Always allowing for the fact that further letters commenting on this subject may yet be discovered, it seems that Diderot's almost total silence can be ascribed to preoccupations of a domestic order, and to the difficult position in which he found himself when Necker began the on-slaught against Turgot which was eventually to bring him to power. How-ever, what we know of these preoccupations and his relations with Necker during this time, with one or two other indications, can help us piece to-gether a fairly accurate idea of Diderot's attitude to the men who held office until the fateful days of May 1776 when they were routed.

Ever the doting father Diderot spent a considerable amount of time trying to further his daughter's and son-in-law's financial interests by using his influence with a number of ministers and high functionaries in order to obtain preferential treatment for them on government contracts. He began his campaign with a letter to Turgot sent from The Hague and continued it on his return with a series of requests made by word of mouth and by letter. Two of Diderot's letters and a reply to a third are extant,[2] but it is certain that more were written. Although Diderot's requests met with little or no success – Turgot's administration did not wish to lay itself open to the charge of nepotism – the tone of the letters on both sides re-flects the mutual high esteem in which they held each other. Despite Di-derot's hostility towards physiocratic theory, dating back to the *Apologie de Galiani*, he was aware that beyond this conflict of ideas both he and Turgot and his team were aiming at the same goal. "Vous travaillez et je travaille aussi," he wrote to Du Pont de Nemours, "Votre travail a le bien pour objet immédiat; le mien n'a cet objet que dans le lointain." [3] The Comte d'Angiviller, although he was unable to satisfy Diderot's petition, nonetheless took the trouble to explain his refusal at length in a letter written in his own hand "à un homme que j'estime et que j'aime, avec le détail que je lui dois à tant de titres que je les lui devrois encore quand je ne connoîtrois de lui que son nom." [4]

Unfortunately it is impossible to tell whether Diderot had any intima-tion of the quite radical proposals for constitutional reform which were at that very moment being worked out by Turgot in conclave with Du Pont.[5] It was not until 1787, after Turgot's death, that the *Mémoire sur*

---

[2] To Sartine, Du Pont de Nemours, and from the Comte d'Angiviller; Letters 861, 868, and 865 respectively in CORR., XIV.

[3] *Ibid.*, pp. 180-181.

[4] *Ibid.*, p. 167.

[5] We cannot agree with J. Varloot's reading of Diderot's letter to Du Pont de Nemours, on which he makes the comment: "Son flair subodore, derrière la porte close, des projets presque aussi "lointains" que les siens," *Ibid.*, p. 180. There is nothing in this letter in our view, which lends itself to this interpretation.

les municipalités, drafted by Du Pont on the former's instigation, and setting out a constitution with elected assemblies, was revealed. Nevertheless it is possible to infer from Diderot's contacts with the administration that he maintained the high degree of confidence in its members that he had openly expressed in the first months. This same note of optimism is contained in a further letter to Catherine II in which he remarks:

Ah! madame, il ne dépend que de ceux qui nous gouvernent de faire encore une grande et belle nation de nous. L'étincelle sacrée qui reste d'un grand brasier n'a besoin qui d'un souffle.[6]

And in an addition to the manuscript of his *Plan d'une université,* equally destined for Catherine, Diderot wrote, fulminating with righteous indignation at Prince Orlof's intemperate and condescending behaviour while visiting him:

Qu'il oublie tant qu'il lui plaira qu'il parle à des hommes sensés, il n'y a pas grand mal à cela. Mais qu'il ne se souvienne jamais qu'il parle à des hommes libres, c'est une inadvertance qui blesse partout et qui est très dangereuse dans ce pays-ci." [7]

In a society where some of the worst restrictions on freedom were already being eliminated – censorship, for example, had been considerably relaxed, and freedom of speech was perhaps greater than at any time during the Ancien Régime – Diderot could with certain justice speak of himself and his compatriots as free men.

It was this same liberalism which allowed Turgot's main antagonist, Necker, to publish his *De la législation et du commerce des grains* in which, following in the wake of Galiani, he attacked the free market policy on grain that the present administration had re-established. Its publication marked the beginning of the serious attempts to oust Turgot and replace him by Necker at the finances. It may be that Necker was used by Conti and the court party as a tool in their intrigues against Turgot.[8] In any case he caused considerable damage to the latter by provoking a split in the philosophic community, the part of the population from whom Turgot should have expected most support. The division of opinion which had produced such acrimonious debate in 1769-1770 had never been properly healed, and once again the differences rose to the surface. Madame d'Epinay wrote approvingly of Necker's book to Galiani,[9] who with her

---

[6] *Ibid.,* p. 176.
[7] A.T., III, p. 535 and CORR., XIV, p. 157 where this letter is correctly dated.
[8] See D. Dakin, *op. cit.,* p. 193.
[9] F. Nicolini, *Gli ultimi anni della signora d'Epinay,* pp. 155 and 157. Quoted in CORR., XIV, pp. 140 and 141.

looked forward hopefully to Turgot's fall and his replacement by Sartine. When Turgot was finally dismissed she communicated the joyful news to her Neapolitan correspondent:

> Qu'aurez-vous dit du départ de monsieur Turgot et Malesherbes? Cela m'a mis du baume dans l'âme, quant au premier." [10]

On the other side Turgot's defence was led by that veteran apologist of physiocratic doctrine, Morellet, who in November of the previous year had at last succeeded in publishing his *Réfutation des Dialogues sur le commerce des Bleds*, written at the height of the first debate five years earlier. It says little for the *philosophes*, who constantly put themselves forward as the champions of progress and reform, that they were so lacking in vision and generosity as to get involved in a polemical dogfight over secondary issues, when the very man who was in a position to implement their principles was starting to fight for his political life. Still less credit is reflected on those *philosophes* who took a positive delight in following if not actually contributing to his declining fortunes.

Necker's book was published on 20th April against a background of rioting provoked by the scarcity of grain and which culminated in an attack on the Paris bakeries. Despite Necker's explanations to the contrary there can be little doubt that the coincidence was deliberate, his intention being to further aggravate a situation which was already causing the administration considerable difficulties. [11] Given the circumstances Diderot's own position was particularly delicate. He was closely associated with Necker through his wife and her *salon*, and some appreciative comment on Necker's thesis would naturally be expected from him, as Galliani's old apologist, from that quarter. At the same time Diderot did not wish to involve himself in the current controversy. Unlike his colleagues he sensed that now was the time for cohesion and not dissension in the philosophic ranks; and indeed throughout the winter when the pamphlet war had been developing he had abstained from all comment. Although Diderot did feel himself obliged to send Necker an appreciation of his book, caution dictated the timing of the letter and its contents. The letter was written in May, but it was not sent to Necker until the 10th June, when civil order had been more or less re-established in Paris and the provinces. Unlike Necker Diderot had no wish to exacerbate the government's difficulties even further.

The letter deals with the subject from an almost entirely theoretical

---

[10] *Ibid.*, p. 178. Quoted in CORR., XIV, p. 200.
[11] See D. Dakin, *op. cit.*, p. 193.

point of view, and is interspersed with an examination of broader literary
and moral issues which Necker's book raises in Diderot's mind. While
Diderot indicates his general agreement with Necker's argument:

Pour un endroit souligné il est resté des vingt pages de suite intactes et
où on liroit à la marge de mon exemplaire: Je voudrais bien savoir ce qu'ils
diront à cela,[12]

references to Turgot and the crisis are restricted to two allusions, one
humorous: Necker's book has provided him with "huit jours de bonheur
continu, et cela à moindre frais qu'il ne m'en coûté pour deux livres de
pain par jour;" and the other, a discreet reminder to Necker that it was
thanks to Turgot's liberalism that he had been able to publish his book at
all.[13] Diderot's response then is courteous but not over-enthusiastic. He
was basically in agreement with Necker's arguments but he was not prepared to appear in public as one of Turgot's detractors. In a letter to
Grimm written six months after Turgot's fall he gave his reasons for not
taking sides.

Plus je vais, plus j'éprouve que le mieux est de marcher droit; à ces conditions, on ne se brouille point avec M. Necker, pour demeurer bien avec
M. Turgot; et l'on ne se tourmente pas ensuite, pour se remettre bien avec
le Turgot ou avec le Neckre lorsque l'un a cessé d'être quelque chose et que
l'autre est tout. L'honnêteté est la meilleure des politiques.[14]

Yet despite Diderot's general endorsement of Necker's views one can
detect that he is less than happy with the latter's manner of publishing his
book and his reasons for doing so. This emerges from a passage in the
letter in which flattery and criticism of his correspondent are mingled in
such a manner that Necker would have noticed Diderot's reservations
but would not have had grounds for taking offence at them, so that the
latter's policy of preserving good relations on both sides of the dispute
is maintained:

Cette cause, remarks Diderot, pouvoit être défendue par de bonnes ou
de mauvaises raisons,

– this is a hint at the ambiguity of Necker's intentions –

Mais, he continues, il étoit difficile de s'en proposer une plus auguste, et
de quelque manière que l'on s'en tirât, on étoit sûr d'en remporter le renom
d'honnête homme et de bon citoyen.[15]

[12] CORR., XIV, p. 147.
[13] Ibid., p. 146.
[14] CORR., XV, p. 17.
[15] CORR., XIV, p. 143.

Without neutralising the effect of his opening sentence Diderot has skilfully disarmed Necker in the second. After praising his correspondent's profundity, eloquence and finesse, Diderot goes on to point out that he has rather more merit in picking out these qualities than Necker might think:

Car avec odorat un peu délicat, on croit s'appercevoir que vous ne faites pas grand cas de la philosophie et des lettres.[16]

A hard-headed man, whose outlook has been fashioned in the narrow spheres of finance, Necker was sceptical about the effective influence of the *philosophes* on the political life of the nation. Diderot rejects the Genevan's shallow pragmatism for a more serious, coherent and farsighted approach to the solution of social problems, more akin to Turgot's own policy:

On dit: Vivre et philosopher ensuite; je dis tout au contraire: Philosopher d'abord et vivre après si l'on peut.[17]

Diderot's final charge against Necker is of playing to the gallery; in aiming his "sublimes leçons de morale" at "la portion opulente, oisive et corrompue de la société" he had cheapened them.[18] Diderot does not seem to have been blind to the fact that Necker's book was less a serious treatise than a weapon of propaganda designed to serve his bid for power by currying favour with the conservatives.

In the last analysis the underlying strictures on Necker's personal attitudes and behaviour more than counter the overt support given to the economic principles which Diderot had first defended in the *Apologie de Galiani*. By refusing to be drawn into the battle against Turgot and by harbouring doubts as to the soundness and integrity of Necker's political views Diderot displayed judgment and insight superior to that of most of his philosophical colleagues.

Apart from a short paper sent through Madame d'Epinay to Galiani in which he expresses his support for the suppression of the corporations,[19] there are no further documents available which record Diderot's impressions of Turgot during the last days of his administration or after his fall. By 1776 the main source for his comment on the contemporary political situation in France, his correspondence, was beginning to dry up. Sophie Volland, his main correspondent, had moved to Paris so that visits had

[16] *Ibid.*
[17] *Ibid.*, p. 144.
[18] *Ibid.*
[19] *Ibid.*, pp. 190-192.

replaced his letters to her. Nevertheless, from the information that we have examined, there can be little doubt that Diderot was deeply disappointed by Turgot's disgrace and that he shared the sentiments expressed by Voltaire in a letter to La Harpe:

Ni eux (Condorcet, d'Alembert) ni moi ne nous consolerons jamais d'avoir vu naître et périr l'âge d'or que M. Turgot nous préparait.[20]

The golden age was finished before it had begun, and the effects of the disappearance of one of the most liberal and forward-looking ministers ever to hold power under the Ancien Régime were soon felt. The achievements of his ministry were quickly undone, and those sections of society which looked backwards reasserted themselves. A little short of a year after Turgot's dismissal Diderot wrote gloomily to Marc-Michel Rey:

L'intolérance augmente de jour en jour. Bientôt on n'y imprimera plus avec privilège que des almanachs et que le *Pater* avec des corrections.
Imaginez qu'on a fait effacer des paragraphes entiers d'une traduction littérale de quelques traités de Plutarque.[21]

The last chance for the renewal of French society through reform had faded. When Maupeou had come to power, sweeping away the *parlements*, the sole protection, it seemed, against naked tyranny, Diderot had turned his gaze away from France towards Russia, where Catherine's intended reforms gave him grounds for believing that all hope was not lost. Now that once more his own country was suffocating under a black pall of reaction he looked abroad again, to North America, for the signs of a new dawn of equity and justice. This time he was to witness a nation being born in the fire of revolution.

II. THE AMERICAN REVOLUTION AND DIDEROT'S DOCTRINE OF REVOLUTION

Diderot's interests in the growing ferment among the colonists in North America was first aroused in 1769 by the publication of a French translation of the *Letters from a Farmer in Pennsylvania to the Inhabitants of the British Colonies* by the Whig pamphleteer, Dickinson. The burden of the *Farmer's Letters* was a call for the modification of the concept of sovereignty in the relations of the metropolis with its colonies. Writing after the passing of the detested Stamp Act and the suspension by the British Government of the legislative powers of the New York Assembly

---

[20] *Voltaire's Correspondence*, XCIV, p. 136.
[21] *Diderot et Catherine II*, p. 514.

for refusing to comply with the requirements of the Quartering Act of 1765, Dickinson argued explicitly that the sovereign body of the empire "need not be supreme everywhere and in all matters in the territory it controlled, but only on some issues and in some ways, and that other, less bodies might exercise absolute and arbitrary powers – sovereign powers in effect – within spheres specifically allotted to them." [22] This cry for liberty, accompanied by a demand for sovereignty, albeit limited, evoked a sympathetic response from Diderot, who was quick to see that Dickinson's arguments had an application much broader than the quarrel between Britain and her colonies. In a review of the pamphlet [23] he wrote:

Je ne connais aucun ouvrage plus propre à instruire les peuples de leurs droits inaliénables, et à leur inspirer un amour violent de la liberté. Parce que M. Dickinson parlait à des Americains, ils (the French censors) n'ont pas conçu que ses discours s'adressaient à tous les hommes.[24]

Although the underlying democratic trend of Diderot's thought at that time had yet to emerge in the abandonment of absolutism and the formulation of a doctrine of popular sovereignty, the central theme of the *Farmer's Letters* appealed to him strongly. Dickinson's call for the replacement of the arbitrary despotism exercised by Britain over her colonies by a shared sovereignty had wider echoes for Diderot. It corresponded closely to his desire to see an end to a similar despotism in France exercised by the King and his government over his subjects, and a new relationship emerge in which the sovereign's rule was guided by the enlightened will of the nation.

Diderot's reaction to the *Farmer's Letters* was essentially intuitive. His political thought had not yet evolved sufficiently to the point where he could fully appreciate the profound constitutional changes between rulers and ruled that the pamphlet envisaged. But he was aware that the work was sowing seeds which over the years would spring up and flourish:

On nous permet la lecture de ces choses-là, et l'on est étonné de nous trouver, au bout d'une dizaine d'années, d'autres hommes. Est-ce qu'on ne sent pas avec quelle facilité des âmes un peu généreuses doivent boire ces principes et s'en enivrer? [25]

The domestic political scene and the journey to Russia were to divert

---

[22] Bernard Bailyn ed. *Pamphlets of the American Revolution. 1750-1776*, I, pp. 128-129.
[23] It is likely that it was intended for the *Correspondance littéraire* but not published.
[24] A.T., IV, p. 88.
[25] *Ibid.*, p. 89.

Diderot's attention from the train of events in North America for a number of years, but the piece on the *Farmer's Letters* does provide an early indication of the influence the struggle of the North American colonies was to exercise on the final shaping of Diderot's political thought. It also contains a surprisingly accurate forecast of the final outcome of that struggle:

C'est une grande querelle que celle de l'Angleterre avec ses colonies. Savez-vous, mon ami, par où la nature veut qu'elle finisse? Par une rupture.[26]

The prediction is all the more remarkable since among the great majority of colonists themselves, including the Whig agitators, the very idea of independence was vehemently rejected until as late as 1775, a discordant note only creeping in in the second half of that year.[27] The very earliest reference to independence came from the pens of Whig extremist journalists in the *Boston Gazette* in 1772.[28] Diderot, of course, had an advantage over the colonists in that he could remain a dispassionate observer of the situation. His judgment unaffected by direct involvement in the conflict, he could see that demographic and economic forces [29] would inevitably lead to a break. A future revolution was in the nature of things. When that revolution came, at a time when Diderot's experience had finally convinced him that despotism was impervious to reform, it provided him with the courage and resolution to draw the necessary conclusions. The only way out of the *impasse*, the only way to prevent his political thought from growing sterile through repeated frustration, was to adopt the most uncompromising radicalism. Blindly and unwillingly the Americans had stumbled on the only effective answer to the arrogant usurpation of power. Diderot was to profit from their discovery and lay the foundations for a similar solution in France.

1776 proved to be the turning point. Turgot was ousted in May, the news of the Declaration of Independence reached Paris in August. These two events brought about a decisive and final reorientation of Diderot's political thought. In the summer of that year "sa politique (déboucha) sur une postulation révolutionnaire." [30]

Turgot's fall brought no written comment from Diderot. There was no point in wasting effort upon a lost cause and exposing oneself to attack

[26] *Ibid.*, p. 86.
[27] Arthur M. Schlesinger, *Prelude to independence*, p. 248, and Moses Coit Tyler, *The Literary History of the American Revolution* 1763-1783, I, pp. 458 *et seq.*
[28] Arthur M. Schlesinger, *op. cit.*, pp. 144-146.
[29] A.T., IV, p. 86.
[30] Jean Fabre, *Lumières et romantisme*, p. 8.

from the triumphant reactionaries in the process. But more than Turgot himself it was the idea of political progress through reform which had lost credit in Diderot's eyes. With the arrival of the news of the Declaration of Independence his prolonged association with the politics and the genuine and false politicians of reform came to an abrupt end. The modern world's first charter of revolution immediately captured Diderot's imagination and his allegiance. Once more he showed his amazing powers of recovery; as a political thinker his career had been marked by a succession of rising hopes followed by deep deceptions, yet now as he neared the end of his life, he espoused the cause of the American Revolution and through it developed a general doctrine of revolution with an unparalleled ardour. The idea of revolution as a means to social and political rejuvenation had been fleetingly entertained by Diderot before the advent of Turgot, but now it was not just an academic hypothesis or a vague hope for the distant future; now, across the Atlantic, it was becoming an objective historical reality.

Unable through age and infirmity to make any direct contribution to the struggle of the American colonists, Diderot appointed himself their apologist, spokesman and counsellor at home. Within a short time of the news of the Declaration of Independence breaking on Paris he had started to write. But because of the subversive nature of his subject he had to wait until 1780, when the third edition of Raynal's *Histoire des deux Indes* was published, to set his thoughts before the public under the safe cover of anonymity which the *Histoire* provided. However, his impatience got a little the better of him, and he gave the public a foretaste of his views by inserting the well-known *Apostrophe aux Insurgents d'Amérique* in the first edition of the *Essai sur les règnes de Claude et de Néron*, published under the title of *Vie de Sénèque*, which appeared in December 1778. Apart from this short passage all of Diderot's writing on the American Revolution is to be found at the end of Book XVIII of the *Histoire*.[31] The text was subsequently recopied from the *Histoire* in a continuous form without division into chapters in a section of the Mélanges XXXVIII of the *Fonds Vandeul*, entitled *Révolution de l'Amérique angloise*.[32]

Written shortly after the events which inspired it the *Révolution de l'Amérique angloise* bears little resemblance to what today goes by the name of contemporary history. Instead we are presented with an inspired

---

[31] Chapters XLII to XLIV, and the penultimate paragraph and the first sentence of the last paragraph of Chapter LII.

[32] MEL., pp. 183-236, HIST., IX, pp. 234-283 and pp. 359-360. For subsequent passages from this section of the *Mélanges* only page references to the *Histoire des deux Indes* are given.

confusion of political philosophy, fictitious speeches, ranging from the tearfully liberal to the brutally despotic, which reflect different British attitudes to the colonial war, an embellished summary of Thomas Paine's *Common Sense*, a fairly literal translation of the main clauses of the Declaration of Independence, a critical analysis of the new federal constitution of the United States, and lastly an address to the people of North America, which resembles the second half of the *Apostrophe aux Insurgents d'Amérique*. The confusion of the *Révolution de l'Amérique angloise* is, however, more apparent than real: despite the heterogenous elements of which it is composed the section does follow a more or less chronological order; but more important than this is the revolutionary theory with which Diderot prefaces his account, and which sets the tone and provides the perspective for the rest of the section. The passage in which Diderot elaborates his theory merits a close examination, for besides containing the most unqualified and intellectually sound justification of revolution since Meslier, it constitutes the final and most radical step in the evolution of Diderot's political thought.

As Yves Benot has remarked, "l'appel aux armes n'est pas lancé par goût de la violence, mais au terme d'une analyse lucide." [33] This analysis follows a familiar pattern. It takes the form of a philosophical investigation into the origins of society, which leads to the elaboration of a doctrine of revolution. There was, of course, nothing new in this method of philosophical history. It had been firmly established by the theoreticians of natural law, and had been used by Hobbes and Locke to formulate their very differing political doctrines. More recently Diderot himself, strongly influenced by Grotius and Pufendorf, had used the by now well-established method in his *Apologie de l'abbé de Prades* and a number of *Encyclopédie* articles, including *Autorité politique*, as had Rousseau in his *Discours sur l'inégalité*. These works, which have been examined in relation to one another in considerable detail by Jacques Proust,[34] provide us with a valuable point of comparison by which to assess the final stage of Diderot's political evolution in the prefatory passage of the *Révolution de l'Amérique angloise*, that we have referred to.

Diderot's description of the origins of society in the *Apologie* and the *Encyclopédie* articles can be summarised as follows. Men were driven together by a natural impulse to form loose groupings or flocks (*troupeaux*). The members of these flocks lived peacefully together, helping one another, and living off the fruits of the earth, with no conventions to bind

---

[33] T.P., p. 50.
[34] *Op. cit.*, pp. 357-384.

them.[35] Over this scene of primitive pastoral bliss, which Diderot dwelt on only very briefly, a spirit of conquest blew which transformed the flock into a horde.[36] The peaceful state of the flock could not be maintained because men are naturally unequal in the talents, physical strength and intelligence they possess. In such a time of ignorance when passions were unrestrained and no conventions existed, it was inevitable that the strong would oppress the weak, and the weak band together to venge themselves against the strong.[37] In order to preserve the human race from extinction a social compact was devised whose aim was to replace the violent anarchy of the horde by conventions ordering and regulating relationships. The compact was in Diderot's eyes eminently reasonable because it established a political equality over men who are naturally unequal, endowing both weak and strong with the same rights and duties. This political equality, as Diderot saw it, was achieved in practice by the fact that all the members of society had submitted themselves entirely to a sovereign.[38]

We have described elsewhere [39] the political doctrine that Diderot developed from this philosophical history. To recapitulate briefly, while in theory he upheld the view that political authority belonged to the nation and was only deposited with the ruler, whose powers were limited by the laws of nature and the fundamental laws of the State,[40] in fact, since he nowhere defined the latter laws, the authority of the ruler was in no way limited throughout the duration of his reign. In other words Diderot, like Rousseau, rejected the concept of shared sovereignty which was the logical outcome of his thought, but, quite the contrary to Jean-Jacques, opted in practice for an absolutism operated by a ruler who represented the general will of the nation.

In the prefatory passage [41] of the *Révolution de l'Amérique angloise* some aspects of Diderot's original philosophical history of the origins of society remain, but some quite radical modifications have taken place. The history is also accompanied by an examination of contemporary society, which was absent from his earlier account. As a consequence the conclusions which he reaches are very different from those summarised above.

In this new philosophical history man again appears on the world's

---

[35] *Apologie de l'abbé de Prades, Agriculture.*
[36] *Agriculture.*
[37] *Apologie de l'abbé de Prades.*
[38] *Autorité politique, Citoyen.*
[39] See Introduction.
[40] *Autorité politique.*
[41] The passage takes the form of an address by the American colonists to their British oppressors, but the ideas expounded evidently belong to Diderot.

stage "Seul et abandonné à lui-même," and, as before, he eventually joins up with his fellows "pour mettre en commun leur force et leur intelligence." [42] But whereas previously the causes of this association were ascribed by Diderot to man's natural sociability, he now puts them down to a conscious realisation by natural man in the face of a hostile environment, that his own preservation depended upon throwing in his lot with other men.[43] By abandoning the Aristotelian theory of natural sociability Diderot has moved appreciably closer to Rousseau's position in the second *Discours*. For in the *Discours* Rousseau had argued that sociability could not exist in the state of nature as it was based upon needs which do not belong to this state, and which require language, the vehicle of reason and itself the product of society to formulate and articulate them.[44] It is false, claimed Rousseau, to suppose that man was reasonable, and therefore sociable from all eternity. It is not man's rationality which explains his sociability but the reverse; his social evolution had allowed him to conquer the power of reason.[45] Diderot, having abandoned natural sociability, is compelled by the same logic which rules Rousseau's argument equally to reject reason in natural man,[46] and he is forced to conclude that in a time "antérieur à toute législation," that is before the foundation of civil society, man was "aussi passionné, aussi déraisonnable que la brute." [47]

With the rejection of the theories of natural sociability and the rationality of natural man Diderot's concept of the social compact which founded civil society and government alters radically. No longer does he see it as a rational and necessary stage in the evolution of the human race, an inevitable development dictated by the natural sociability inherent in man. He has carried out what appears to be a complete *volte-face* in his views on the social compact. It is implicit in his thinking that the compact is no longer consecrated by reason and hallowed by nature, but something purely artificial, evolved at a particular time to meet a particular set of circumstances. The similarity of Diderot's and Rousseau's views is again apparent. Can Diderot therefore be accused of abandoning a materialistic interpretation of society for an idealist one? It is a question that we shall consider later. First we must examine the consequences of his rejection of a natural social compact for one based on convention.

By demolishing the idea of a natural social compact Diderot has re-

---

[42] HIST., IX, p. 235.
[43] *Ibid.*
[44] *Discours sur l'inégalité*, pp. 90-92.
[45] *Ibid.*, p. 93.
[46] *Ibid.*, p. 98.
[47] HIST., IX, p. 237.

moved the last ideological barrier preventing him from formulating a doctrine of revolution. As the compact is a pure artifice created by men to satisfy a given set of needs, it follows that whenever these needs change it can also be changed. More particularly it is the compact as manifested in the form of government which rules a society, that is open to alteration by that society. There are, then, no grounds for arguing that an existing society must be bound to a form of government which was chosen by its forefathers:

Mais ces formes de gouvernement, du choix et du choix libre des premiers aïeux, quelque sanction qu'elles puissent avoir reçue, ou du serment, ou du concert unanime, ou de leur permanence, sont-elles obligatoires pour leurs descendans? Il n'en est rien.[48]

This view is reinforced by Diderot's definition of the nature and function of government which follows on from his analysis of the origins of society:

La société est née des besoins des hommes, le gouvernement est né de leurs vices. La société tend toujours au bien; le gouvernement doit toujours tendre à réprimer le mal. La société est la première, elle est dans son origine indépendante et libre; le gouvernement a été institué pour elle et n'est que son instrument. C'est à l'une à commander, c'est à l'autre à la servir.[49]

In its origins and purpose government is necessarily subordinate to society and can never legitimately assume the upper role. But the history of civilised society shows that the function of government invariably becomes corrupted; government, instead of serving society by maintaining the artificial equality for the establishment of which society was founded, constantly seeks to dominate and oppress the governed. The sword of justice, ideal in itself, when it is held by a real person, as indeed it must be if it is to operate, is all too frequently misused. As a result all the pages of history "sont teintes de sang, les unes du sang des oppresseurs, les autres du sang des opprimés." [50] Whatever form of government may have been instituted in the beginning, "dans une même société, il n'y a aucune condition qui ne dévore et qui ne soit dévorée." [51] As explanations of the historical evolution of society and of the relationship of government to society this account contains some glaring weaknesses. Unlike Rousseau, Diderot fails to recognise that social differences brought about by the development of

---

[48] *Ibid.*, pp. 238-239.
[49] *Ibid.*, p. 236.
[50] *Ibid.*, p. 238.
[51] *Ibid.*

agriculture and metallurgy were present at the birth of civil society itself, and that legislation far from setting out to establish an artificial equality among all its members, was ever thereafter consciously directed through the arm of government toward protecting and furthering the advantage of the economically privileged.[52] Notwithstanding these criticisms the effect of Diderot's three part analysis is to completely undermine what may broadly be called the legitimist position, not only as regards North America, but anywhere a ruler usurps the rightful authority of his subjects, not least in France.

So far we have broadly emphasised the closeness of Diderot's views to the doctrine which Rousseau had preached much earlier in the second *Discours*. But Diderot had not only caught up with his erstwhile friend, he had overtaken him. For whereas Jean-Jacques constantly refused to spell out the revolutionary implications of his political philosophy, shrinking back from the very thought of revolution, Diderot had no such qualms. On the contrary, having begun his analysis, he was determined to take it to its logical conclusion:

> Je vais (...) suivre mon objet, sans en redouter les suites.[53]

And so he goes on to state in bold terms the conclusion towards which he has been moving:

> Si les peuples sont heureux sous la forme de leur gouvernement, ils le garderont. S'ils sont malheureux, ce ne seront ni vos opinions, ni les miennes; ce sera l'impossibilité de souffrir davantage et plus long-tems qui les déterminera à la changer, mouvement salutaire que l'oppresseur appellera révolte, bien qu'il ne soit que l'exercice légitime d'un droit inaliénable et naturel de l'homme qu'on opprime, et même l'homme qu'on n'opprime pas.[54]

Since the social compact is no more than a convention the individual at all times retains the right with his compatriots to alter the government under which they live whenever it fails to serve the purpose for which it was intended, namely the happiness of the people. In other words the people by rebelling against their oppressors are re-establishing their sovereignty and with it the freedom which, as we have seen [55] is the absolute prerequisite of their happiness.

In this key passage a further important feature of Diderot's revolu-

---

[52] For a fuller critique of Diderot's theory see Y. Benot, *Diderot, de l'athéisme à l'anticolonialisme*, pp. 236-237 and p. 243.
[53] HIST., IX, p. 239.
[54] *Ibid.*
[55] Part I, Chap. III.

tionary doctrine emerges. A revolutionary conflict, it is clear, arises spontaneously and inevitably; it cannot be artificially stimulated. It is, in Diderot's view, a stage in the ineluctable cycle of birth, growth, decline, dissolution and regeneration which affects all living organisms, societies being no exception to this all-encompassing law of nature.[56] Within this cycle the advent of tyranny is a sign that a society has reached senility, revolution is the means by which it is dissolved and regenerated. Elsewhere in the third edition of the *Histoire des deux Indes* Diderot underlines this point with the violent image he had used some time before in the *Réfutation d'Helvétius*:

Une nation ne se régénère que dans un bain de sang. C'est l'image du vieil Æson, à qui Médée ne rendit la jeunesse qu'en le dépeçant et en le faisant bouillir.[57]

But if revolution is the result of an historical necessity what role can the *philosophe* play in it? In the same passage Diderot expresses his belief that the *philosophe* living in a senile society is condemned to impotence in his attempts to reinvigorate it:

C'est un architecte qui se propose de bâtir sur une aire couverte de ruines. C'est un médecin qui tente la guérison d'un cadavre gangrené. C'est un sage qui prêche la réforme à des endurcis. Il n'a que de la haine et des persécutions à obtenir de la génération future; il produira peu de fruit avec beaucoup de peine pendant sa vie, et n'obtiendra que de stériles regrets après sa mort. Une nation ne se régénère que dans un bain de sang ... Quand elle est déchirée, il n'appartient pas à un homme de la relever.[58]

Even when a nation has entered the revolutionary phase itself, the fulfilment of the revolution is independent of the *philosophe*. But this does not mean that Diderot considers the *philosophe*, and by inference himself, superfluous to the revolutionary process. It is simply that he is at pains to stress the autonomy and hence the natural origin of that process; fearful too perhaps that by placing too great an emphasis on the role of the *philosophe* he might prepare the ground for the usurpation of the revolution itself by an individual or a small group. The *philosophe* does have a part to play, and Diderot had already outlined it in the *Mémoires*:

Il éclaire les hommes sur leurs droits inaliénables ... Il dit aux peuples qu'ils sont les plus forts ... Il prépare aux révolutions qui surviennent toujours à l'extrémité du malheur des suites qui compensent le sang répandu.[59]

[56] Viz. P.D., pp. 75-78, HIST., X, pp. 21-23.
[57] P.D., p. 72. HIST., VI, p. 22. This image first appeared in a letter to Wilkes dated 14th November 1771, CORR., XI, p. 223.
[58] *Ibid.*
[59] MEM., p. 235.

His function is to articulate and consolidate the revolutionary drive of the
people by reminding them of their rights and laying the foundations for
the subsequent reconstruction of society. It could also be the *philosophe's*
task to call the people to arms, thus setting the revolution in motion, but
Diderot remains discreetly ambivalent on this point as on others, preferring not to minimise the initiative of the people whose reaction against
tyranny is as inevitable as it will be violent.

Il faut que tôt ou tard la justice soit faite. S'il en arrivait autrement je
m'adresserais à la Populace: "Peuple, dont les rugissements ont tant de fois
fait trembler vos maîtres, qu'attendez-vous? Pour quel moment réservez-vous
vos flambeaux, et les pierres qui pavent vos rues? arrachez-les... Mais les
Citoyens honnêtes, s'il en reste quelques-uns, s'élèveront en fin.[60]

There are times when the dilatoriness of the people in rising against their
oppressors wrenches from him an anguished cry of despair:

Peuples lâches! peuples stupides! puisque la continuité de l'oppression ne
vous rend aucune énergie; puisque vous vous en tenez à d'inutiles gémisse-
mens lorsque vous pourriez rugir; puisque vous êtes par millions et que vous
souffrez qu'une douzaine d'enfants, armés de petits bâtons, vous mènent à
leur gré; obéissez. Marchez sans nous importuner de vos plaintes; et sachez
du moins être malheureux, si vous ne savez pas être libres.[61]

But as Yves Benot has noted,[62] this and other passages in a similarly
pessimistic vein which recur frequently in the 1781 edition of the *Histoire*
serve to guard against any tendency to indulge in naive illusions. The
people may be exasperating in their unwillingness to move to action, in
their continuing readiness to submit to oppression, nonetheless without
them there can be no radical change. The *philosophe* must recognise the
fact, and pursue his task of enlightening them as to their true destiny, free
from illusion and without faltering. He can propose, it is for the people
alone to dispose.

But in the last analysis it is not what Diderot wrote about the role of the
philosophe in preparing the revolution which is important, but the way
in which he himself enacted it. As director of the *Encyclopédie* he had
transformed what at the outset had been a minor commercial venture, the

---

[60] P.D., p. 329, HIST., II, pp. 253-254.
[61] HIST., VI. p. 414. We have been unable to find this passage in any of the manuscript conflations of Diderot's contributions to the *Histoire des deux Indes*.
[62] *Op. cit.*, pp. 219-220. See also p. 256. We do not, however, share Benot's view
that Diderot rejects a belief in the natural progress of humanity, replacing it by a tragic
view of history. Revolution is for him part of that process whereby society, in keeping
with the natural order to which it belongs, constantly renews itself.

translation of Chambers' *Cyclopedia*, into a vast intellectual, scientific and technological revolution, which swept throughout France and parts of Europe. As an increasingly important contributor to Raynal's *Histoire des deux Indes* he transformed it in the course of its three editions from a fairly run-of-the-mill attack on the colonizing endeavours of the European powers into a barely covert revolutionary manifesto, couched in a powerful oratorical style which contrasts sharply with the staid reasonableness of Raynal's and Pechméja's prose. By the final edition the colonies had become something of a pretext; any Frenchman reading the *Histoire* in the tense political atmosphere of the 1780's could not fail to realise that he was being called upon to recognise the fact that a radical turning-point had been reached in the destinies of France and Europe, and that this active participation was required to usher in a new order. As Benot has written, "Du fait que Diderot a remanié, complété, enrichi la troisième et dernière édition, sa contribution revêt une signification capitale, puisque c'est lui qui a définitivement orienté dans un sens révolutionnaire l'oeuvre de Raynal, qui doit au Philosophe d'avoir été revêtu du titre usurpé de 'Père de la Révolution'." [63] If Rousseau was the spiritual father of the French Revolution, Diderot truly called it into being.

Before finally considering in what terms Diderot envisaged a post-revolutionary society based upon a doctrine of popular sovereignty, we must first try to discover whether, in setting up a revolutionary doctrine, he had been forced to abandon his materialist theory of the origin and nature of society for an idealist one.[64] From the standpoint of contemporary historical materialism even the most advanced thinkers of the eighteenth century were inevitably prisoners of the conceptual limitations of their age. J.-L. Lecercle has commented that "Les philosophes du XVIIIe siècle, dont les plus avancés ont été matérialistes dans leur conception de la nature, s'en sont tenus à l'idéalisme dans leurs vues sur l'histoire et la société." [65] Seen in this light it was inevitable that Diderot should advance an idealist interpretation of the origins of society formulated in terms of philosophical history and the related theory of contract. However, at first he had tried to bend this idealist framework to the service of his materialism by the introduction of a theory of natural sociability on which his conception of the origins of society rested, and which itself was inherently materialist. In so far as it was possible then,

[63] "Diderot, Pechmeja, Raynal et l'Anticolonialisme," p. 138.
[64] This philosophical problem is so closely bound up with Diderot's revolutionary theory that we must perforce examine it here rather than in the first part of this study where it more naturally belongs.
[65] Introduction to *Du Contrat Social*, p. 35.

given the conceptual tools at his disposal, Diderot's theory of society, as it was set out in the *Apologie de l'abbé de Prades* and the *Encyclopédie* articles was essentially materialist. But once the theory of natural sociability has been removed, as is the case in the prefatory passage of *Révolution de l'Amérique angloise*, can it be argued that Diderot's view of society and history remains in any sense based upon the philosophy of materialism, which continues unblemished in other compartments of his thought? The question is extremely problematical, and the solution to it is rendered even more difficult by the fact that in a passage which also appears for the first time in the third edition of the *Histoire des deux Indes* Diderot unambiguously reiterates his old view on natural sociability:

On fait la satire des premiers fondateurs des nations, par la supposition d'un état sauvage, idéal et chimérique. Jamais les hommes ne furent isolés, comme on les montre ici. Ils portèrent en eux un germe de sociabilité, qui tendait sans cesse à les développer.[66]

There is no getting away from the fact that Diderot has contradicted himself. But why? The conclusion which seems to make sense is that, while he was aware of the imperative need for a revolutionary doctrine, he found himself unable to elaborate one that was consistent with his materialism. So rather than abandon the task, he preferred to poach in the idealist reserve for the necessary theoretical material. This is understandable when it is remembered that materialism has only been able to lay claim to a consistent doctrine of revolution since annexing the Hegelian dialectic of history. If there is a real link between Diderot's revolutionary doctrine and his materialism it is not to be found in his understanding of the origin and development of society but in his concept of the individual.[67] By his very nature the individual is pledged to seek his happiness through the simultaneous fulfilment of his own potentialities and his social duties. Such a fulfilment can only be achieved in a society whose freedom is guaranteed by each individual as citizen. Wherever this freedom is denied, and reform is ineffective, revolution is the only way open for men to regain their usurped rights.

III. SOCIETY AFTER THE REVOLUTION

Once the authority of the people had been re-established a new social order would arise out of the ruins of the old. That Diderot felt confident enough to lay down the ground-rules for the new society in his contribu-

[66] P.D., p. 54, HIST., X, pp. 17-18.
[67] See Part I, Chap. III.

tion to the final edition of the *Histoire des deux Indes* was in large part due to his diligent efforts since the *Apologie de Galiani* to acquaint himself in depth with the complex administrative, social, and economic problems necessarily associated with the running of a complex and multifaceted society. The time spent in Holland and Russia had given him ample opportunity to study these problems in detail; and in the *Voyage de Hollande* and the *Mémoires pour Catherine II* we have seen how he tried to extract from his observations and experiences a coherent policy on a number of major issues such as constitutional government, citizenship and property. Many of the ideas expressed in these two works are taken up again in the third edition of the *Histoire*, but with a new urgency and in many cases woven into a searching criticism of the existing situation in France.

The other main influence affecting the final formulation of Diderot's views on the new society was, of course, the American Revolution; and it was particularly on the issue of representation that events in North America had most effect on his thinking. He had returned from Holland convinced of the value, not only of representative government, but of the particular type practised in the United Provinces where the representative was simply a delegate of the electors and had few discretionary powers of his own. Diderot had been sufficiently impressed by this form of representation, which maintained the greatest degree of popular sovereignty compatible with practical considerations, to suggest to Catherine II its adoption in a suitably modified form in the Russian Empire.[68] But the experience of the Americans led him to change his mind, and in the *Révolution de l'Amérique angloise* he argues that even in the early days of a new republic it is both impractical and unnecessary to demand that "tous les citoyens soient sans cesse au conseil, à l'armée, dans la place publique, et qu'ils aient les yeux toujours ouverts sur les représentans à qui ils ont confié leur destinée."[69] It is impractical, in the case of the United States at least, because of the vast size of the territory, but more important it is unnecessary because:

Ce n'est jamais dans la naissance d'une constitution et au milieu des grandes fermentations de la liberté, que l'on doit craindre qu'un corps de représentans trahisse, par corruption ou par faiblesse, les intérêts qui leur sont confiés. C'est plutôt dans un pareil corps que l'esprit général et s'exalte et s'enflamme. C'est là que réside, dans sa vigueur, le génie de la nation.[70]

[68] See MEM., *De la commission formée pour la confection des lois.*
[69] HIST., IX, p. 290.
[70] *Ibid.*, p. 291.

But a body of representatives has another even more important justification in Diderot's eyes which makes it vastly superior to any body of mere
delegates. He is no starry-eyed populist, confident in the ability of the
people to keep up their revolutionary fervour against all temptations to
exchange their independence, which can only be maintained through
constant danger and sacrifice, for a return to subjugation and peace. He
knows only too well that the people are short-winded, pusillanimous and
fickle, and that in the long term men of sterner stuff are needed to safeguard the nation's hard-won sovereignty. There lies the task of the body of
representatives, that small groups of men "choisis et faits pour servir de
chefs" in whom "résident ces résolutions constantes et vigoureuses qui mar-
chent d'un pas ferme et assuré vers un grand but, ne se détournent jamais
et combattent avec opiniâtreté les malheurs, la fortune et les hommes." [71]
It is clear that Diderot intends the representatives to be chosen from among
those men whose model reappears constantly throughout his work, from
Saunderson to Bordeu to Seneca, the *sages*.

Representation apart, Diderot's views on the constitution of the new
society lack precision. With regard to France at least he does not seem
to envisage the replacement of the monarchy by a republic. Rather he
sees the monarch becoming a constitutional head of state who uses his
limited powers to maintain peace and harmony in the nation:

Le chef de l'état (...) protégeroit les différens ordres, et en seroit adoré.
Il auroit conçu qu'aucun des membres de la société ne pourroit souffrir sans
quelque dommage pour le corps entier et il s'occuperoit du bonheur de tous. [72]

It is, however, not clear what powers he would retain in order to carry
out this high-sounding but rather loosely defined task.

For the rest Diderot leaves constitutional matters alone and confines
himself to defining the functions of the different orders of citizens who
should form the backbone of the new society, and to setting out reforms
which would have to be implemented if certain existing barriers to justice and material progress, and the good of the nation generally, are to be
removed. Among the population there are a number of groups of citizens whom Diderot esteems highly:

J'ai élevé dans mon coeur un autel à quatre classes de Citoyens: au philosophe qui cherche la vérité qui éclaire les nations, et qui prêche d'exemple
la vertu aux hommes: au magistrat qui sait tenir égale la balance de la justice: au militaire qui défend sa patrie, et au commerçant honnête qui l'en-

[71] *Ibid.*, p. 293.
[72] P.D., p. 65, HIST., IX, p. 2.

richit et qui l'honore. J'oubliais l'agriculteur qui la nourrit et je lui en demande pardon.[73]

The first two categories of citizen, the *philosophe* and the magistrate are more or less interchangeable for Diderot, and we have discussed them elsewhere.[74] As for the soldier he does not have much else to say about him. While Diderot shared the contempt of the other *philosophes* for the aristocrats' pursuit of war as a delectable path to personal glory and honour,[75] he recognised that the citizen state would still need protection from its enemies. But more particularly it was the citizens' property at home and in transit on the seas which would require protection by the arm of the military. Diderot shows some hesitation in the course of a stirring exhortation to the military to protect the goods of citizens:

Apprenez que la gloire de conserver, vaut encore mieux que celle de détruire [76]

but it does little to diminish the impression that he, with most of his like-minded contemporaries, had simply exchanged dynastic and aristocratic militarism for economic militarism. He has equally little to say about the agricultural worker, whom he includes in his list almost as an after-thought, though he is deeply moved by the plight of the poorer peasant whose land is taken from him, who is over-burdened with taxes, and who with his wife, children and animals, is pressed into service for the *corvée* with no return for his labours.[77] No doubt Diderot held that agriculture had powerful enough defenders in the physiocrats, and was not prepared to champion a cause which he believed from an economic point of view was overstressed. The category of citizen which interested Diderot most and to which he devoted most of his attention and reforming zeal is the merchant class, in which he saw the greatest source of wealth and prosperity for the nation.

In his contributions to the first two editions of the *Histoire des deux Indes* Diderot had written at length on the central importance of trade to a free and prosperous society. His insistence on the inseparability of political freedom and a flourishing commerce whose operations are un-inhibited by restrictive legislation echoes the views which Voltaire had

[73] P.D., pp. 216-217, HIST., X, pp. 237-238.
[74] Part I, Chap. III, pp. 85-86.
[75] P.D., p. 175, HIST., X, p. 169.
[76] P.D., p. 205, HIST., IX, p. 331.
[77] MEL., pp. 7-8, HIST., II, pp. 388-389.
[78] P.D., p. 384, HIST., III, p. 233. The passage appears in the first edition of the *Histoire*.

expressed much earlier in his *Lettres philosophiques*. Since human society exists, argues Diderot,[78] to satisfy the common interest and is sustained by the reciprocal interests of its members, an increase in happiness
must result from their intercourse. It is within this context that he sees
trade as the mainstay of society:

> Le commerce est l'exercice de cette précieuse liberté, à laquelle la nature
> a appellé tous les hommes, a attaché leur bonheur et même leurs vertus.
> Disons plus; nous ne les voyons libres que dans le commerce; ils ne le de-
> viennent que par les loix qui favorisent réellement le commerce: et ce qu'il
> y a d'heureux en cela, c'est qu'en même tems qu'il est le produit de la liberté,
> il sert à la maintenir.[79]

In this text Diderot appears as a typical representative of the middle-class
Enlightenment, who saw in trade, with its international exchanges, and
the new knowledge and technical progress which it stimulated, a natural
ally against the despotism of the monarchy and the obscurantism and militant orthodoxy of the Church. But as the seventies progressed Diderot's
enthusiasm for trade was gradually qualified. An increase of wealth in
itself, he came to realise, did not necessarily make for happiness:

> En même tems que le commerce favorise la population par l'industrie de
> mer et de terre, par tous les objets et les travaux de la navigation, par tous
> les arts de culture et de fabrique; il diminue cette même population par tous
> les vices qu'amène de luxe. Quand les richesses ont pris un ascendant géné-
> ral sur les âmes, alors les opinions et les moeurs s'altèrent par le mélange des
> conditions.[80]

These remarks first appeared in the 1774 edition of the *Histoire* at the
beginning of a long analysis of the corrupting effect of luxury and riches
on a nation. Diderot tried to solve the problem by distinguishing between *mauvais luxe*, a sign of the ostentation of the rich and a mask hiding
the wretchedness of the poor who emulate them, and *bon luxe*, which
would develop in a society endowed with, among other things, an effi-
cient and equitable administration and tax system.[81] He puts the matter
succinctly in the *Réfutation d'Helvétius*:

> Si l'on suppose une répartition plus égale de la richesse et une aisance na-
> tionale proportionnée aux différentes conditions, si l'or cesse d'être la repré-
> sentation de toutes les sortes de mérite, alors on verra naître un autre luxe.[82]

[79] *Ibid.*
[80] P.D., pp. 231-232, HIST., X, p. 313. See also previous chapter pp. 186-187 and
192-193.
[81] See T.P., p. 129.
[82] A.T., II, p. 415.

But Benot has remarked very pertinently [83] that the *bon luxe* argument is utopian because it is based on the supposition of a more equal distribution of wealth, and Diderot provides no indication as to how this is to be achieved. And indeed he could not, for as Benot again remarks, "Il ne peut pas suggérer d'intervention extérieure dans ce domaine: ce serait porter atteinte à ses propres principes de liberté." [84] Diderot was unable to transcend the contradiction with which trade presented him: on the one hand it was the great bastion of freedom and civil virtue, on the other it was the source of corruption, which had turned the opulent Dutch, whom he had once so much admired, away from the democratic freedoms which they had earlier adhered to with so much tenacity. In an apostrophe to the Dutch people, published for the first time in the third edition of the *Histoire*, he writes,

Bataves, la destinée de toute nation commerçante est d'être riche, lâche, corrompue et subjuguée. [85]

To the big international merchant who is prepared to see everything perish, his own country and the country with which he trades, fellow citizens, foreigners and associates, as long as he is free to enrich himself, [86] Diderot can only proffer pious exhortations to honour and virtue. [87]

Yet despite these contradictions and hesitations Diderot in the main continued to be an enthusiastic apologist of trade and commerce, and seen in perspective his position is understandable. It was inevitable that his opposition to the *dirigisme* of an intellectually and socially discredited régime should crystallise into support of the rising merchant middle class, which embodied the individualism which was to be the foundation of the new liberal society. And it would be somewhat naive to criticise him for failing to foresee the vices inseparable from free-enterprise capitalism, which only became obvious after the Industrial Revolution. Indeed, as we have seen, Diderot was convinced that the abuses which trade and commerce produced could be almost entirely ascribed to the shortcomings of absolutism. In particular, he believed, not without reason, that existing fiscal practices were responsible for many of these abuses:

Partout le fisc avide et rampant encourage à des injustices particulières par les injustices générales qu'on le voit commettre. Il opprime le commerce par

[83] T.P., p. 181, n. 3.
[84] *Ibid.*, p. 57.
[85] P.D., p. 376, HIST., I, p. 473.
[86] P.D., p. 330, HIST., II, p. 254.
[87] P.D., pp. 213-216, HIST., X, pp. 233-237.
[88] P.D., p. 218, HIST., X, p. 239.

les impôts sans nombre dont il le surcharge; il dégrade les négocians par les soupçons injurieux qu'il ne cesse de jeter sur leur probité. Il rend en quelque sorte la fraude nécessaire par la funeste invention des monopoles.[88]

Diderot evidently intended that fiscal reform should be the means by which a "répartition plus égale de la richesse" should be brought about, and in a section of the *Mélanges* entitled *Sur l'impôt et le crédit public* he prefaces his proposals for reform with an attack on the amassing of great fortunes and a call for a more equal spread of wealth.[89] But when one looks at the reforms proposed one gains the impression that he is in fact not so much concerned with spreading wealth more equally as with minimising the state's intervention in the financial affairs of its citizens. According to Diderot a tax on private income and resources is an act of violence against the privacy of the individual; it is "une vexation individuelle sans utilité commune... un esclavage affligeant pour l'homme, sans profit pour l'état." [90] Purchase tax has a deleterious effect upon agriculture and industry,[91] and if it is levied on goods of prime necessity, it amounts to an attack on the very existence of the individual.[92] Import and export taxes can only harm trade and industry by raising prices and reducing production.[93] In fact the only tax which Diderot is prepared to admit as justifiable is one on land which would be levied equitably on all landowners with no privileged exceptions.[94] No doubt these reforms are laudable when set against the practices of the Ancien Régime, but to assume that a land tax alone could make up for the vast differences of wealth in the population smacks of a certain ingenuousness on the part of Diderot. It is also an indication of how strongly he was still influenced, despite certain disagreements of principle, by the prevailing economic theory of the physiocrats, for he supports his land tax with the following argument:

On ne trouvera jamais de revenu annuel que celui des terres. Il n'y a qu'elles qui restituent chaque année les avances qui leur sont faites, et de plus un bénéfice dont il soit possible de disposer. On commence depuis longtems à soupçonner cette importante vérité. De bons esprits la porteront un jour à la démonstration et le premier Gouvernement qui en fera la base de son administration, s'élèvera nécessairement à un degré de prospérité inconnue à toutes les nations et à tous les siècles.[95]

[89] MEL., p. 109, HIST., X, p. 317.
[90] MEL., p. 114, HIST., X, p. 322.
[91] MEL., p. 115, HIST., X, p. 323.
[92] MEL., p. 115, HIST., X, p. 322.
[93] MEL., pp. 116-117, HIST., X, pp. 323-324.
[94] MEL., pp. 118-119, HIST., X, p. 325.
[95] *Ibid.*

In the final analysis Diderot's attitude towards taxation and fiscal reform must be judged in the light of the contemporary situation. Throughout the Ancien Régime taxation had been one of the prime means by which the monarchy had exercised its despotic control over the nation, the main burden of taxation being born by the underprivileged middle classes and peasantry. It was they who had to finance the huge extravagances of the court and the aristocracy; it was they too who had to make up the frequent deficits of the royal purse. No wonder then, that for Diderot and for so many of his contemporaries taxation was synonymous with despotism, and that it hardly occurred to him that even a democratic state required a fiscal system rather more sophisticated than one based simply on a land tax, if it were to bring about the more equal distribution of wealth that he considered necessary. But if Diderot lacked vision in this respect, by placing fiscal legislation, control and administration in the hands of the representatives of the nation [96] he did at least make provision for a greater flexibility in taxation than existed under the Ancien Régime, where the tax system was hamstrung by a multitude of traditions and time-honoured abuses.

Not surprisingly one area in which Diderot strongly advocates state intervention and control is in ecclesiastical affairs. The Church he sees as the greatest danger to the sovereignty of the nation, a view common to all the *philosophes*, and which since the expulsion of the Jesuits from France was not entirely foreign to the existing régime either. Diderot justifies the right of the state to regulate religious practices and institutions, though not personal religious convictions,[97] on the principle that the State was not made for religion but vice versa, that the general interest is the measure by which all things in the state must be judged, and that it is the people or the sovereign authority acting as a depositary of the people's authority, who are solely authorised to judge the conformity of any institution with the public interest.[98] Stern principles indeed, which are logically in accordance with Diderot's general doctrine of popular sovereignty, but which he nowhere invokes so vigorously nor applies so literally. The State, in Diderot's opinion, must exercise its right of control over every aspect of the Church's doctrinal teaching and activities; over its dogmas "pour s'assurer, si, contraires au sens commun, ils n'exposeraient point la tranquillité à des troubles d'autant plus dangereux que les idées d'un bonheur à venir s'y compliqueront avec le zèle pour la gloire de Dieu et la

---

[96] MEL., p. 127, HIST., X, pp. 334-335.
[97] MEL., p. 102, HIST., X, p. 135.
[98] MEL., p. 98, HIST., X, p. 131.

soumission à des vérités qu'on regardera comme révélées;" over its discipline "pour voir si elle ne choque pas les moeurs régnantes, n'éteint pas l'esprit patriotique, n'affaiblit pas le courage, ne dégoûte point de l'industrie, du mariage et des affaires publiques, ne nuit pas à la population et à la sociabilité, n'inspire pas le fanatisme et l'intolérance . . .," [99] and so it goes on. The catalogue of baleful influences exercised by the Church over the nation, and which it will be the business of the new citizen-state to prevent, has not changed since the *Pensées philosophiques*. The clergy will also be subject to profound reforms. Ecclesiastical courts will be dissolved, since a legal system and tribunal exclusive to one section of the community is injurious to the equality of citizens.[100] All immunities and other privileges enjoyed by the clergy will be abolished.[101] The state must also be able to control the conduct of the clergy, by reserving the right to appoint and dismiss them.[102] Finally Diderot considers that religious vows should be prohibited; the reasons that he gives are revealing:

> Le voeu de chasteté répugne à la nature et nuit à la population; le voeu de pauvreté n'est que d'un inepte ou d'un paresseux; le voeu d'obéissance à quelqu'autre puissance qu'à la dominante et à la loi, est d'un esclave ou d'un rebelle.[103]

As with Rousseau it is on the issue of religion that the shadow of dogmatism, intolerance and illiberalism falls across the thought of a man whose political doctrines were otherwise devoted to its eradication by the bright light of freedom and justice. But can Diderot be blamed for introducing a policy of *étatisme* on religious matters into his reforms? All ideologies, with the exception of anarchism, advocate state control over those areas of community life, which in the eyes of the ruling class pose a potential threat to the authority of the State. Some liberal bourgeois systems have given the impression of not practising any kind of state control, and of ruling by consensus, when in fact the ruling class has exercised its power in a covert way through a social and political phenomenon which has come to be known as the "establishment." Diderot in his proposals for the reform of the relationship of the Church with the State must at least be given credit for avoiding this form of hypocrisy.

We would not wish to end this study of the evolution of Diderot's political thought by giving the impression that he was in the last resort

---

[99] MEL., pp. 98-99, HIST., X, pp. 131-132.
[100] MEL., pp. 99-100, HIST., X, p. 133.
[101] MEL., p. 100, HIST., X, p. 133.
[102] MEL., p. 100, HIST., X, p. 134.
[103] MEL., pp. 100-101, HIST., X, p. 134.

only concerned with the destiny of his own country. We hope to have shown that he did not look upon the features and events of the political life of other nations simply as a source for ideas, comparisons and information which would enable him more fully to understand the political character of France and plan for her future. Inevitably, since he was a citizen of that country his political ideas were predominantly influenced by the particular needs and nature of French society. But when he turned his attention to Russia, Holland, the American colonies, or any other country on which his interest happened to alight, it was with the hopes, aspirations and happiness of the people of those countries, with which he was particularly concerned. For Diderot, despite the fact that his political thought was to contribute to the constricting nationalism of the nineteenth century, was a citizen of the world in the great tradition of the eighteenth century. If final proof of his total dedication to not only a country but a world founded upon the principles of individual freedom and human dignity is needed, it can be found in his attitude towards slavery.

This aspect of Diderot's thought has been dealt with very competently by Yves Benot,[104] so we will complete our study of the post-revolutionary society proposed by Diderot by underlining some of Benot's conclusions which emphasise the generosity, breadth and visionary nature which continued to characterise Diderot's political thought right to the end of his life. Almost all of his thoughts on slavery and the slave trade are to be found in Book XI of the third edition of the *Histoire des deux Indes*.[105] Raynal had originally recruited a *philosophe* by the name of Pechméja to pad Book XI, and in the process of fulfilling his commission Pechméja had shifted the point of view from the moderate reformism adopted by Raynal in common with Montesquieu and Voltaire to a radical opposition to slavery. Diderot's additions in the 1780 edition reinforce and extend Pechméja's arguments with an inimitable eloquence, and contribute in the words of Benot, "à faire pencher la balance contre le réformisme de Raynal, du côté de la suppression pure et simple de la traite et de l'esclavage." [106]

Diderot is particularly sarcastic about the hypocrisy and inconsistencies to be found in the attitude of enlightened Europe towards the question of slavery:

[104] "Diderot, Pechmeja, Raynal et l'anticolonialisme" and *Diderot, de l'athéisme à l'anticolonialisme.*
[105] These contributions make up a section of the *Mélanges* entitled *Sur l'esclave des nègres.*
[106] *Op. cit.*

L'Europe retentit depuis un siècle des plus sublimes maximes de la morale. La fraternité de tous les hommes est établie de la manière la plus touchante dans d'innombrables écrits. On s'indigne des cruautés civiles ou religieuses de nos féroces ancêtres, et l'on détourne les regards de ces siècles d'horreurs et de sang ...

But he continues,

Il n'y a que la fatale destinée des malheureux nègres qui ne nous intéresse pas. On les tyrannise, on les mutile, on les brûle, on les poignarde, et nous l'entendons dire froidement et sans émotion. Les tourments d'un peuple à qui nous devons nos délices ne vont jamais jusqu'à notre coeur.[107]

Behind the façade of a concern for morality and justice there lurks a disreputable compound of unacknowledged racialism and economic expediency. Europeans who consider themselves to be enlightened will support any number of reforms of slavery and the slave trade to salve their consciences and satisfy the demands of reason. For Diderot reformism cannot be the answer to tyranny and oppression, for it is the mask which allows self-interest to mascarade as realism, and moral cowardice to pass as moral rectitude.

In order to drive home the unmitigated evil of slavery to his European reader Diderot identifies the political situation of the peoples of the Old World with the condition of the negro slaves of America:

Mais en Europe comme en Amérique les peuples sont esclaves. L'unique avantage que nous ayons sur les nègres, c'est de pouvoir rompre une chaîne pour en prendre une autre.

Il n'est que trop vrai. La plupart des nations sont dans des fers. La multitude est généralement sacrifiée aux passions de quelques oppresseurs privilégiés. On ne connaît guère de région où un homme puisse se flatter d'être le maître de sa personne, de disposer à son gré de son héritage, de jouir paisiblement des fruits de son industrie ...[108]

But he adds that the plight of the Negroes is even worse than that of the Europeans, because they are denied even the name of freemen, and have no hope of ever obtaining it. No hope, that is unless they take it upon themselves to free themselves from their bondage. For Diderot had reached the sombre conclusion, more than borne out by the history of the modern world, that the oppressed, whether they are subjects of European absolutist régimes, inhabitants of colonies, or slaves, can count only upon them-

[107] MEL., pp. 333-334, HIST., VI, pp. 157-158.
[108] MEL., p. 347, HIST., VI, p. 199.

selves to throw off the yoke of tyranny that burdens them. Regarding slavery he is convinced that the day must come when a great leader will arise who will gather his companions around the sacred standard of liberty; and in an exalted tone Diderot goes on to prophecy the wars of liberation which will come about, a prophecy which nearly two hundred years later is only beginning to be fulfilled:

> Plus impétueux que les torrents, ils laisseront partout les traces ineffaçables de leur juste ressentiment. Espagnols, Portugais, Anglais, Français, Hollandais, tous les tyrans deviendront la proie du fer et de la flamme. Les champs Américains s'enivreront avec transport d'un sang qu'ils attendaient depuis si longtemps, et les ossements de tant d'infortunés entassés depuis trois siècles tressailliront de joie.[109]

Diderot was perhaps too optimistic in his belief that "l'ancien monde joindra ses applaudissements au nouveau. Partout on bénira le nom du héros qui aura rétabli les droits de l'espèce humaine, partout on érigera des trophées à sa gloire." [110] The various struggles for freedom throughout the world in modern times have never succeeded in producing anything more than a shadow of the solidarity and mutual encouragement among the nations which he envisaged. Once they have gained their own freedom men, as groups if not as individuals, tend to grow indifferent towards the suffering and oppression of others. Rare are the men like Diderot, whose generous concern for "les droits de l'espèce humaine" is never diminished by the more urgent and pressing demands of their own country, their own family, or their own personal interests. To the service of this ideal Diderot devoted his life's energies. He was not naturally drawn to politics, but when in the later years of his life he came to realise that tyranny, injustice and misery needed a political solution, he addressed himself selflessly to the task, diverting his talents from other areas of endeavour, which would have more certainly assured his reputation for posterity. A cautious and moderate man in public matters, he nevertheless went against his natural inclinations, rejecting reformism as being totally impotent in the face of tyranny, to become the first effective advocate in the modern world of social and political reconstruction through violent revolution.

---

[109] MEL., p. 355, HIST., VI, pp. 207-208.
[110] MEL., p. 355, HIST., VI, pp. 207-208.

CONCLUSION

Although the revolutionaries of 1789 found inspiration in the writings of all the major intellectual figures of the French Enlightenment, only Diderot can be truly counted as their spiritual contemporary. It has been rightly contended that Montesquieu, Voltaire, the *philosophes*, and even Rousseau, while they were opposed to the glaring injustices and abuses of the Ancien Régime, sought to alter its inequitable practices through the processes of reform alone. It is therefore remarkable that Diderot, who in so many ways epitomised the philosophical and moral preoccupations of his generation and shared many of its social and political objectives, should have late in life rejected reform for revolution. His apparently anomalous position within the general context of the political thought of the French Enlightenment cannot be adequately explained by referring to his temperament or social position. Although his early release from family restraint and a natural impetuousness combined to form an attitude of ebullient independence towards convention, at a deeper level he was cautious, at times to the point of timidity. And it is caution which prevailed in his relations with authority. Doubtless the deep sense of social responsibility inherited from his father contributed to his hostility to a régime which he looked upon as being socially irresponsible, and to his frustration over his own political impotence within a system which denied the right of the citizen to have a say in the running of society; but this alone cannot account for his adoption of a revolutionary stance when others in a similar position to himself continued to opt for reform. Socially the middle-aged Diderot was a wealthy, respected, and influential member of the upper bourgeoisie, who had assured his daughter's future and social respectability by marrying her to a member of the minor aristocracy: hardly what one might expect of a potential revolutionary. The key to Diderot's emergence as the only significant theorist of revolution before 1789 lies elsewhere: in his ability to develop from his materialism a

new understanding of the relationship of the individual to society, and
to adapt the latest techniques of empirical investigation to the study of
the structure and mechanisms of society.

From the beginning the focal point of Diderot's preoccupation was
morality, but it was clear to him that as a means of determining the rightness and desirability of human action it required a firm philosophical
foundation, without which it must necessarily degenerate into a list of
arbitrary preferences and desiderata. The initial effect of Diderot's transference of philosophical allegiance from deism to materialism was however to deprive his moral philosophy of its prescriptive dimension and
reduce it to a purely descriptive science of manners. The ambiguities inherent in such a situation which opened the door to nihilism and moral
anarchy could not be ignored. Only by the prolongation of morality into
the realm of political philosophy could these dangerous ambiguities be
countered; the solution proposed was enlightened absolutism, the only
doctrine consonant with the rigid and oversimplified view of human nature which Diderot held at the time. While the weaknesses of such a
utopian doctrine are evident, it nonetheless marks an important development: for the first time a logical continuity between philosophy, morality,
and politics existed. With the subsequent shift in emphasis from the species to the individual, rendered possible by a literary investigation into
the complexities of human behaviour, Diderot's materialism in alliance
with the latest discoveries in medicine and physiology led him to discover through an analysis of the workings of the human consciousness
that human happiness is achieved through a dynamic and positive relationship between the individual and society, in which self-fulfilment and
social duty are identified. This identification by its very nature is only
feasible in an atmosphere of freedom which allows the individual to satisfy the needs of his personality through the fulfilment of his social duties
without direction or hindrance from outside. The elaboration of the doctrine of popular sovereignty, the political theory to which this principle
corresponded, was made possible by the rejection of a rationalist approach
to politics for one which made an objective study of the facts of political
life. Furthermore, an empirical analysis of the nature of absolutism and
the psychology of the absolute ruler convinced Diderot that reform as a
way of transferring sovereignty, usurped by the ruler, back to the people
was destined to fail. Revolution alone could achieve the desired aim of
restoring to men control over their own lives, individually and collec-
tively, without which their happiness must remain an unattainable goal.

In assessing the originality of Diderot's political thought it is tempting to conclude that at the end of his life he had reached a similar position to that held by Rousseau twenty years earlier. There is a certain amount of truth in this view, but it ignores the areas where Diderot's audacity carried his thinking into realms in which Jean-Jacques did not care to venture. It also fails to appreciate that Diderot's political doctrine enjoys the support of a more sturdy philosophical foundation than the one that Rousseau was able to provide for his in many ways more impressive structure. It is these two areas of Diderot's political thought which require final consideration if we are to establish his originality in comparison with the man who has constantly overshadowed all other theorists of his generation.

As we have seen in the course of this study the two men had a very different approach to politics and the elaboration of political theory, which reflected their opposing temperaments. For Rousseau objective political realities formed a catalyst which set off a subjective process of a highly intimate and personal nature, which in due course produced a complex and original response in the form of a new order which was a rejection of the old. In the last resort the Rousseauesque society of the contract makes its appeal not so much by a description of what society could be, based upon an objective analysis of its potentialities, but more by an emotive portrait of what it ought to be, which appeals strongly to a non-rational millenarian sentiment. The channel of communication which Rousseau establishes between himself and his reader is a subjective one. He uses facts and rational analysis, it is true, but they are not determinative in his political thinking, which is in the profoundest sense creative. With Diderot, on the other hand, the political gaze is always outward. This is true of him even before his thought managed to break out of the dead-end utopianism of enlightened absolutism which ensnared him until Galiani came to his rescue by showing him the rich possibilities that an empirical approach to politics could open up. For during this time his attention was directed in the first place towards the leaders of the great political debate which had been going on in Europe for the past hundred years, not in order to subject them to searching and often damaging criticism as does Rousseau, but to learn from them; in the second place towards the enlightened monarchs of the age and of history, such as Catherine II and Henri IV, around whom he believed, mistakenly as it happened, he could construct a doctrine of practical application. Once the bubble of utopian illusions had been burst Diderot's attraction to the facts and realities of political life is indisputable; from his first excursion into the difficult field of economics where his sober realism contrasts favourably with the doctrinaire babble of the physiocrats, to the revolutionary call of the *Histoire des deux Indes* which arises out of a convincing analysis of the politics of oppression, the dominant formative influence on his thought is the real world, where men's fortunes and aspirations, indeed their lives, are dependent on the shifting patterns of power within society.

The difference in the modes of political thought of Diderot and Rousseau accounts for some of the weaknesses of the former, but it also points to his strengths. Since the evolution of Diderot's ideas was inextricably linked to the progress of external events he could not accomplish the sudden and vast conceptual leaps which enabled Rousseau to produce works of such dense and sweeping intuition. While Rousseau's society of the contract may be seen as an answer to many of his private obsessions, frustrations, and longings, Diderot's revolutionary bourgeois democracy was the outcome of a long process of observation, analysis, and testing of the facts of political life. For a man whose respect for the complex and multifaceted nature of objective truth in the field of science and technology led him to devote twenty years of his life to the *Encyclopédie*, it is not surprising that he should devote another twenty years to the search for political truth. Unfortunately such a concern for objective truth, coupled with a refusal to indulge in the sophistries of which he frequently accused Rousseau, resulted in such a fragmentation of his ideas that he has failed to gain anything approaching a reputation as a political theorist, while lesser men of his generation such as Morelly and Mably have managed to earn themselves a place in the history of French political thought. It is this fragmentation of Diderot's political views and their dispersion over so many different writings which place him at a disadvantage when set against not only Rousseau but all the minor thinkers who succeeded in expressing their ideas in a more sustained, cogent and economic manner. Nowhere does he provide us in one work, or even in two or three related works, with a proper exposition of his doctrine; though, had he had the time and inclination towards the end of his life to write a fully-fledged treatise in which his ideas were coherently presented, it is not idle to suppose that he would now enjoy a reputation as the most important political philosopher of his generation after Rousseau.

Diderot's achievement is to have related the principles of political theory which he holds in common with Rousseau to a searching critique of existing institutions. In this sense his political thought provides a valuable complement to Jean-Jacques'. Whereas Rousseau's conceptions of popular sovereignty, the general will and civil liberty are drawn from a highly abstract and general analysis of the origins and evolution of human society, Diderot's are much more closely linked to an examination and refutation of the contemporary power structure with its inherent abuses and injustices. Indeed an important contribution to political history would be made if it could be established to what degree Diderot, particularly through the *Histoire des deux Indes*, opened the way to the application by the men of 1789 of the theories contained in the *Contrat social*. It would be forcing an historical analogy to breaking-point to pretend that he played a pre-revolutionary Lenin to Rousseau's Marx, but it is not too much to assume that in the critical period leading up to the French Revolution and during the Revolution itself, when the political writings of the Enlightenment were consumed more avidly than at any previous time, the *frères ennemis* were posthumously united in providing both theory and directions for its practical application.

Diderot transcends Rousseau, however, in the revolutionary aspect of his politics. Although Jean-Jacques takes up a more radical stance in such key notions as economic equality and democracy, unlike Diderot he could not bring himself to accept that the only way to the realisation of his political beliefs lay through the violent overthrow of the existing order. Where Rousseau failed to face up to the inevitability of violent change, partly because of his naïve belief in the power of education and persuasion to change men's minds, Diderot with an implacable logic born of experience courageously rejected the empty attractions of reform, which had been tried and found wanting, for the dangers of revolution. But it would be wrong to end with a picture of Diderot handing down to the next generation a full and detailed programme for revolution. Apart from a general call for the destruction of the existing order he does not proffer any advice on the strategy and tactics to be adopted. Neither does he furnish more than the broad outlines of the political structure of the new order that the revolution will usher in. These gaps may be counted as major inadequacies within the general framework of his revolutionary doctrine; on the other hand it can be argued that his refusal to tie the revolution to a strict programme, thereby allowing it a reasonable flexibility, was the consequence of his political empiricism which made him keenly aware that success must depend on the ability to adapt to the swiftly changing conditions that were bound to occur. When it is remembered that so many subsequent revolutionary movements have failed to live up to their noble aims because of their unbendingly doctrinaire attitudes, Diderot's prudence is commendable.

It is something of a paradox that Diderot's commitment to revolution should go hand in hand with a relative absence of dogmatism regarding the course it should take, whereas the fearfulness displayed by Rousseau towards the very idea of violent political upheaval does not preclude some brutal assertions of an unambiguously totalitarian nature in the *Contrat social*. Such a contrast reinforces the impression that, philosophical considerations apart, Diderot's politics flow from a generous and humanitarian sentiment, while Rousseau is fired by a puritanically austere and righteous fervour. The one adopts extreme measures which are in contradiction to his natural inclination to moderation, while the other eschews them despite the fact that the radical nature of his thought could be argued to draw him logically in their direction. It is consequently hard to escape the conclusion that on the issue of revolution Diderot may be admired not only for his audacity but for his moral courage, while Rousseau may be criticised for a lack of consistency which verges on hypocrisy.

It must be left to the political historian to determine whether an ideology is more successful in its appeal if it is firmly rooted in a philosophy of the human condition which can make a substantial claim to intellectual plausibility. From a purely analytical point of view one of the main weaknesses of Rousseau's politics, and one of the reasons why they have been open to such varied interpretations, is that they lack any such firm philosophical grounding, stemming as they do from a semi-inchoate idealism. Diderot's final political position, however, is the culmination and highest expression of a materialism which has evolved to provide a thorough and coherent explanation of the needs of the individual and the means by which man may satisfy these needs through a readjustment of the social order. From the description of matter, via the explanation of man's physiological organisation and the theory of consciousness, to the analysis of the interaction of the individual and society, and the justification of the principle of popular sovereignty, each link is connected with the one preceding it, forging an unbroken chain. However, with the doctrine of revolution, which rests on premises which deny some of the basic tenets of his materialist view of the origins of society, the continuity of Diderot's thought appears to be disrupted. But as we have seen [1] the reason for this is the inadequacy of his conceptual apparatus which forced him to make concessions to idealism. The break is one of logic and not of structure as was subsequently demonstrated by Marx's solution to the problem by his adaptation of the Hegelian dialectic of history. This is not to say that Diderot was an historical materialist *avant la lettre*, for

[1] Part II, Chap. IV.

right to the end his politics remained tainted with an ineradicable pessimism: revolution may bring about a new age of justice and equality in which men are free to determine their own lives, but it cannot last; the best men can hope to do is to slow down the inevitable progress towards dissolution which affects all societies. Although Diderot's belief in the cyclical theory of history, which he shared with d'Alembert, had its counterpart in his biological transformism, he never successfully integrated it into an overall materialist view. This pessimistic attitude towards the evolution of society finds an echo in Montesquieu's conviction that all forms of government are destined to inevitable decline and in a similar though more hesitant belief expressed by Rousseau, and it marks the one point at which Diderot's politics remained incongruously within the idealist tradition.

Among the political theorists of the French Enlightenment whose ideas had some influence during the course of the Revolution only Morelly and Mably are unmarked by any trace of pessimism. The extreme nature of their optimism is matched by an equally extreme radicalism which makes Diderot seem singularly cautious in contrast. If, however, we compare the essentials of their political views with those of Diderot we will discover that their greater audacity is more apparent than real.

For many years Morelly's *Code de la nature* was wrongly ascribed to Diderot as it had been erroneously included in one of the first editions of his works. It is difficult to explain why this case of mistaken identity should have persisted so long after overwhelming evidence had been supplied to show that not only was Diderot not the author of the *Code* but that he had never even read it. One possible reason may be that his reputation as a materialist and a militant atheist inclined people to believe that he was capable of advocating a society run on communist lines, which is the book's main conclusion. There are, it is true, certain views that the two men hold in common as a consequence of their materialism. Morelly, like Diderot, believes that man is naturally sociable and that an irresistible force brings individuals together to live in society so that the citizens of a republic exist in a state of mutual dependence. But this is where the similarity ends, for Morelly with a naïve logic of which Diderot is not guilty, sees the solution to man's present miseries in the abolition of property, which is the essential obstacle to the complete socialisation towards which his whole being tends, and the setting up of a perfect communist utopia in which the state provides for and controls the lives of the citizens. How men are ever to reach this happy state Morelly does not say, for nowhere does he envisage sudden change or violent revolution. Both men start out with the same philosophical premises, they both reject the perversion of human nature, the injustice, misery, and oppression of which contemporary society is the cause, but whereas Morelly escapes into a dream world of wish-fulfilment without practical consequence, apart from the Babouvist aberration, Diderot avoids the temptation of a mathematically perfect but completely unrealistic doctrine for the much more arduous task of aligning theory with practice. In one respect only, had he opened the *Code de la nature*, might he have profited from his reading, for Morelly held that the human race was constantly evolving towards a higher degree of perfection, thus imposing upon the historical process a more consistent materialist interpretation than did Diderot.

Although not a materialist, Mably was strongly influenced by the sensualist philosophy of his half-brother, Condillac, and in his logical conclusion that a sensualist morality founded on personal interest must lead to communism he showed greater audacity than Diderot. Unlike Morelly, however, he counterbalanced his utopianism by an analysis of the contemporary situation and the outline of a strategy aimed at the destruction of monarchical despotism, which took the form of a revolutionary doctrine. The similarities with Diderot are evident, particularly the emphasis on the direct experience of politics buttressed by a knowledge of the past, as the means by which men may discover how to regain their lost liberties. Like Diderot he was in advance of his contemporaries who for the most part still argued about society in terms better suited to physics and geometry. His justification of revolution also bears a close similarity to Diderot's, for he argues that sovereign power lies with the people who are free at any time to reinterpret their contract with their rulers, and change the laws which govern their lives. With Diderot too he believes that the role of political writers is to enlighten the nation on its rights and prepare it for the day when the Third Estate will come to power. But although Mably had a revolutionary doctrine he did not know how to apply it, for he failed to realise that the revolutionary ideas require revolutionary forces to put them into effect. Although Diderot was intent on bringing the property-owning middle classes to power, his call to insurrection is made to the nation as a whole, whereas Mably's suspicion of the masses and his fear that the handing of power to the populace would lead to civil war and the aggravation of despotism deprived him of the means of bringing about the revolution. While Diderot was aware of the corrupting effect that commerce and industry could have on a nation's morale, he knew that they were the principal means by which the middle classes could consolidate their political power. In contrast Mably's desire to impose limits on commerce and industry would hinder the development of the very class that was supposed to direct the revolution.

By refusing to succumb to the temptations of the utopianism which vitiates the ideas of Morelly and Mably, Diderot arguably limited his vision of the evolution of society. His politics, within the European context at least, are restricted to the formulation of a bourgeois property-owning ideology. But in contrast to the millenarian he has the considerable merit not only of defining the principles but of describing the means by which social and political change can be initiated. However, beyond the immediate concern for the liberation of the middle classes, Diderot's politics do contain the germ of a doctrine of much broader application. By insisting that integration within a free social structure is essential to the fulfilment of the individual at the deepest moral and psychological level, and that the citizen can count on no-one but himself to establish and maintain this freedom, Diderot is a forerunner of all those who see the source of human unhappiness first and foremost in the political, economic, and physical exploitation of the weak by the strong, and for whom the solution lies in the overthrown of the oppressors by the oppressed.

The oversimple picture of the French Enlightenment as an age of optimism and unqualified belief in the progress of the human race is in the process of being drastically revised. It is now increasingly recognised that the men of the 18th century were less unaware of the huge obstacles which lay in the path of the advancement towards the good life than has generally been considered the case. The evolution of Diderot's politics bears out this conclusion. With maturity he came to realise that an understanding of man's needs and a knowledge of present realities were in themselves insufficient to remove the errors and injustices from which man living in society suffered. A clear definition of aims and a frank realisation of the obstacles which lay in the way of their fulfilment must be reinforced by a knowledge of how to exploit and direct the potential dynamic for change existing within society. "Savoir *comment les choses devraient être*," wrote Diderot, "est d'un homme de sens; *comment elles sont*, d'un homme expérimenté; *comment les changer en mieux*, d'un homme de génie." [2] His politics, we believe, reveal a further notable dimension of his genius.

---

[2] MEM., p. 110.

BIBLIOGRAPHY

A. MANUSCRIPT SOURCES
(Bibliothèque Nationale)

N. a. fr. 13.766. Diderot, *Mélanges*, Vol. XXXVI of the bound volumes of the Fonds Vandeul, containing *Sur la civilisation de la Russie* (Cf. H. Dieckmann, *Inventaire*, pp. 87-90).

N. a. fr. 13.768. Diderot, *Mélanges*. Vol. XXVIII of the bound volumes of the Fonds Vandeul (Cf. H. Dieckmann, *Inventaire*, pp. 92-95).

N. a. fr. 24.939. *Pensées détachées sur divers sujets extraites des manuscrits remis à l'abbé Raynal par Mr. Diderot*, Fond Vandeul (Cf. H. Dieckmann, Inventaire, pp. 136-141 and H. Wolpe, *Raynal et sa machine de guerre*, pp. 210-252).

N. a. fr. 24.940 I and II. Fragments imprimés tirés de l'*Histoire des deux Indes*, Fonds Vandeul (Cf. H. Dieckmann, *Inventaire*, pp. 151-155 and M. Duchet, *"Diderot collaborateur de Raynal: à propos des Fragments imprimés du Fonds Vandeul"*).

B. PRINTED SOURCES

L'Année littéraire, ed. Elie Fréron, Amsterdam and Paris, Lambert (then Panckoucke, Lacombe, Delalain, Le Jay), 1754-1790, 202 vols.

BAUDEAU, Nicolas, *Lettres d'un amateur "à l'abbé G."* Paris, 1770.

Correspondance littéraire, philosophique et critique, par Grimm, Diderot, Raynal, Meister, etc., ed. M. Tourneux, Paris, Garnier 1877-1882, 16 vols.

DESCHAMPS, Dom Léger-Marie, *Le vrai système ou le mot de l'énigme métaphysique et morale*, ed. J. Thomas and F. Venturi, Paris, Droz, 1939.

—. *La voix de la raison contre la raison du temps, et particulièrement contre celle de l'auteur du Système de la Nature, par demandes et réponses*, Brussels, 1770.

DIDEROT, Denis, *Contes*, ed. Herbert Dieckmann, London, University of London Press, 1963.

—. *Correspondance*, ed. G. Roth, vols. 13 to 16 with the collaboration of J. Varloot, Paris, "Les éditions de minuit," 1955-1969, 16 vols.

—. *Diderot et Catherine II*. ed. M. Tourneux, Paris, Calmann-Lévy, 1899.

—. *Les Eleuthéromanes*, avec un commentaire historique, A. Ghio, 1884.

—. *Mémoires pour Catherine II*, ed. P. Vernière, Paris, Garnier, 1966.

—. *Observations sur l'Instruction de sa Majesté Impériale aux députés pour la confection des lois,* ed. P. Ledieu, Paris, 1920. (This edition contains the original text of Catherine's *Instruction*).

—. *Oeuvres complètes,* ed. J. Assézat and M. Tourneux, Paris, Garnier, 1875-1877, 20 vols.

—. *Oeuvres philosophiques,* ed. P. Vernière, Paris, Garnier, 1956.

—. *Oeuvres politiques,* ed. P. Vernière, Paris, Garnier, 1963.

—. *Oeuvres romanesques,* ed. H. Bénac, Paris, Garnier, 1951.

—. *Pages inédites contre un tyran,* ed. F. Venturi, Paris, G.L.M., 1937.

—. *Quatre contes,* ed. J. Proust, Geneva, Droz, 1964.

—. *Rêveries à l'occasion de la révolution de Suède,* published by H. Dieckmann in "Les contributions de Diderot à la "Correspondance littéraire" et à l''Histoire des deux Indes,' " *Revue d'histoire littéraire de la France,* 1951, pp. 417-440.

—. *Salons,* ed. J. Seznec and J. Adhémar, Oxford, Clarendon Press, 1957-67, 4 vols.

—. *Supplément au Voyage de Bougainville,* ed. G. Chinard, Paris, Droz, 1935.

—. *Supplément au Voyage de Bougainville,* ed. H. Dieckmann, Geneva, Droz, 1955.

—. *Sur la liberté de la presse;* ed. J. Proust, Paris, Editions sociales, 1964.

—. *Sur la Russie,* published by H. Dieckmann in "Les contributions de Diderot à la 'Correspondance littéraire' et à l''Histoire des deux Indes,' " *Revue d'histoire littéraire de la France,* 1951, pp. 417-440.

—. *Textes politiques,* ed. Y. Benot, Paris, Editions sociales, 1960.

Encyclopédie, ou Dictionnaire raisonné des sciences, des arts et des métiers, Paris, Briasson, etc., 1751-1780, 32 vols.

La Signora d'Epinay e l'abate Galiani, Lettere inedite (1769-1772), ed. F. Nicolini, Bari, Laterza, 1929.

FREDERICK II, *Examen de l'Essai sur les préjugés* in *Oeuvres,* IX, pp. 131-152, Berlin, Decker, 1848.

GALIANI, Ferdinando, *Correspondance,* ed. L. Perey and G. Maugras, Paris, Calmann-Lévy, 1881, 2 vols.

—. *Dialogues sur les commerce des bleds,* ed. F. Nicolini, Milan, Ricciardi, 1959.

—. *Récréations économiques, ou lettres de l'auteur des représentations aux magistrats, à M. le Chevalier Zanobi,* Paris, 1770.

GROTIUS, Hugo, *Le droit de la guerre et de la paix,* Bâle, E. Thourneisen, 1746, 2 vols.

HEMSTERHUIS, François, *Lettres sur l'homme et ses rapports* avec le commentaire de Diderot, ed. G. May, New Haven, Yale U.P., Paris, P.U.F., 1964.

HOBBES, Thomas, *Leviathan,* ed. A. R. Waller, Cambridge, Cambridge University Press, 1904.

HOLBACH, Paul Thiry baron d', *Essai sur les préjugés,* London, 1770.

—. *Système social, ou principes naturels de la morale et de la politique, avec un examen de l'influence du gouvernement sur les moeurs,* London, 1773.

LA RIVIERE. See MERCIER DE LA RIVIERE.

LOCKE, John, *Two Treatises of government*, London, 1728.

MABLY, Gabriel Bonnot de, *Observations sur l'histoire de France*, Geneva, Compagnie des Libraires, 1765, 2 vols.

—. *Oeuvres complètes*, London, 1789, 13 vols.

MERCIER DE LA RIVIERE, Paul-Pierre, *L'intérêt général de l'Etat ou la liberté du commerce des bleds*, Paris, 1770.

—. *L'ordre naturel et essentiel des sociétés politiques*, London, J. Nourse, 1767.

MONTESQUIEU, Charles-Louis de Secondat, baron de, *Oeuvres complètes*, ed. R. Caillois, Paris, Gallimard, 1949, 2 vols.

MORELLET, André, *Réfutation de l'ouvrage qui a pour titre Dialogues sur le commerce des blés*, London, 1770.

MORELLY, *Code de la nature ou le véritable esprit de ses lois*, ed. G. Chinard, Abbeville, F. Paillat, 1950.

Pamphlets of the American Revolution, 1750-1776, ed. B. Bailyn, Cambridge, Mass., Belknap Press of Harvard University Press, 1965, 2 vols.

PUFENDORF, Samuel, *Le droit de la nature et des gens, ou système général des principes les plus importants de la morale, de la jurisprudence, et de la politique*, trans. by J. Barbeyrac, Amsterdam and Paris, Briasson, 1733, 2 vols.

—. *Les devoirs de l'homme et du citoyen tels qu'ils sont prescrits par la loi naturelle*, ed. J. Barbeyrac, H. Schelte, 1707.

RAYNAL, Guillaume Thomas François, *Histoire du Stadthoudérat*, The Hague, 1747.

—. *Histoire philosophique et politique des établissements et du commerce des Européens dans les deux Indes*, Paris, Berry, An II (1793-1794), 10 vols.

ROUSSEAU, Jean-Jacques, *Correspondance générale*, ed. T. Dufour and P.-P. Plan, Paris, Collin 1924-1934, 20 vols.

—. *Discours sur l'origine et les fondements de l'inégalité parmi les hommes*, ed. J.-L. Lecercle, Paris, Editions sociales, 1958.

—. *Du contrat social*, ed. J.-L. Lecercle, Paris, Editions sociales, 1956.

—. *Profession de foi du vicaire savoyard*, ed. H. Falcon, Paris, Pauvert, 1964.

—. *The political writings of Jean-Jacques Rousseau*, ed. C. E. Vaughan, Cambridge, Cambridge University Press, 1915, 2 vols.

VOLTAIRE, François-Marie Arouet de, *Correspondence*, ed. Th. Bestermann, Geneva, Institut et musée Voltaire, 1953-65, 107 vols.

—. *Oeuvres complètes*, ed. Molan, Paris, Garnier, 1883-1885, 52 vols.

—. *Oeuvres historiques*, ed. R. Pomeau, Paris, Gallimard, 1957.

—. *Politique de Voltaire*, ed. R. Pomeau, Paris, Colin, 1963.

C. SECONDARY SOURCES*

I. Studies on Diderot

ALEXANDER, Ian W., "Philosophy of organism and philosophy of consciousness in Diderot's speculative thought," in *Studies in Romance Philology and French literature presented to John Orr*, Manchester University Press, 1953, pp. 1-21.

BENOT, Yves, *Diderot, de l'athéisme à l'anticolonialisme*, Paris, Maspero, 1970.

—. "Diderot, Pechmeja, Raynal et l'anticolonialisme," Europe, Jan.-Feb. 1963, pp. 137-153.

BESSE, Guy, "Observations sur la *Réfutation d'Helvétius* par Diderot," in FELLOWS, *Diderot Studies*, VI, pp. 29-45.

BONNEVILLE, Douglas A., *Diderot's "Vie de Sénèque": A Swansong Revised*, University of Florida Monographs – Humanities 19, Gainesville, University of Florida Press, 1966.

BRUGMANS, H. L., "Autour de Diderot en Hollande" in Fellows, *Diderot Studies*, III, pp. 55-71.

CHOUILLET, Jacques, "Le mythe d'Ariste ou Diderot en face de lui-même," *Revue d'histoire littéraire de la France*, 1964, pp. 565-588.

COTTA, Sergio, "L'illuminisme et la science politique: Montesquieu, Diderot et Catherine II," *Revue internationale d'histoire politique et constitutionnelle*, 1954, pp. 273-287.

CREIGHTON, D. C., "Man and Mind in Diderot and Helvétius," Publications of the Modern Language Association, 1956, pp. 705-724.

CROCKER (KRAKEUR), Lester G., "Diderot and the idea of progress," *Romanic Review*, 1938, pp. 151-159.

—. "Diderot et la loi naturelle," Europe, Jan.-Feb. 1963, pp. 57-65.

—. "*Jacques le Fataliste* an 'expérience morale' " in Fellows, *Diderot Studies* III, pp. 79-100.

—. "*Le Neveu de Rameau*, une expérience morale," Cahiers de l'A.I.E.F., XIII, pp. 133-155.

—. *The Embattled Philosopher; a biography of Denis Diderot*, East Lansing, Michigan State College Press, 1954.

—. *Two Diderot studies. Ethics and aesthetics*, Baltimore, John Hopkins Press, 1952.

DIECKMANN, Herbert, "Diderot, Grimm et Raynal," *Revue d'histoire littéraire de la France*, 1951, pp. 417-440.

—. "Diderot's Conception of genius," *Journal of the History of Ideas*, 1941, pp. 151-182.

—. *Inventaire du fonds Vandeul et inédits de Diderot*, Genève, Droz, 1951.

* *Abbreviations:*

Cahiers de l'A.I.E.F.: *Cahiers de l'Association internationale des études françaises*, XIII, Paris, Société d'édition "Les Belles Lettres," 1961.
Studies on Voltaire   : *Studies on Voltaire and the Eighteenth Century*, ed. Theodore Bestermann, Geneva, Institut et Musée Voltaire, 1955.
Transactions   : *Transactions of the first international congress on the Enlichtenment*, 4 vols. in *Studies on Voltaire . . .*, XXIV-XXVII.

—. "Les contributions de Diderot à la *Correspondance littéraire* et à *l'Histoire des deux Indes,*" *Revue d'histoire littéraire de la France,* 1951, pp. 417-440.

—. "The presentation of reality in Diderot's tales" in Fellows, *Diderot Studies* III, pp. 101-128.

DUCHET, Michèle, "Diderot collaborateur de Raynal: à propos des Fragments imprimés du fonds Vandeul," *Revue d'histoire littéraire de la France,* 1960, pp. 531-556.

—. "Le *Supplément au Voyage de Bougainville* et la collaboration de Diderot à l'*Histoire des deux Indes,*" Cahiers de l'A.I.E.F., XIII, pp. 173-187.

DULAC, Georges, Review of Diderot, *Mémoires pour Catherine II,* ed. P. Vernière, *Revue d'histoire littéraire de la France,* 1968, pp. 661-663.

DUTOURD, Jean, "Le prolétaire errant," *Nouvelle revue française,* 1958, pp. 684-689.

FELLOWS, Otis and O'GORMAN, Donal, "Another addition to the *Salon de 1767*" in Fellows, *Diderot Studies* III, pp. 215-217.

FELLOWS, Otis, *et al.* ed. *Diderot Studies,* Syracuse University Press and Paris, Droz, 14 vols. between 1949 and 1970.

FEUGERE, A., "La doctrine révolutionnaire de Raynal et de Diderot d'après l'*Histoire des Indes,*" *Mercure de France,* 1913, pp. 498-517.

GUY, Basil, "The Prince de Ligne and Diderot," *Romanic Review,* 1962, pp. 260-268.

HAVENS, G. R., "Diderot, Rousseau and the *Discours sur l'inégalité*" in Fellows, *Diderot Studies* III, pp. 219-262.

HERMAND, Pierre, *Les idées morales de Diderot,* Paris, P.U.F., 1923.

HINTERHAUSER, Hans, *Utopie und Wirklichkeit bei Diderot; Studien zum "Supplément au Voyage de Bougainville,"* Heidelberg, Carl Winter, 1957.

HYTIER, Adrienne, "Le philosophe et le despote: histoire d'une inimitié" in Fellows, *Diderot Studies* VI, pp. 55-58.

JANET, P., *La philosophie de Diderot. Le dernier mot d'un matérialiste,* Nineteenth Century, 1881, pp. 695-708.

LEFEBVRE, Henri, *Diderot,* Paris, "Les éditeurs réunis," 1949.

LOUGH, John, *Essays on the Encyclopédie of Diderot and d'Alembert,* London, University of Durham Publications, Oxford University Press, 1968.

LOY, J. Robert, *Diderot's Determined Fatalist: A critical appreciation of "Jacques le Fataliste,"* New York, King's crown press, 1950.

—. "L'Essai sur les règnes de Claude et de Néron," Cahiers de l'A.I.E.F., XIII, pp. 239-254.

LUPPOL, I. K., *Diderot: ses idées philosophiques,* Paris, Editions sociales internationales, 1936.

MAUZI, Robert, "Diderot et le bonheur" in Fellows, *Diderot Studies* III, pp. 263-284.

MORLEY, John, *Diderot and the Encyclopaedists,* London, Chapman and Hall, 1878, 2 vols.

MORNET, Daniel, *Diderot, l'homme et l'oeuvre,* Paris, Boivin, 1941.

MORTIER, Roland, "Diderot et la notion du peuple," *Europe,* Jan.-Feb. 1963, pp. 78-88.

—. "Diderot sous le prisme de la critique marxiste," Proceedings of the second Congress of the International Comparative Literature Association, Chapel Hill, 1959, pp. 679-691.

NIKLAUS, Robert, "Diderot et le conte philosophique," Cahiers de l'A.I.E.F., XIII, pp. 299-315.

—. "The mind of Diderot. An enquiry into the nature of Diderot's understanding and thought," Filosofia, 1963, pp. 926-938.

OESTREICHER, Jean, La pensée politique et économique de Diderot, Thèse de la Faculté de Droit, Vincennes, Imprimerie Rosay, 1936.

PERKINS, J. A., "Diderot's concept of virtue" in Bestermann, Studies on Voltaire ..., XXIII, pp. 77-91.

PROUST, Jacques, Diderot et l'Encyclopédie, Paris, Colin, 1962.

—. "La contribution de Diderot à l'Encyclopédie et les théories du droit naturel," Annales Historiques de la Révolution Française, 1963, pp. 257-286.

SANDOMIRSKY, L. N., "The Ethical Standard of the Genius in Diderot's Neveu de Rameau," Symposium, 1964, pp. 46-55.

SCHALK, Fritz, "Diderots Essai über Claudius und Nero" in Studien zur französischen Aufklärung, Munich, Hueber, 1964.

SEE, Henri, "Les idées politiques de Diderot," Revue historique, 1897, pp. 46-60.

SEILLIERE, Baron Ernest, Le péril mystique dans l'inspiration des démocraties contemporaines, Paris, "Renaissance du livre," 1918.

SEZNEC, Jean, Essais sur Diderot et l'Antiquité, Oxford, The Clarendon Press, 1957.

SMILEY, J. R., "A List of Diderot's articles for Grimm's Correspondance littéraire," Romanic Review, 1951, pp. 189-197.

SPINK, J. S., "La vertu politique selon Diderot ou le 'Paradoxe du bon citoyen,'" Revue des sciences humaines, 1963, pp. 471-483.

STRANGE, M., "Diderot et la société russe de son temps," Annales historiques de la Révolution française, 1963, pp. 295-308.

STRENSKI, Ellen M., "Diderot for and against the physiocrats" in Transactions ..., III, pp. 1435-1455.

—. "The Problem of inconsistency, illustrated in Diderot's social and political thought" in Fellows, Diderot Studies XIV, pp. 197-216.

SZIGETI, József, Denis Diderot, une grande figure du matérialisme militant du 18e siècle, Budapest, Akadémiai Kiadó, 1962.

THIELEMANN, L., "Diderot and Hobbes" in Fellows, Diderot Studies II, pp. 221-278.

THOMAS, Jean, Diderot in Histoire des littératures, III, Littératures françaises, connexes et marginales, Paris, Gallimard, 1958.

—. L'humanisme de Diderot, Paris, Belles-Lettres, 1938.

VERNIERE, Paul, "Diderot et l'invention littéraire: à propos de Jacques le fataliste," Revue d'histoire littéraire de la France, 1959, pp. 153-167.

WALDAUER, Joseph L., "Society and the freedom of the creative man in Diderot's thought" in Fellows, Diderot Studies V.

WILSON, Arthur M., "The concept of 'moeurs' in Diderot's social and political thought" in The Age of the Enlightenment. Studies presented to Theo-

dore Bestermann, ed. W. H. Barber, etc., (St. Andrews University Publications, No. LVII), Edinburgh - London, Oliver and Boyd, 1967.

—. "The development and scope of Diderot's political thought" in *Transactions*..., IV, pp. 1871-1900.

II. Other Studies

BARNI, J., *Histoire des idées morales et politiques en France au 18e siècle*, Paris, Alcan, 1886.

BAYET, Albert and ALBERT, François, *Les écrivains politiques du XVIIIe siècle*, Paris, Colin, 1935.

BESTERMAN, Theodore, "Voltaire, absolute monarch and the enlightened monarch" in BESTERMANN, *Studies on Voltaire*..., XXXII, pp. 7-21.

BIOLLAY, Léon, *Le pacte de famine*, Paris, Guillaumin, 1885.

BOXER, C. R., *The Dutch Seaborne Empire 1600-1800*, London, Hutchinson, 1965.

BROOME, J. H., *Rousseau, a study of his thought*, London, Arnold, 1963.

BURGELIN, Pierre, *La philosophie de l'existence de J. J. Rousseau*, Paris, P.U.F., 1952.

COBBAN, Alfred, *A History of Modern France*, Harmondsworth, Penguin Books, 1965, 2nd Edition, 3 vols.

—. *Rousseau and the modern state*, London, Allen and Unwin, 2nd edition, 1964.

COE, R.N.C., "The Fortunes of the *Code de la Nature* between 1755 and 1848," French Studies, 1957, pp. 117-126.

CROCKER, Lester G., *An Age of Crisis; Man and World in 18th-Century French Thought*, Baltimore, John Hopkins Press, 1959.

—. *Nature and Culture; ethical thought in the French Enlightenment*, Baltimore, John Hopkins Press, 1963.

DAKIN, Douglas, *Turgot and the Ancien Régime in France*, London, Methuen, 1939.

DELBEZ, M., "Les sources philosophiques de l'individualisme révolutionnaire," *Revue internationale d'histoire politique et constitutionnelle*, 1956, pp. 241-258.

DERATHE, Robert, *Jean-Jacques Rousseau et la science politique de son temps*, Paris, P.U.F., 1950.

—. "Les philosophes et le despotisme" in FRANCASTEL, *Utopie et institutions au dix-huitième siècle*, pp. 57-75.

DULAC, G., "La question des blés," Europe, Jan.-Feb. 1963, pp. 103-109.

ECHEVERRIA, Durand, *Mirage in the West: A History of the French Image of American Society to 1815*, Princeton, Princeton University Press, 1957. Reprinted 1966 by Octagon Books, New York.

FABRE, Jean, "Deux frères ennemis: Diderot et Jean-Jacques" in FELLOWS, *Diderot Studies III*, pp. 155-213.

—. *Lumières et romantisme*, Klincksieck, 1963.

FRANCASTEL, Pierre et al., *Utopie et institutions au dix-huitième siècle*, Paris - The Hague, Mouton, 1963.

GAY, Peter, *The Enlightenment: An Interpretation*, London, Weidenfeld and Nicolson, 1967.

—. *Voltaire's Politics*, Princeton, Princeton University Press, 1959.

GREEN, F. C., *The Ancien Régime. A Manual of French Institutions and Social Classes*, Edinburgh, At the University Press, 1958.

HAMPSON, Norman, *The Enlightenment*, Harmondsworth, Penguin Books, 1968.

HAZARD, Paul, *La pensée européenne au dix-huitième siècle; de Montesquieu à Lessing*, Paris, Boivin, 1946, 3 vols.

HUBERT, René, *Les sciences sociales dans l'Encyclopédie*, Travaux et mémoires de l'Université de Lille, nouvelle série, section Droit-Lettres, No. 9, 1923.

KAWANO, K., "Prototypes idéologiques de la Révolution française," *Europe*, Nov.-Dec. 1961, pp. 160-163; 166-167.

KOCH, P., "The Genesis of Galiani's *Dialogues sur le commerce des blés*," *French Studies*, 1961, pp. 314-323.

LABRIOLLE-RUTHERFORD, M. R. de, "L'évolution de la notion du luxe depuis Mandeville jusqu'à la Révolution" in *Transactions . . .*, III, pp. 1025-1036.

LABROUSSE, C. E., *La crise de l'économie française à la fin de l'Ancien Régime*, Paris, P.U.F., 1943.

LARIVIERE, Ch. de., "Mercier de la Rivière à Saint-Pétersbourg en 1767," *Revue d'histoire littéraire de la France*, 1897, pp. 581-602.

LECERCLE, Jean-Louis, "Utopie et réalisme politique chez Mably" in *Transactions . . .*, II, pp. 1049-1070.

LORTHOLARY, Albert, *Le mirage russe en France au dix-huitième siècle*, Paris, Boivin, 1951.

MATHIEZ, A., "Les doctrines politiques des physiocrates," *Annales historiques de la Révolution française*, 1936, pp. 193-203.

—. "Les philosophes et le pouvoir au milieu du XVIIIe siècle," *Annales historiques de la Révolution française*, 1935, pp. 1-12.

MAUZI, R., *L'idée du bonheur dans la littérature et la pensée françaises au 18e siècle*, Paris, Colin, 1960.

MORNET, Daniel, *La pensée française au 18e siècle*, Paris, Colin, 1951.

—. *Les origines intellectuelles de la Révolution française, 1715-1787*, Paris, Colin, 1934.

MURRIS, R., *La Hollande et les Hollandais au dix-septième et au dix-huitième siècles vus par les Français*, Paris, Champion, 1925.

NAVILLE, Pierre, *Paul Thiry d'Holbach et la philosophie scientifique de son temps*, Paris, Gallimard, 1943.

PERKINS, Jean A., *The Concept of the Self in the French Enlightenment*, Geneva, Droz, 1969.

RENIER, Gustaaf Johannes, *The Dutch Nation: an historical study*, London, Allen & Unwin for the Netherlands Government Information Bureau, 1944.

SCHLESINGER, Arthur M., *Prelude to Independence: the newspaper war on Britain, 1764-1776*, New York, Knopf, 1958.

SÉE, Henri, *L'évolution de la pensée politique en France au XVIIIe siècle*, Paris, Giard, 1925.

STELLING-MICHAUD, Sven, "Lumières et politique" in *Transactions . . .*, IV, pp. 1519-1544.

TOUCHARD, Jean, *Histoire des idées politiques*, Paris, P.U.F., 1962.

TYLER, Moses Coit, *The Literary History of the American Revolution, 1763-1783*, New York, Ungar, 1957 reprint, 2 vols.

VAUGHAN, C. E., *Studies in the History of Political Philosophy before and after Rousseau*, Manchester, Manchester University Press, 1925, 2 vols.

—. *The political writings of Jean-Jacques Rousseau*, Cambridge, Cambridge University Press, 1915, 2 vols.

VENTURI, Franco, "Galiani tra enciclopedisti e fisiocrati," *Rivista storica italiana*, 1960, pp. 45-64.

VERCRUYSSE, J., "Les Provinces - Unies vues par Voltaire" in *Transactions* ..., IV, pp. 1715-1722.

VYVERBERG, Henry, *Historical Pessimism in the French Enlightenment*, Cambridge, Mass., Harvard |University Press.

WALDINGER, René, *Voltaire and reform in the light of the French Revolution*, Geneva, Droz, 1959.

WEULERSSE, G., *Le mouvement physiocratique en France*, Paris, Alcan, 1910, 2 vols.

WILSON, A. M., "Why did the political theory of the Encyclopedists not prevail?" French historical studies, 1960, pp. 283-294.

WOLPE, Hans, *Raynal et sa machine de guerre*, Paris, Editions M. Th. Génin, 1957.

III. Unpublished thesis

STRENSKI, Ellen M., *Diderot's political thought*, Thesis submitted for the degree of Ph. D. in the Faculty of Letters, University of Reading, 1967.

INDEX

Lightning Source UK Ltd.
Milton Keynes UK
178535UK00001B/3/A